Remaking America

James A. Joseph

Remaking America

How the Benevolent Traditions of Many Cultures Are Transforming Our National Life

Jossey-Bass Publishers • San Francisco

Substantial discounts on bulk quantities of Jossey-Bass books are available to corporations, professional associations, and other organizations. For details and discount information, contact the special sales department at Jossey-Bass Inc., Publishers. (415) 433-1740; Fax (800) 605-2665.

For sales outside the United States, please contact your local Paramount Publishing International Office.

TCF Manufactured in the United States of America on Lyons Falls Pathfinder Tradebook. This paper is acid-free and 100 percent totally chlorine-free.

Credits are on page 256.

Library of Congress Cataloging-in-Publication Data

Joseph, James A. (James Alfred), date.
    Remaking America : how the benevolent traditions of many cultures are transforming our national life / James A. Joseph. — 1st ed.
        p.   cm. — (Jossey-Bass nonprofit sector series)
    Includes bibliographical references (p.   ) and index.
    ISBN 0-7879-0095-8 (acid-free paper)
    1. United States—Civilization—1970–   2. Minorities—United
States.   3. Benevolence—Social aspects—United States.
4. Pluralism (Social sciences)—United States.   I. Title.
II. Series.
E169.12.J666   1995
973.92—dc20   94-49403

HB Printing   10 9 8 7 6 5 4 3 2 1   FIRST EDITION

Contents

Preface ix

The Author xix

Introduction: The Search for an American Identity 1

Native Americans

1. The Tribe as Benevolent Community 23
2. Chief Seattle: Every Part of the Earth Is Sacred 37
3. Reuben Snake: Walking on the Prayers of Our Grandmothers 49
4. Zikala-Sa: On the Razor's Edge Between Tradition and Change 59

African Americans

5. The Cosmology of Connectedness 73
6. Thomy Lafon: Black Aristocracy and Benevolent Wealth 87
7. Maggie Walker: Self-Help and Social Reform 97
8. Madame C. J. Walker: Entrepreneurial Philanthropy 109

Asian Americans

9. The Bridging of Cultures 121
10. Le Ly Hayslip: When Heaven and Earth Changed Places 137
11. Patrick Okura: In Quest of Justice 147
12. An Wang: Humanity Without Benevolence Invites Destruction 159

Latinos

13. The Primacy of Family and Church   171
14. Patrick Flores: The Mariachi Bishop   185
15. Sister Isolina: The Mother Teresa of Puerto Rico 193
16. Cesar Chavez: Apostle of Nonviolence   203
    Conclusion: A New American Paradigm   213
    Notes   229
    Recommended Readings   245
    Index   251

Preface

In the bayou country in Louisiana where I was born, the rivers of compassion ran deep. We were poor, but when we were hungry we shared with each other. When we were sick we cared for each other. We did not think of what we gave to others as philanthropy, because sharing was an act of reciprocity in which both the giver and the receiver benefited. We did not think of what we did for others as volunteering, because caring was as much a moral imperative as an act of free will.

Despite this long tradition of self-help and attending to each other's needs, when most Americans think about African Americans and the civic culture, they are more likely to think of recipients of charity than of members of a community with a long tradition of benevolence. Although the charitable giving of prominent African Americans is gaining increased public attention, the primary focus remains on the pathologies of those in the community who are on the margins of the economy, rather than on the practices of those who are moving toward the mainstream.

Even so, writing a work of this magnitude has to be driven by something other than a desire to demythologize prevailing perceptions or to put one's thoughts in print. My motivation for embarking on this venture begins with memories of what it was like to grow up black in Louisiana in the 1950s. Some of my memories are romantic—vivid images of moss-covered oak trees, the almost mystic influences of the Creole and Cajun cultures, and the vitality of schools and churches that were rigidly segregated but whose members refused to be rigidly subservient.

My other memories are less romantic and less mystical. I also remember a time and place in which I walked miles past the white school to go to the "colored" school on the other side of town, in which I studied from hand-me-down books in hand-me-down buildings.

My experience of segregation—picking cotton in hot, dusty fields because all other summer jobs were reserved for white teenagers, enduring the indignity of "whites only" signs when I desperately needed a drink of water—became a tempering agent that forged a determined will to succeed. Yet in the end, what has served me best has not been simply the personal drive but the strength of character that enabled me to rise above the hostility that could have so easily consumed me with rage.

This book is thus the product of a lifelong curiosity about what happened to me and to so many others in myriad groups who not only refused to hate, but embraced the stranger—even the oppressor—in ways that now make community possible.

Forming a More Perfect Union

The historical concept of the American society is of a people forming a more perfect union, a society that is neither fixed nor final, a nation that is always in the making. But rarely has there been as much concern, even anxiety, about the remaking of America. The argument over what constitutes the national identity has led to a breakdown of civility, with zealots of all sorts clinging tenaciously to old myths out of fear that some of their most cherished traditions might be discarded or discredited. Many want to return to an age when the assimilation of a "received" tradition was regarded as the primary path to the American dream.

Racial minorities in America share neither a common historical experience nor a common religion or race. Each group has its own cultural heroes, its own unique identity, and its own sense of how best to define itself as part of American society. Yet, despite the wide chasm these differences seem to reflect, each group has traditions of self-help, voluntarism, and associational life that if properly understood and affirmed could reinvigorate present efforts to find common ground.

This is a defining moment in American history. We will soon enter a new century in which it will no longer be possible to define the meaning of America or describe the beliefs and practices that shape our character without reference to the civic traditions that give American society its vitality. Many elements of these traditions are shared in common not only by those Americans who trace their ancestry to Europe but by all of our citizens: European, African, Asian, Latino, and Native American alike. Yet neither Alexis de Tocqueville, in his classic *Democracy in America,* nor Robert Bellah, who reintroduced de Tocqueville's notion of "habits of the heart" 150 years later, included the benevolent traditions of America's racial minorities in their highly celebrated writings on the civic virtue and civic habits of the American people.

Citing the constraints of a small research team and a limited budget, Bellah was quite open in admitting that he and his associates decided to concentrate on "white, middle class America," thus limiting the ability to illustrate "much of the diversity that is so important a part of our national life."[1] The problem is more profound than Bellah and his associates assumed. As Vincent Harding, an African-American historian, was to observe later, illustrations of racial diversity are not the primary loss. Missing is a major portion of the richness of the American past that will be so important to understanding and shaping the American future.

In an earlier book, I examined the relationship between wealth and social conscience in communities and cultures outside the United States in order to demonstrate the universality of the charitable impulse. I have wanted since to write about the benevolent traditions of racial minorities in this country to help dispel the notion that the service ethic and the civic habits Americans celebrate are found primarily among the white majority.

Benevolent Traditions

This book is an attempt to identify and analyze the benevolent traditions of America's minority population groups, and compare them to the much celebrated traditions of the majority. It does not claim that one tradition is better than another, but shows that beneath all that seems to divide racial minorities from the majority population, there is a strong consensus about the relationship between the individual and society, between the private and public good.

The English word *benevolence* has a checkered history. In fifteenth-century England it referred to a compulsory gift extorted by various English kings from their subjects without the consent of Parliament. This usage of the word was altered by later generations who followed the Platonic philosopher Henry More in affirming a new "axiom of benevolence" which suggested that "if it be good that one man should be supplied with the means of living well and happily, it is doubly good that two should be so supplied and so on."[2]

Some writers restrict the meaning of benevolence to what is most often called "charity," alleviating human suffering. This connotation, which has its genesis in religion, is associated closely with the Latin term *caritas* used by Augustine and others to suggest that one should love one's neighbor as one loves oneself. This notion of benevolence is significant in that it describes "other-regarding" sentiments of compassion, but it is far too limited to describe the full scope of the traditions of the racial minorities included in this study. Faced with a need to change their circumstances as well as ameliorate the consequences of their political and economic status, they expanded the idea of benevolence to include both charity and social reform.

In this study, the term *benevolence* refers to community service, philanthropy, voluntarism, and myriad forms of self-help, not to private entrepreneurship, although the development of ethnic enterprise has been a primary means of community development for some groups. The emphasis here is on voluntary activity for the well-being of the community rather than on private action to achieve individual wealth. This more limited focus is not intended to suggest that private entrepreneurship is not an important strategy for community betterment. It means that the concern of this study is how minorities have used the intermediate space between government and business to improve their predicament and to provide dignity and meaning in the process. An obvious exception is made for Korean Americans whose system of *keh*, while focused on small enterprise development, reflects a special form of community bonding.

The racial minority groups studied here are African Americans, Asian Americans, Latinos, and Native Americans. These generic terms are ambiguous and sometimes confusing, but for the purposes of this work they identify minorities who are increasingly grouped together for analysis and study.

The term *Native Americans* is used interchangeably with *American Indians* to refer to a loose residue of tribes rather than a distinct community with a common culture or consciousness. Yet this very diverse group shares many commonalities. The term *Asian* has replaced the now disfavored *Oriental* to describe Americans of Japanese, Chinese, Korean, Indian, Burmese, Thai, or Philippine descent. But while those whom we describe as Asian Americans may prefer that title, they did not choose it for themselves. They are more likely to refer to national identities than to the pan-ethnic designations. Americans of Hispanic or Latino heritage include among their members persons of almost pure European ancestry as well as individuals of African or Native descent. Like Asian Americans, many members of this group choose to emphasize their national and cultural identity rather than traits associated with Hispanics or Latinos. The term *African American*, a late bloomer on the racial landscape, tends to be used interchangeably with *black American;* however, the latter is more inclusive, embracing Afro-Caribbean and Afro-Hispanic Americans.

For white Americans, group identity has more varied layers. The same person, for example, might be simply an American when traveling abroad, self-consciously white when visiting the central city, and proudly Italian American on returning to his neighborhood. But this choice of adding or discarding layers is not available in the same way to those minorities whose boundary marker is skin color. All those interested in revitalizing American public life and finding common ground should be pleased to learn that people who have suffered the ravages of American individualism so harshly have managed to maintain a strong commitment to community.

This work is a small installment in a much-needed effort to capture a vision of community struggling to be born and to put it to work for a society that must soon recognize that the fear of difference is a fear of the future, that diversity need not divide, and that pluralism rightly understood and rightly practiced is a benefit, not a burden.

Audience

The book was written with many audiences in mind: serious students in the new philanthropy courses now being offered in colleges and universities; leaders of nonprofit organizations faced with the need to understand the traditions of the racial minorities who have increasing influence on the civic infrastructure of their communities; students in history, political science, and theology; and members of racial minorities who are not themselves fully aware of the richness of their own traditions and practices.

Overview of the Contents

The work begins with a historical perspective on the search for an American identity, examines why so many Americans are saying a fervent "no" to the assimilationist vision, analyzes the civic habits and civic cultures of America's racial minorities, and concludes with a new paradigm of community.

The introduction reviews current attempts to redefine the national identity, to liberate the past from highly selective recall, and to develop a new American creed. It examines three ideas that have their roots in widely different communities and cultures: (1) the idea of a civil society, (2) the idea of a good society, and (3) the idea of a transforming society.

The first section, on Native Americans, explores the impact of Native American traditions on the stream of ideas that shaped the early American vision of community. It examines why political philosophers as different as Thomas Paine and Karl Marx saw the Indian tribe as a model of social organization, benevolence, and communal life.

The second section, in which the African-American tradition is the focus, makes a special attempt to trace the moral sentiments of African Americans back to the African cosmology stored away in the minds of the early slaves through the communal ethic of the slave quarters, the black church, black voluntary associations, and protest politics.

As the third section demonstrates, Asian Americans fit no special mold, but they share a common commitment to taking care of their own. This section examines the civic culture of the Japanese Americans, whose activist principles such as charity and volunteering are relative latecomers to the lexicon of civic virtues; of the Chinese Americans, whose neo-Confucian ethic interprets benevolence as a characteristic element of humanity; of the Korean Americans, whose practices of self-help are aided by an ancient tradition called *keh*; and of those Vietnamese Americans who, as Buddhists, believe that because Buddhahood is innate in each individual, all people inherently possess a life of great goodness and are, therefore, deserving of respect.

The last section, on Latinos, identifies basic Latino values that have their genesis in and derive their authority from the primacy of church and family in Latin cultures. This section examines the civic traditions of Mexican Americans, Puerto Ricans, Central Americans, and Cuban Americans.

The conclusion sets out my belief that both a national identity and a national culture are still possible if we are willing to get away from the notion of a received tradition and acknowledge that our national identity is forever evolving. It proposes a new paradigm of community based on shared values, a universal compassion, a new spirituality, and a compelling vision.

The methodolgy used in gathering information for the profiles contained in this book included both direct interviews and literature research. Patrick Okura, Sister Isolina, Le Ly Hayslip, and Reuben Snake were interviewed by the author. Information for the other profiles was drawn from primary and secondary sources, including biographies, autobiographies, newspapers, and other writings contemporaneous with the individuals profiled.

Acknowledgments

In writing this work, I had the encouragement and support of many people who remain nameless and faceless; some of them were not even aware that they were helping me to probe the motives and values that lead to sentiments of compassion and acts of generosity; others helped with the research or kept the pressure on to complete what could have easily remained an unfinished manuscript. My research assistant, Karin Stanford, falls into both categories. I will be forever in her debt for caring as much about the subject as I do. Janice Windle, director of the El Paso Community Foundation and author of a recent book of her own, provided research funds in memory of Karl O. Wyler, who was pleased enough with my first book to read it twice. Mary Braxton, Myrtle Mark, Terry Lavoie, and Robin Hettleman at the Council on Foundations were of enormous help.

I am grateful to those persons who agreed to be interviewed, especially Le Ly Hayslip, Reuben Snake, Sister Isolina, and Patrick Okura. I also owe a lot to my family: my late wife Doris, my son Jeffrey, and my daughter Denise, for the time they gave up that I might be free to pursue my fascination with this subject.

Falls Church, Virginia   James A. Joseph
February 1995

The Author

James A. Joseph, president and chief executive officer of the Council on Foundations, has had a distinguished career in public service, business, education, and philanthropy. Before joining the Council, a national organization of more than thirteen hundred foundations and other grantmakers, Joseph spent four years as the undersecretary of the interior in the Carter Administration. He presently serves as chairman of the board of directors of the Corporation for National Service, a position to which he was appointed by President Clinton.

Born in Opelousas, Louisiana, Joseph received his B.A. degree in 1956 from Southern University, Louisiana, and his M.A. degree in 1963 from Yale Divinity School. He is also the recipient of numerous honorary degrees, including doctor of divinity, doctor of public service, doctor of laws, and doctor of humane letters. He has taught at Yale, Claremont, and Stillman, and has served as a visiting fellow at Nuffield College, Oxford University. While at Stillman, he was one of the leaders of the local civil rights movement in Tuscaloosa, Alabama, during the 1960s. A contributor to a wide variety of books and journals, he is author of the *The Charitable Impulse* (1989), a study of wealth and social conscience in communities and cultures outside the United States.

Joseph served for ten years as vice president of Cummins Engine Company and president of the Cummins Engine Foundation. An ordained minister, he was also chaplain of the Claremont Colleges and a member of the faculty of the Claremont School of Theology before becoming executive director of the Irwin-Sweeney-Miller

Foundation in 1970. Joseph is a frequent lecturer and writer on public service, the civic culture, and philanthropy.

Joseph serves on the board of directors of The Brookings Institution, the Children's Defense Fund, Africare, the National Endowment for Democracy, and the Points of Light Foundation. A member of the Council on Foreign Relations and the Overseas Development Council, he was appointed by President Bush to the President's Advisory Committee on Historically Black Colleges and served on the Advisory Committee to the Agency for International Development.

Joseph lives in Falls Church, Virginia. He has two children.

Remaking America

Introduction: The Search for an American Identity

In the United States, like many other countries, a struggle to redefine the national identity is taking place. Multiple visions of community compete for intellectual, cultural, and political dominance. The best known and longest enduring is the notion of the "melting pot." As George Washington and others in his time envisioned it, the United States would take the new settlers from varied nations and religions and fuse them into a people with one national identity.

In *Letters from an American Farmer*, Hector St. John de Crevecoeur, a Frenchmen who came to America in 1759, described an American, "this new man," as "one who leaves behind all ancient prejudices and manners to become a new person who acts upon new principles. . . . Here," he said, "individuals of all races are melted into a new race of man."[1] Crevecoeur's book was a best-seller in Europe.

From the beginning, this vision of the American was challenged by new arrivals with a disinclination to blend into a uniform national type. But the prevailing portrait of America remained that of an Anglo-Saxon Protestant country—an image that not only fit the original English colonists but also accommodated later European immigrants who, despite their differences, found enough common ground to make the melting pot notion credible.

Crevecoeur's vision of the American community is once again under serious challenge. According to a 1993 study by researchers at Johns Hopkins University,[2] a new generation of Americans is saying a fervent "no" to the assimilationist vision. The long-standing assumption that immigrants had to give up their heritage, their hyphen, in order to be truly American is now being disavowed by more Americans than was earlier assumed. Fifty years ago, the children of European immigrants accepted without question that they had to reject the old world in order to get ahead in the new. In his essay "An American Writer," Richard Rodriguez wrote that "America is the country where one stops being German, stops being Chinese. Where grandmothers stand at windows, mistrusting, deploring."[3] Today it is no longer only grandmothers who are concerned about losing the cultural boundaries that once defined family life. Today's immigrant children, who are primarily Hispanic, Asian, and Caribbean, want an American identity, but they also want to see the history and culture of their parents respected and affirmed.

This new vision of community "stands the cultural blueprint for the advancement of immigrant groups in American society on its head," says Alejandro Portes, the sociology professor who directed the Johns Hopkins study.[4] In 1990, there were about 24.8 million children of immigrants in this country, of whom roughly 7.7 million were born to immigrants who arrived after 1960.[5] Neither racism nor widespread poverty seems to have daunted the hopes of many to achieve social mobility, but most expect to do so while retaining some of the culture and practices of their parents' homeland. They are not un-American. Quite the contrary; they want very much to be considered Americans, but they want also to be able to maintain their ethnic identity and the pride that comes from respect for heritage.

The most eloquent chronicler of this new vision was Alex Haley, the author of *Roots*,[6] who emphasized the importance of history and the celebration of heritage. His book, and the popular television series it spawned, ignited a sentimentality about history that went far beyond the content of his own work. We now have the irony of communities around the world becoming more alike—with their economies more interdependent, their lifestyles, values, and aspirations more similar—yet more people turning inward, seeking to return to smaller, more intimate centers of meaning and belonging.

While this juxtaposition appears at first glance to be a contradiction, it may be a natural part of the search for common ground—a search for beginnings. As John Naisbitt and Patricia Aburdene argue in *Megatrends 2000*,[7] the more humanity sees itself as inhabiting a single planet, the greater becomes the need for each culture on the globe to assert its heritage. This tension between the larger community of meaning and the smaller community of memory appears to be a natural outgrowth of the search for a new American identity. Yet, even noted scholars like Arthur Schlesinger, the author of *The Disuniting of America*,[8] decry the preoccupation with ethnic identity and the use of history as a therapeutic tool. They worry about whether the melting pot will give way to the Tower of Babel and the disuniting rather than the uniting of America.

The Uses of History

With due respect for the excellent contribution Schlesinger makes to the national discourse about pluralism and multiculturalism, it is possible that the longing for roots, the concern with history, is an integral part of the search for common ground. History has always been therapeutic. It provides the resource for dignity and the capacity for self-assertion. While we must insist that it be accurate and inclusive, the nature of the craft is that those who write history will be influenced by their own story. There is an old African proverb that says, "If lions had historians, tales of hunting would no longer glorify the hunter."

Instead of debating who owns the past, we may be able to accomplish more by liberating it from partisan and selective recall. The practice of cultural amnesia is in no one's long-term interest. Dietrich Bonhoffer, the German Protestant theologian hanged by the Nazis, wrote from prison in 1942 that he had learned to see the great events of world history from below, from the perspective of those who were excluded, under suspicion, ill-treated, powerless, oppressed, and scorned—in short, those who suffer.[9] The contro-versy surrounding the historic voyage of Christopher Columbus in 1492 reminds us that American history would be different if it were written from the perspective of the victims: the Native Americans who saw 90 percent of their population destroyed; the Japanese Americans who were systematically gathered up and relocated into prison-like enclaves; the African Americans who were promised, but never received, the forty acres and a mule that might have given them an equal opportunity in a harsh and unforgiving economy.

It is right and good that those in power tell their story, but like Dietrich Bonhoffer, we need to begin to see the great events of world history from below. We need to hear another side of history, the perspective of those who were excluded, scorned, and made powerless. For several decades, the role of history and tradition in American life has been undergoing a huge transformation. The emphasis has shifted from one tradition to many, with racial minori-ties claiming, as Fortinbras did to Horatio in *Hamlet*, "I have some rights of memory in this kingdom/ which now to claim my vantage doth invite me."[10]

It is true that there are shrill voices making inaccurate and unre-alistic claims in every community, and permitting them to drown out the authentic and accurate reporting of those whose only bias is toward accuracy over advocacy would be a mistake. What is remembered and chronicled as history by the dominant civic cul-ture has been too often mobilized to serve parochial purposes. Yet, it is still possible to honor one's history without dishonoring the his-tory of others.

Howard Thurman, the African-American theologian, mystic, and poet, was fond of saying, "I want to be me without making it difficult for you to be you."[11] It is not too dramatic to say that if

Thurman, who spent much of his life in search of common ground, were alive today, he would be deeply disturbed by the new tribalism that is polarizing and balkanizing communities around the globe, making pluralism and social cohesion uneasy bedfellows.

Where are we, then, to find common ground? Where are we to find the social glue, the civic ethic that can bring a diverse society together? When Alexis de Tocqueville wrote about the uniqueness of the American society half a century after the founders had pledged to form a more perfect union, he thought he had stumbled onto the unifying element: civic participation. He mused about everyone "taking an active part in the government of society."[12] But several centuries later, Robert Bellah, lamenting the decline of civic participation, warned of the threat of a democracy without citizens. His concern was not so much with a threat to democracy as with the potential decline in the civic infrastructure that makes democracy viable.[13] It was almost as if he foresaw the United Way controversy that arose a few years later, with allegations of misuse of funds by the organization's leading officials and the resulting erosion of public confidence in voluntary organizations.

Another foreigner and keen observer of American life was Gunnar Myrdal, the Swedish economist and sociologist, who wrote *American Dilemma*. He saw the unifying element as "the American creed,"[14] that cluster of ideas, institutions, and habits that affirm the ideals of the essential dignity and equality of all human beings, of inalienable rights to freedom, justice, and opportunity. Others have found the potential for common ground in America's civil religion. But the Protestant ethic that once undergirded it is waning. James D. Hunter, who teaches the sociology of religion at the University of Virginia, is but one of many voices who argue persuasively that the civil religion that once united America is dead. He sees instead an increasing conflict over fundamental conceptions of moral authority; conflicts over different ideas and beliefs about truths, the good, obligations to one another, the nature of community and so on. Dr. Hunter describes these conflicts as "culture wars,"[15] further polarizing an already polarized society.

The idea of a unifying American creed is obviously in trouble. The bonds of social cohesion and community are increasingly fragile. Moral theologians, political philosophers, and opinion leaders of all sorts are once again in search of common ground. Yet they have been simply looking in the wrong place, assuming that the American creed was a fixed and final orthodoxy.

A New American Creed

In examining the benevolent traditions of America's minorities, we have identified some common elements that can be used to affirm and advance the connectedness of humanity. Not only do they provide the basis for a new American creed, but they also point to civic values and civic habits shared in common with America's majority. They remind us that America as a civil community is still a multicultural experiment. Unlike the European immigrants of earlier years, who were able to assimilate into a common culture once they discarded their language, their culture, and their general "foreignness," today's racial minorities tend to have identifying marks that cannot be so easily melted away. It is revealing that Gunnar Myrdal saw the combination of race and color in America as essentially a caste condition making it difficult for blacks to escape their birth.[16] The German, Italian, and other European immigrants learned English and adopted American democratic values, thus melting away their differences. This is not an option for those whose color or physical traits maintain visible differences. After compiling a wealth of information regarding racial differentials and American attitudes, Andrew Hacker, the widely respected author of *Two Nations*, concluded that of all the human divisions in American society, the most pervasive and penetrating is the division between black and white, surpassing even gender and ethnicity in intensity and subordination.[17]

It is increasingly true in the United States, as in Latin America, that "money whitens," but even the black middle class must deal daily with the perception of many Americans that black people are associated with a higher incidence of crime or lower educational attainment. As Hacker points out, "If you are black, white reactions brand you as a carrier of contaminations. No matter what your talents or attainments, you are seen as infecting a neighborhood simply because of your race."[18] Taxi drivers who refuse to stop for black riders are not making distinctions about who is educated or who is well off. Like their wealthier counterparts in private golf clubs, they see the race of the person and respond according to cultural and psychological conditioning. Making quick judgments and acting on limited impressions is not restricted to cab drivers or members of exclusive private clubs. Most white Americans, whether they are willing to admit it or not, make judgments and engage in actions influenced by the badge of skin color and the baggage it carries. All the arguments that America is a nation of individuals rather than groups cannot remove the fundamental reality that for African Americans it is membership in the group, and not their individual nature, that often determines how others will relate to them.

In his last book, *Man's Nature and His Communities*, the great moral theologian Reinhold Niebuhr suggested that the chief cause of our inhumanity to each other is the tendency to set up "we" groups and to place them over and against "they" groups that we assume are outside the pale of our humanity.[19] Once we are able to persuade ourselves that a group's difference in status is actually a difference in kind, neither our conscience nor our religious faith is disturbed when we ignore them, exploit them, or leave them hopeless.

There was never really strict adherence to the melting pot myth, nor was there ever a time when Americans looked exactly alike, spoke the same language, or believed the same things. This has always been a heterogeneous country, although less so in the past than today. Whatever cohesion early Americans enjoyed, much of it was based on mutual respect. And that, not surprisingly, is today's missing element. Unless mutual respect is restored, the American society will continue to unravel. No responsible voice in minority communities is asking that the past be remade or that new myths replace old ones. The simple demand is that history be accurate and balanced and that the collective memory include the richness of the civic values and civic habits of all the various traditions that constitute the American society.

What distinguishes this moment in American history from all others is the opportunity for a new American creed. Three ideas are converging to demonstrate the universality of the civic impulse, emphasizing in very important ways what Americans share in common rather than what divides us. Each can be found in the benevolent traditions of racial minorities as well as in the majority tradition represented by John Winthrop's vision of a "city on a hill."[20]

The first of these ideas is the concept of a civil society, that cluster of ideas, ideals, and social arrangements through which a people gains its voice, promotes self-sufficiency, and mobilizes itself for a public good. Few Americans are aware of the extent to which voluntary groups provided a means of economic survival for racial minorities and helped them to make sense of their realities by serving as vehicles for self-help, social cohesion, and a positive group identity.

As early as 1598, Mexicans in the Southwest formed *confraternidades* (lay brotherhoods) to assist members with their basic needs. These self-help groups closely resembled the Chinese *hui kuan*, the benevolent fraternal orders that provided the Chinese-American community with an unofficial supragovernment that met the needs of its members and represented them in their dealing with outside groups. In the African-American community, voluntary groups and mutual aid societies became so prominent in the nineteenth century that several states enacted laws banning all black voluntary or charitable organizations. Examples of generosity in Native American culture are also deeply rooted. They include Indian giveaways, which reached an advanced form in the potlatch ceremonies of the Northwest tribes as well as the custom of Chippewa mothers who used to tell their young daughters to take a dish of food to a neighbor simply to teach the child to give and share. These early manifestations of the charitable impulse among racial minorities were remarkable, not simply in how they served the illiterate and poor in their midst but also in the consistency of the civic values they affirmed with the ideals and aspirations of the larger society.

The second idea creating the potential for a new American creed is the concept of a good society, the notion that a benevolent community depends as much on the goodness of individuals as it does on the soundness of government and the fairness of laws. America's racial minorities have never regarded private action as a substitute for government, but most have seen it as an important alternative to government. Many of their voluntary groups have been social and fraternal, but some have been reformist and political as well. An example is the groups involved in the civil rights movement of the 1960s, who took matters into their own hands; they recognized that while some governments at some levels were working well for some of their citizens, no government at any level was working well for all of its citizens, especially those on the margins.

The commitment to a benevolent community has taken many forms, with neighbors and friends rolling up their sleeves and pitching in to help one another, credit unions multiplying the impact of individuals' limited financial resources, benevolent societies taking care of the sick, and burial societies taking care of the dead. Denied admission to the social and civic institutions of the larger society, they had to rely on the generosity and goodness of members of their own community.

If these benevolent practices of racial minorities summon images of settlers helping to build each others' barns, gathering for quilting bees, and volunteering as firefighters, it is because the American tradition of philanthropy, voluntarism, and other forms of caring is a shared tradition as common to African, Asian, Hispanic, and Native Americans as it is to the majority population. And equally important is that the charitable, voluntary impulse expressed in self-help and associational activities was not an attempt to mimic the majority community, but was a central expression of their own traditions of benevolence.

The third idea that is converging to create a new American creed is that of a transforming society. People around the world are learning that when you get involved with the needs of others, both those who help and those who are helped are transformed. But this is no new discovery for America's racial minorities whose only mode of survival was through neighbors helping neighbors and even strangers helping strangers. Engagement in one another's lives provided a positive and reassuring vision of themselves and their community, influencing even their understanding of the purpose of the human journey. Their stories are tales of both duty and destiny. They go beyond survival and solidarity to embrace fundamental social theories and religious theologies as well.

African Americans, for example, have always believed that society transcends the state and that the patriot is one who is willing to defend his country even from his own government. They have long sought the freedom to use the intermediary space between the state and the individual as a place where private energy could be spontaneously generated and exercised. Left out of the American story with its morality tales of civic values and civic virtues, they, like other racial minorities, have alternated between enthusiasm and suspicion as they have watched the growing emphasis on nonprofit, voluntary activities as a separate and distinct sector. It is not simply that their own transforming experiences were omitted, but as concerned observers they wondered whether the American society was creating a conceptual myth—a nonprofit sector that was increasingly profit-generating, a voluntary sector that was increasingly professional, an independent sector that was dependent on government funding for a major part of its revenues. Some observed that since voluntary activities promoting the general welfare existed before there were governments, it might be more appropriate to speak of the vast array of voluntary activities as the first sector rather than the third.

Despite the prevailing image of some racial minorities as the recipients of charity rather than as members of communities with their own rich traditions of benevolence, these groups have much to contribute to the preservation and revitalization of community service, voluntarism, and philanthropy as an essential element of democratic systems. Just as American democracy in its first two centuries was a product of the traditions and values of many immigrant groups largely from Europe, so it will evolve and change in the next century. As the new groups reshape the demographics of American society, they are likely to redefine the civic culture. This study maintains that the concerns for neighbor, the forms of benevolence that promote the well-being of others, have no racial or cultural boundaries. The caring impulse is triggered whenever people see themselves as part of a community, whether it be the family, the tribe, the neighborhood, or the nation. As the notion of community expands, so does the scope of benevolence. We do not know how much of the caring impulse has been damaged by the denial, rejection, and indignity that has been the lot of racial minorities; but some of this concern is left. Its existence is observable in the growing participation of minorities in the philanthropic and voluntary organizations that serve the larger society.

There is much talk of the need to reinvent government, but those who speak of the need to reinvent the larger society are often met with skepticism and ridicule. All of us can benefit from a polite reminder that the American Revolution was not so much an event in our past as a process that continues into our future. It is still true, as Thomas Paine wrote in *Common Sense*, that "we have it within our power to begin the world all over again."[21]

The Changing Boundaries of Community

To reinvent America, to find the coherence needed to act as a single community again, we need to fuse the varied traditions of our people as the founders fused democracy and capitalism. This does not mean that we need to reject the past or deny differences. Rather, we need to build on the rich diversity of our history, respect its varied forms, and understand the many ways in which the boundaries of community are changing. The most important change may be conceptual, a paradigm shift from the notion of a network of neighbors to the metaphor of a company of strangers. There seems to be a renewed effort to romanticize "the good old days" when social cohesion and civic solidarity came from a common race, a common religion, or a common culture—when neighbors came together to build each other's barns. But as Parker Palmer points out in his book, *The Company of Strangers,* the foundation of community is no longer the intimacy of friends but the capacity of strangers to share a common territory, act on common problems, and even celebrate their unity without, in many cases, ever becoming friends.[22] The word *stranger* may be too strong a metaphor, but it reminds us of the need to find civic cohesion and social solidarity from something other than a common race, a common religion, or a common culture.

The idea of neighborhood benevolence—of neighbors looking after one another—is still alive in much of America, but a sentiment of generosity that stops as distance and differentness increase no longer serves either our needs as a nation or our ideals as a people. Writing in *Tales of a New America*, Robert Reich reminds us that even if they had the time or the inclination to get to know their neighbors, most Americans would meet people who share the same standard of living as they.[23] If they are poor, their neighborhood is likely to be populated by other poor people; if very rich, by others who enjoy the good things in life; if young and professional, then by others who are young and professional. Reich argues that the idea of community as neighborhood offers a way of enjoying the sentiment of benevolence without the burden of really acting on it. If responsibility ends at the borders of one's neighborhood, and most Americans can rest assured that their neighbors are not in dire straits, the apparent civic requirement of helping the neighbor can be exhausted at small cost. This notion of neighborhood benevolence, of seeing America as a nation of local communities, too easily leaves the poor clustered in their own neighborhood outside the boundaries of communal obligation.

As Disraeli said more than a century ago, "modern society knows no neighbors."[24] Yet the individual was not meant to stand alone. There is a need, an urge to belong to something or someone. It is only where we find a sense of belonging that we find people prepared to deny themselves for the good of others. "Without it," argues Charles Handy in *The Age of Paradox*, "duty and conscience have no meaning."[25] Jung went even further, concluding that it is only through others that we fully discover ourselves. In modern America, where so many of the connections that establish a sense of belonging have broken down, we no longer know clearly where we connect or where we belong. The essential question may not be why so many people are turning to crime and other forms of antisocial behavior, but why more are not. "Think of a person," said John Rawls, "without any sense of justice. He would be without any ties of affection, friendship or mutual trust, incapable of resentment or indignation. He would barge into a line if he could get away with it and expect everyone else to do the same. He would be less than human."[26]

The boundaries of community are changing demographically as well. Many Americans are familiar with statistics on the changing social, economic, and ethnic profile of their communities, but only a few have considered seriously the demographic implications of life in an increasingly interdependent world. According to Donella Matthews, author of *Limits to Growth*, if you lived in a representative global village of 1,000 people, 584 citizens would be Asians,

124 Africans, 95 East and West Europeans, 84 Latin Americans, 55 former Soviets, 52 North Americans, and 6 Australians and New Zealanders.[27]

The people of the village would have a difficult time communicating: Mandarin would be spoken by 165, English by 86, Hindi by 83, Spanish by 64, Russian by 58, and Arabic by 37. There would be 329 Christians (187 Catholics, 84 Protestants, and 31 Orthodox), 178 Muslims, 167 "nonreligious," 132 Hindus, 60 Buddhists, 45 atheists, 3 Jews, and 86 from other smaller religious groups. Of the people in the village, 330 would be children, with only half of them immunized against preventable infectious diseases. Half of the 670 adults would be illiterate. In this group of 1,000, only 330 would have access to clean, safe, drinking water, 20 percent would receive 70 percent of the total income, 500 would be hungry, and 600 would live in shantytowns.

It is, therefore, no surprise to find many people, in many parts of the world, asking how we shall deal with the pluralism of the new world order. Is there a common ground, a social glue, a civic ethic that transcends the many boundaries that divide us into "we" and "they" groups? One of the ironies of our time is that as communities around the world are becoming more alike—with our economies more interdependent and our lifestyles, values, and aspirations more similar—people are increasingly turning inward, seeking to return to smaller, more intimate forms of community. Hispanic Americans want to be both Hispanic and American. African Americans want to affirm both their African roots and their American identity. This may appear at first to be a contradiction, but what some fear as a new form of tribalism may in fact be a natural part of the search for common ground, a search for beginnings.

The boundaries of community are changing not only conceptually and demographically but also functionally. In the past, Americans have thought of their society as divided between three sectors: a public sector driven by the ballot, a private sector driven by profit, and a voluntary or third sector driven by compassion. But just as many other nations are beginning more formally to develop a voluntary or social sector, the old boundaries are becoming ambiguous, with the private sector engaged in the delivery of social services for a profit and voluntary organizations turning to profit-making measures to compensate for the loss in government revenues.

The functional problems of a benevolent community can be seen on another level as well. The traditions of private benevolence we have been examining in minority communities served them well when they were denied equal access to the resources of the American society, but they are the first to point out that when we seek to meet human and social needs primarily through private means, we run into some very serious limitations.

The first is financial insufficiency. The central shortcoming of private benevolence is its inability to generate resources on a scale that is both adequate and consistent enough to cope with the social needs of an advanced industrial society. Whenever the burden of coping with the social needs of a society is largely dependent on private action, the resources made available will almost certainly be less than what a truly benevolent community considers optimal.[28]

The second limitation of private action is individual preference. Those who use private resources for public purposes will rarely do so in such a way as to benefit all segments of the community equally. Thus, serious gaps may occur in the coverage of categories of need as well as groups in need. The emphasis is usually on meeting particular needs rather than addressing the general welfare.

The third limitation is democratic process. Excessive dependence on private benevolence to meet social needs and solve social problems may place the influence over defining needs and determining which are to be met in the hands of those commanding the greatest resources. The nature and extent of the society's benevolence becomes shaped not by the general citizenry but by the wealthier members of the society.

Does this suggest, then, that private benevolence is of dubious value in maintaining a caring community? Quite the contrary; it

..phasizes the importance of developing compassionate values and encouraging private generosity. But it puts it in perspective by emphasizing that in a truly benevolent community the consensus welfare needs of the society are met by the people in common while philanthropic individuals and institutions—true to their voluntary status—selectively choose which public purpose they will serve. They may choose to provide housing for the homeless. They may choose to feed those who are hungry. They may choose to heal the sick. But if we truly intend to promote the general welfare, we cannot leave it to the private choices and preferences of those who elect to be benevolent.

From this, we come to the central question of the twentieth century: how do we define community geographically? What is a border? The changing boundaries of community in the Pacific Rim, the increasing prospects for change in the Middle East, and the continuing out-migration of indigenous population groups in Latin America all challenge our ability to sustain the notion of communities defined by old geographical boundaries. But in the end, the decline of the nation-state as the primary custodian of the civic culture may have greatest implication for those who seek to define community geographically. Many cities are spilling into multistate jurisdictions and many people who live on national borders are simply ignoring them as a defining boundary.

The Continuing Barriers to Community

While the boundaries of community are changing, many of the old barriers continue. Three are especially threatening to the many efforts to form a more perfect union: (1) the resurgence of racism, (2) the resurgence of nativism, and (3) the emergence of a social deficit that is just as troubling as the twin deficits of international trade and the federal budget.

Perhaps few changes are as unsettling as the decline of European dominance abroad and the declining influence of the descendants of Europe at home. Just as American culture today is the amalgamation of Anglo-European and Mediterranean populations (German, Irish, Italian, Slavic) of the 1800s, so it will be redefined by the new population groups of the twentieth and twenty-first centuries.

That inevitable evolution in the American culture, unfortunately, raises discomfort and concern in many quarters of society. Racism and nativism are once again permeating our private and public interactions. To the extent we allow these destructive attitudes to continue, they will heighten the possibility of discord and make civic solidarity and social cohesion impossible.

In *Race Matters*, Cornel West has persuaded many Americans that our society is a long way from the color blindness many prefer.[29] Even national polls support the West thesis. A 1993 USA Today/CNN/Gallup poll found that a majority of Americans, both black and white, believe that race relations "will always be a problem" in the United States. Among African Americans, this opinion represented a significant change from 1963 when only 26 percent agreed with this statement. Now 55 percent of blacks and 53 percent of whites share this growing pessimism about the future of race relations.[30] Derrick Bell of Harvard has also proclaimed the permanency of racism. According to Bell, "Racism in America is not a curable aberration—as we all believed at some earlier point. Rather, it is a key component in this country's stability."[31] One does not have to be as pessimistic as Bell to conclude that the astonishing disappearance of race from public discussion is testimony to just how painful and distressing a serious engagement with the subject is.[32] Race does matter and it is likely to continue to be a barrier to community for some time to come.

Nativism, the discomfort with the foreign born who appear to be different, is an equally important barrier to community. It is not new, however. It appeared in the 1860s when Irish immigration hit its peak after the potato famines of the 1840s; in 1880 when the railroads reached the west coast and the large numbers of Chinese workers employed to build them were no longer needed; in the 1920s when the National Origin Quota System was enacted to restrict those who didn't "look American." In the 1990s we are seeing a repeat reaction, but this time to the arrival of so many new groups in the 1980s. Nativism in any guise, but especially when combined with racism, delays and retards our ability finally to form a more perfect union. Delay in the social and upward mobility of these new groups and the indigenous minorities who compete with them for a place on the margins will severely affect our ability to foster pluralism and at the same time maintain enough coherence to act as a single community.

In addition to racism and nativism, another troubling barrier to community is the large social deficit that we have allowed to accumulate alongside the twin deficits of international trade and the federal budget. This social deficit, with its high poverty levels and the growing isolation and alienation of those left behind, is a loud signal of impending danger to the social cohesion of the nation. Whatever we may think about the Great Society programs initiated in the 1960s, they signaled, despite the success of some and the failure of others, a strong element of hope and optimism in the very poor and a pride in their collective identity. Even in the darkest days of the Ku Klux Klan's terrorizing of African Americans, deportations of Hispanics from the Southwest, incarceration of Japanese Americans, and the many manifestations of racism in this century, we did not have the profound levels of alienation and despair found in many American ghettos and barrios today. To the extent that the descendants of these groups give up on American social and cultural life, we are likely to see the social fabric continue to unravel.

Subsequent chapters of this book present overwhelming reasons to believe that the historic pragmatism that has seen generation after generation of Americans balance private generosity with public benevolence will continue. When Americans think of paradigms of community, they are likely to recall John Winthrop's vision of a city on a hill in which "we delight in each other, seek to make other's condition our own, rejoice together, labor and suffer together, always having before our eyes our community as members of the same body."[33] Others, both Christians and non-Christians, point to the vision of the Apostle Paul who spoke of a community in which "Jews or Greeks, slaves or free" were to have "the same care for one another. If one member suffers, all suffer together; if one member is honored, all rejoice together."[34] And still others are likely to be influenced by the dreams of Mahatma Ghandi and Martin Luther King, Jr., who, like Thoreau at Walden Pond, built castles in the sky and then set out to put foundations under them.

But as this work demonstrates, we need to make room for the visions of Chief Seattle, the legendary Suquamish Indian leader, who sought to transform a young nation's vision of national community into a new form of earth community in which humanity seeks to live at harmony with itself, with nature, and with the cosmos; Thomy Lafon, an African-American aristocrat, who contributed so much of his own money to the building of New Orleans that the nineteenth-century Louisiana legislature authorized the creation of a bust in his likeness to honor him for his philanthropy; Sister Isolina Ferre, whose work among the poor in Ponce caused her to be called the "Mother Teresa" of Puerto Rico; and Le Ly Hayslip, a Vietnamese-American woman who experienced the worst wounds of war, but despite everything has been able to establish the West Meets East Foundation to convey the message of forgiveness and reconciliation while aiding the bruised and battered in her home country. There are many others like Patrick Okura, who was placed in an American detention camp for Japanese Americans during World War II, but used the reparation payment he received years later to begin a foundation to help other Americans; and Reuben Snake, a spiritual leader in the Native American Church, who combined its peyote sacrament with a pan-Indian ethic of "brotherly union." These are but a few of the Americans whose life and legacy are contributing to a new civic culture and defining a new civic ethic. Their visions of community come out of their own unique experiences, but, as the following pages reveal, the values they affirm are consistent with those of the cultural heroes better known and more widely celebrated.

Native Americans

Chapter One

The Tribe as Benevolent Community

Few Americans are aware of the impact Native Americans had on the stream of ideas that shaped the early American vision of community. From the first enduring English settlement in North America to the present, the perception of the Native American has evolved from the Puritans' devil-man, to the autonomous "Noble Savage," to the acknowledgment that "the native peoples lived in confederations governed by natural law so subtle, so nearly invisible, as to be an attractive alternative to monarchy's overbearing hand."[1] The advanced democratic practices of the Iroquois, for example, fitted very well with the abstract principles of democracy already forming in the minds of the European settlers. But the Native American concept of community contained elements that went far beyond the theories of civil society espoused by Locke, Rousseau, Hegel, and other European thinkers.

From the beginning, American Indians and the European settlers had very different cognitive maps. The epistemology and worldview of the Europeans, their science, their technology, and their theology were based on group-validated experiences of the human community. The cultural disposition of the Native American by contrast was much more subjective, much more influenced by individual experiences with nature, the spirits, and the power beings that inhabited the natural world. Most Americans of European origin, for example, associate land with the idea of property rights that comes from English Common Law and the Magna Carta. Native Americans, on the other hand, see land as existing in itself rather than as something to be owned. They see animals as power beings with a spirit; to them, even plants have their own unique essence. Thus, to abuse the land is to abuse or dishonor all the spirits that exist there. The reverse is also true. To respect and work in harmony with nature is to ensure the benevolence of its spirit and power. For them, not only human beings but all living things have the capacity for benevolence.

The 1.7 million Native Americans who live in the United States speak 200 languages and come from more than 500 tribes and native groups. When a second category, Americans of Indian descent, is included, the population swells to seven million. The remarkable heterogeneity to be found in both groups reflects the astonishing variety in American-Indian tradition and culture. Some of the aboriginal tribes were farmers with stable community life while others were hunters constantly on the move. Primary communities of heritage were sometimes linked together by male descent, others by female. The people of each culture had their own relationships to the supernatural, their own heroes from the past, their own perceptions of proper and improper behavior, and their own name for themselves, often meaning something like "the people" or "original beings."[2]

Despite these important differences, the aboriginal tribes shared in common the belief that the earth is sacred and all things on it are holy. In human relationships, as well as in the relationship with nature, the emphasis was on reciprocity and connectedness. Each person was expected to live and work in harmony not simply with members of the family or the tribe but with all living things—"the deer, the horses, things that crawl, things that fly, things that grow in and on the ground."[3]

This feeling of oneness with the world is best exemplified by the worldview of the Pueblo tribes in the southwestern United States. According to the creation myth of the Pueblos, Indian life began in a primordial home where men, gods, and animals lived together in community. In that distant time, humans were not the masters of nature, but mediators of complex relationships among all living things. Jay Miller, one of the contributors to *America in 1492*, points out that to most native inhabitants on the eve of the sustained contact with Europeans, humans were regarded as the nexus or link in the interplay of immortals (the supernaturals of a locale) and mortals (all the species that lived, died, and were reborn in the habitat).[4] Through special relationships, renewed generation after generation, particular immortals and members of special human families worked to maintain the spiritual and ecological balance of a region.[5] When local resources were used, of whatever kind and for whatever purpose, the appropriate immortals were compensated through appropriate prayers, offerings, procedures, and rituals.

Yet, while animals and some plants had a human-like essence and trees and streams had spiritual energy, the touchstone for all interaction was the human community. There is, thus, as much to be learned from the cosmology of Native Americans about living in harmony with the human environment as there is about the natural and moral environments. Every school child learns that the indigenous people Christopher Columbus encountered in the Americas had ideas about mind and spirit that were alien to the early settlers. They are not usually taught, however, that deeply ingrained in the political culture, civic habits, and even the soul of America are social ideas that had their genesis in tribal communities.

Political philosophers as different as Thomas Paine and Karl Marx saw the Indian tribe as a model of social organization and communal life. Paine was enamored particularly of the Indians' personal liberty, their freedom from rulers and social classes. Marx idealized their economic lives, communal ownership of property, and placement of group interest over individual interest. Writing later about Marx's fascination with the Indian tribal community, Engels described life among the Iroquois as a condition in which there "cannot be any poor or needy—the communal household and the gens know their responsibility toward the old, the sick and those disabled in war."[6] In Marxist theory, the final communist society would be an industrialized version of the Iroquois social system in

which "all are free and equal—the women included."[7] Eventually
Marx and Engels translated the Iroquois image into a European one
that fit their own materialist theories and, thus, the ideas embodied in communism lost all connection to the Iroquois or any other
Indian group.

The democratic and egalitarian nature of most Indian tribes
caught the attention of political philosophers and journalists in
both America and Europe. Sir Thomas More wrote about it in his
1516 book *Utopia*, and Michel de Montaigne, the French essayist,
was specifically attracted to the tribes' lack of magistrates, forced
services, riches, and poverty.[8] Benjamin Franklin, however, was the
first to see in the communal life of Native Americans important features that could be a model for a new form of community among
the European settlers. While serving as Indian commissioner for the
colonial government of Pennsylvania, Franklin became intrigued
with the political and civic culture of the Iroquois. Speaking to the
Albany Congress in 1754, he called on the delegates of the various
English colonies to unite and emulate the civic habits of the Iroquois who had, at that time, the world's only true democracy—a
supreme chief, a legislative council, and a judicial branch as well as
universal suffrage and direct representation.[9]

This fascination with Native American models of community
did not go unnoticed by Indian leaders anxious to develop more
respect for their traditions. Charles Eastman, speaking in 1919 to a
conference of fellow Indian leaders, described his conception of the
Indian contribution to America:

> We Indians laid the foundation of freedom and equality and democ-
> racy long before any Europeans came and took it up but they do not
> give us credit. . . . We did not take anybody's land, we never
> enslaved anybody . . . we developed man, man was man, and he
> loved his God. . . . We all believe in one God. That too was our con-
> tribution to this country . . . we were that character, the original
> American character. . . . We must keep our heads and our hearts

together. Keep our old characteristics that we have contributed to this country—those characteristics that have been put into the Constitution of the United States itself.[10]

Some of the scholars and historians who write about early Native American life are now beginning to give these people credit for their sophisticated political and economic organization, but little attention has yet been paid to their tradition of sharing and reciprocity that predated the practices of charity and philanthropy of the European settlers. The Indians were in fact the first American philanthropists. The Europeans would not have survived their initial winter without gifts of corn, squash, and beans as well as herbal medicine and planting and fertilizing techniques from the Indians. Moved by their generosity, Columbus wrote in his journal that "no request of anything from them is ever refused, but they rather invite acceptance of what they possess, and manifest such a generosity that they would give away their own hearts."[11]

The generosity to the new settlers was not an isolated act of benevolence. The early Indian tribe was by its very nature a benevolent community in which sharing was a primary virtue and selfishness a primary vice. The exchange of goods and services according to carefully prescribed norms was the key to social relationships. One common custom that exemplifies this is called the *giveaway*, an elaborate ceremony for the sharing of possessions. As a form of reciprocity, it assures the giver social recognition and acknowledges the receiver as a person of worth. The person who accomplishes something significant will accumulate things to give away with the intent to honor the community that fostered the individual and the achievement.[12] In Native American tradition, wealth is generated for its distribution, not its accumulation. The good of the community takes precedence over the good of the individual. Even the tribal chief accumulated wealth in order to meet his responsibility to widows, orphans, and others. This practice often made him the poorest member of the community.

The most highly developed example of the giveaway is the *potlatch*. Widely practiced among northwest coast Indians, it is a gathering to which the host group invites other groups, with which it has some relationship, and gives to them huge quantities of goods. Each potlatch sets up obligations of reciprocity by the invited guests, who must match the display of wealth in order to maintain their own status. While all contributions, no matter how small, receive community recognition, the number and value of the goods an individual gives away determine his or her status within the comity.

In earlier days, members of the tribe often competed with each other to give away the most. This produced economic as well as social benefits by distributing goods widely through the community. The purpose of accumulating possessions was not to maintain them permanently, but to acquire them in order that they might be shared.

Gift giving took many forms. The rites performed for an individual at birth, puberty, marriage, death, and other major ceremonies were often accompanied by a feast. There was usually a host family group and a guest group of nonrelatives who were invited to attend the celebration. The hosts provided the guests with food as long as the ceremony lasted. At some later date, the roles were reversed; the guests became the hosts and the hosts became the guests.

The uniqueness of benevolence in the Native American tradition is that it is a form of sharing rather than a form of charity.[13] A gift, in fact, focusing on the gift distorts the dynamics involved, since the proper focus is the exchange. The exchange itself is an acknowledgment of relationship and of contribution to the community. Thus, the manner in which something is given and the manner in which it is received is of paramount importance. *I honor you* by giving; it is not done to make you feel beholden and small. *You honor me* by receiving the small token of my esteem for all you have contributed. Giveaways, therefore, are not so much person to person as they are person to community in recognition of member-ship.[14] Even providing housing for the elderly cannot be regarded as welfare because it is "honoring," supporting the elderly in the present for their past contributions.

The giveaway best reflected the Native American tradition of benevolence and the social utility of wealth. This penchant for giving continues in intertribal powwows that feature a blend of the old and the new. People arrive in vans rather than on foot or on horses and they use public address systems and electrical lighting for their ceremonies. In *Indian Givers*, Jack Weatherford reports on a gathering in Fargo, North Dakota:

> Between one set of dances, a family comes to the fore to distribute presents in honor of their teenage daughter, who has taken her grandmother's Indian name. The young girl presents gifts of blankets, embroidered pieces of Indian bead jewelry, cartons of cigarettes, and money to people who have helped her mature to this stage of life. She then leads off a dance in their honor. Between dances, someone occasionally rises to honor another person, commemorate an event, announce an upcoming powwow, or welcome a group that has traveled particularly far to participate in that night's festivities. . . . Today the powwow blends traits of a dozen different Indian groups together with items borrowed from white culture, just as some of the Indians have blond hair and green eyes. Some have "typical" Indian names while others have Norwegian, Irish or French names. Despite all the blending however, some very basic Indian values dominate.[15]

Paramount among these values is the tradition of sharing. Giving is not charity but honoring the community, not even a matter of altruism but of mutual responsibility. Native Americans covet the freedom of the individual, but the good of the community takes precedence. Gift-giving is a unifying cultural trait in which both the giver and the receiver are honored and their equal status validated.

The Benevolent Practices of Urban Indians

After European colonization, the social structure of tribal societies was practically destroyed and the bonds of family and kinship changed. The notion of community, once reflected primarily in tribal terms, took on a pan-Indian character as many Native Americans settled in cities and towns. Here they developed voluntary groups and self-help associations that largely resembled those of the population groups they found there. Some were mysterious and included an elaborate ritual. Others were cloaked in secrecy. Most, however, were fraternal and social clubs established to help retain an Indian identity or to extend a benevolent hand to the members of the community most in need.

One of the earliest fraternal groups was the Teepee Order founded in 1915. It was a curious blend of ideas and rituals from white Masonic clubs and Indian life. Reflecting the prevailing attitudes of the time, only Indians and whites of the United States, Canada, and Latin America were eligible for membership.[16] The American Indian Association, established in 1922 as a branch of the Teepee Order, made a special effort to enlist eminent whites in its ranks, but it barred blacks.[17] The Order's reasons for excluding blacks took on a somewhat defensive tone. "We have nothing against the black race, but we do not allow any member of Negro strain to be a member of our organization. We take the same stand, very strictly, regarding this point that the white race does in white organizations. So long as the white race holds this, we will."[18]

This was a far different position from that taken by tribal Indians who earlier befriended escaped slaves, welcomed them into their ranks, elevated them to positions of leadership, and celebrated them in folklore as great warriors. Black Indians played a major role in the early days of Florida history, forming a powerful African-Seminole Alliance that developed very successful settlements and fought the U.S. military to a standstill for forty years. It was, thus, no surprise that even the Teepee Order retreated from its position taken in the 1920s when white associates sought to convince Indian fraternal groups that mingling with blacks was contrary to the laws of nature.

Most of the local Indian voluntary groups seemed to mushroom, flourish for a time, and then fade away, sometimes to rise again in new forms.[19] But like the many benevolent acts among whites that deTocqueville described as "habits of the heart,"[20] voluntary activity among urban Indians was a fundamental part of urban life. Some groups like the Wigwam Club were founded to help Indian boys and girls. Others like the "Wa-Tha-Huck" (Brings Light Club) were exclusively for women. The activities of the various clubs were quite similar—fraternal, social, and educational—and the leadership of the clubs tended to be both Indian and white.

While the earliest form of voluntary Native American organizations off the reservation were primarily fraternal and social, later groups were reformist and political. With the hopes of pan-Indian armed resistance or supernatural deliverance now dashed on the reservation, an Indian reform movement aimed at more benevolent public policies began to take shape. Groups like the Society of American Indians, formed in 1910, became explicitly political, using legal and other means to investigate Indian problems and to obtain remedies. They were also in the forefront of efforts to define a new Indian consciousness that went beyond the limitations of mere tribal communities. At the third annual conference of the Society in Denver in 1913, a young Indian named Oliver Lamere addressed the issue of Indian self-reliance, self-help, and community in a new way. The members of the society had chosen as their theme "What the Indian can do for himself, for his race, and for his country." Lamere, who was descended from French ancestors on his father's side and Winnebago on his mother's, spoke for the pragmatists who wanted to forge a "union with the civic life of America."[21] He sought to integrate the most positive and usable elements of Indian life and of the larger American society. What, then, he asked, should the Indian take from America? "Her practical sense, her energy, the courage with which she faces the problems of life and conquers them, . . . and ethical ideals, even though she has failed lamentably from practicing them."[22]

What elements of Indian life should be incorporated into this new civic union? For Lamere, it was "a love of nature and an acquaintance with nature which few whites know; ethical and moral teachings fully as high as those of Christianity, and in fact coinciding with them . . . and lastly, but not least, Indian art."[23] Lamere argued that this vision of a new community did not mean that Indian elements and American elements would become so intertwined that they would lose their individual identity. Rather, he believed that there could be "a union of parts and still a separate individual existence of these parts."[24] He was convinced that although the result of the union was one distinctive culture, the parts composing it could still retain their distinctive life and ideals.

In addition to fraternal and reform groups off the reservations, a religious pan-Indianism emerged that led to the development of new forms of voluntary association among the traditionalists who had remained on the reservation. The earliest form of pan-Indian religion was the Ghost Dance of the late nineteenth and early twentieth centuries. A messianic movement with a message of amenity and peace, it contained a personal as well as a collective ethic. The dance ritual united its participants in an effort to hasten the return of aboriginal time when tribal communities were meaningful expressions of the dignity, aspirations, culture, and self-sufficiency of a proud people. The appeal of the Ghost Dance was its doctrine rather than the dance itself. It was predicated on the belief in an Indian millennium or "return of the ghosts," when the Ghost Spirit would liberate the Indians from white dominance. A new community was to emerge with the decimated ranks reinforced by the resurrection of all the Indians who had ever died. There would be a new heaven and a new earth with boundless prairies covered with green grass and populated by great herds of buffalo and other game. The doctrine of the Ghost Dance included not simply a widely accepted eschatology but a moral ethic as well. According to James Murray, an anthropologist who investigated the Ghost Dance religion in the late 1880s for the Bureau of American Ethnology, its moral code was as pure and simple as anything found in religious systems from the days of Gautama Buddha to the time of Jesus Christ.[25] It emphasized such virtues as honesty, "do not tell a lie"; goodwill, "do no harm to anyone"; and a communal ethic, "do right always."

The Ghost Dance was succeeded by an intertribal cult that used peyote in its rituals. The peyote cult's identity as a pan-Indian rather than a tribal or a white man's religion enabled its adherents to play a greater role in the development of an intertribal consciousness than occurred with any of the other varieties of pan-Indianism. It was, thus, a social as well as a religious force creating community across traditional tribal boundaries. The virtues associated with this new religion were not unlike those enunciated by Christianity: love, faith, hope, charity, and the avoidance of adultery, drunkenness, stealing, and lying.

The use of peyote in the Ghost Dance ritual, however, engendered such strong opposition to its practice that even the reform organizations that originally opposed it felt compelled to come to its defense as a legitimate compromise between the old ways and the new. Christian missionaries saw it less as a religion than as a subterfuge for the use of peyote. Officials in the Bureau of Indian Affairs, then known as the Indian Bureau, were opposed because of their fear of any expression of Indian independence. Even the old-time medicine men opposed it because of its obvious threat to their own practices. But despite opposition that extended all the way to the U.S. Congress, the peyote religion attracted such a strong following that some of its believers incorporated it in 1918 as the Native American Church. In choosing the term *Native American Church*, they were emphasizing the intertribal solidarity of the new religious community as well as hoping to gain the same guarantees of religious freedom as those granted the Christian church. By 1934, the peyote religion had become the traditional religious faith of many Indians, something in which they could take pride because they created and operated it themselves, something that linked them with an Indian past while allowing them to function in a new and changed present.

Voluntary, self-help, and associational life among Native Americans was, thus, reformist, religious, and fraternal. In this regard, the civic infrastructure in Indian communities paralleled the civil institutions of the larger society. Although many of the old ways have been lost, giveaways continue and community members still take responsibility for each other, and the honor of giving and receiving is still recognized.

New Forms of Self-Help

After years of neglect, poverty, and the social experiments of the Bureau of Indian Affairs, many Indian tribes began in the 1970s and 1980s to develop new strategies for economic development, self-help, and benevolence. Some tribes turned to entrepreneurship. As under secretary of the interior, I was privileged to be a part of the land-claim settlement with the Pasmaquoddy Indians of Maine who used the $81.5 million they shared with the Penobscot tribes to develop tribal enterprises with a vigor and success that won even Wall Street's admiration. Their goal from the beginning was to use the land-claims money to solve unemployment, create and use wealth for the well-being of the community, and to change their dependency status. The Mississippi Choctaws, the Salt-River Pima Maricopa of Arizona, and the Jicarilla Apache of New Mexico have likewise built successful tribal enterprises. Responding to the energy crisis of the 1970s, tribes with oil and other natural resources formed the Council of Energy Resource Tribes (CERT) to achieve similar objectives. Those fortunate enough to have valuable resources on their reservations found themselves with large infusions of cash. But in the 1980s, oil prices plunged and Indian mineral revenues with them.

A recent trend has been to set up lucrative gambling operations on reservations. The tribes who have chosen this option have found themselves in the middle of a national debate about the freedom of tribes to choose their own strategies for economic development, self-help, and communal life. The Shakopee Mdewakanton Sioux, a federally recognized tribe of 250 members on a self-governing reservation in Minnesota, probably best represent this blend of old communal values with new forms of economic life. This small tribe has used revenue from gaming not only to provide for its members but also to make donations to other tribes as well as to surrounding non-Indian communities, schools, and charities.

By 1991, gaming was bringing to Indian reservations more than $1.3 billion a year. In Minnesota, home of the Minnesota Sioux, it created 4,500 jobs and reduced Indian welfare rolls by 16 percent. Yet major questions are raised by many who attack the social improvement spawned by gaming as tainted benevolence. Some Native American activists regard gaming as a quick fix that makes tribes vulnerable to exploitation by smooth-talking salesmen. Leonard Prescott, the tribal chair of the Shakopee Sioux, also serves as chair of the National Indian Gaming Association and was instrumental in the development of the Federal Indian Gaming Regulatory Act of 1988. According to members of his staff, he believes that gaming not only provides badly needed cash, but also fuels other forms of self-sufficiency, permitting tribes to do for themselves what neither the federal government nor tribal neighbors have been willing to do.

The Native American desire for independence and self-help remains deeply imbedded in the culture of the group as well as the psyche of the individual. The strong dependence on government is not of their own choosing and is clearly at odds with the aspirations, inclinations, and civic traditions of their community. But only

about one in ten tribes today has any means of producing a significant amount of revenue. Conventional capital sources like the
American Indian Bank and philanthropic resources like the Seventh Generation Fund are all part of the landscape of new strategies for self-help. But without the capital and skills needed to
compete in a complex interdependent economy, a rich tradition of
sharing and caring for the common good is threatened by the
pathologies that powerlessness and hopelessness inevitably breed.

At present, giving patterns among Native Americans differ
depending on whether a person is socialized in an urban or reservation environment. Reservation-based Native Americans tend to
give more to family and community while those in urban areas give
more to an intertribal network or pan-Indian activities. However,
despite the high poverty rate in Native American communities,
their members are considered by many to be the most generous people in America.

For five hundred years we have underrated and often ignored
the real contributions of American Indians to the cultural, social,
and political life of our nation. It is time that we move away from
viewing them primarily as objects of study and begin to see them as
a people with much to teach. The three profiles that follow provide
a helpful start in this regard. They are living testimonies to the wisdom of the Native American vision of community and the benevolent tradition it reflects.

Chapter Two

Chief Seattle:
Every Part of the Earth Is Sacred

It has become fashionable to denigrate the life and stature of the legendary Suquamish Indian chief Seattle, who, until recently, occupied a special place on the list of Native American cultural heroes. The license taken with Seattle's nineteenth-century speech by a screenwriter more than one hundred years later has sometimes obscured the many reliable accounts of his life that preceded the more recent "eco-homilies" placed in his mouth.

Chief Seattle devoted most of his life to promoting peace and community; first, among warring tribes whom he brought together in an alliance known as the Dwamish Confederacy; later, with white settlers who brought strange ideas, habits, and expansionist ambitions to his village. And through it all he maintained that land and people were a united whole, bound together by bonds going back to the creation of the world. Like most Native Americans of his time, he saw society as an all-encompassing moral order whose members included many species and living forms, only some of whom were humans. Every terrain was saturated with the spirits that were the custodians of the landscape. Every hillside, every valley, and every plain were suffused with sacredness. The Sioux called this holiness *wakan*, the Ojibwa and other Algonkian peoples called it *manitu*, and the Iroquois called it *orenda*.[1] But while this vision of holiness was a part of the religion and philosophy of every tribe, no one gave it the clarity and eloquence that Chief Seattle provided. Described by all who knew him as a powerful orator, his translator reported that his words were like poetry. Writing in the *Seattle Sunday Star*, October 29, 1887, Henry A. Smith said, "When rising to

37

speak in Council or tendering advice, all eyes were turned upon him, and deep-toned, sonorous and eloquent sentences rolled from his lips like the ceaseless thunder of cataracts flowing from exhaustless fountains."[2] He added that Chief Seattle's eloquence, dignity, and grace were as native to his manhood as are needles and cones to a great pine tree.[3] James Vernon Metcalfe, son of the first attorney general for the Territory of Washington, gave the same testimony in his writings at the turn of the century. A historian and president of the Pioneer Association of the State of Washington for twelve years, he wrote an autobiography in which he described Chief Seattle as an "exemplar of the theme Peace on Earth."[4]

Seattle's idea of community combined the spiritual vision he experienced as a young man with the wisdom he demonstrated in old age. While he was still a boy, wandering along the edge of the sound he knew as the Whulge but later called Puget Sound, a seagull appeared to him as if in a dream—what the Suquamish called a *ta-man-a-wis*. The gull was a symbol of peace to the Suquamish, and its appearance in a vision to young Seattle indicated that he was to spend his life in search of peace and harmony. And so it was that he spent forty-three years as chief of the Suquamish, making peace while others were waging war. Ironically, Seattle first distinguished himself as a warrior, when as a young man he planned and led an alliance of six coastal tribes against inland "horse tribes." It was this military triumph that won him the position of chief of the Allied Tribes (the Dwamish Confederacy).

With his compelling oratory and mighty influence, Chief Seattle could have aroused and united a force capable of wiping out every settler north of California, but he became a peacemaker instead, leaving it to future generations to ponder why. His instincts for making allies out of adversaries may have been inherited or inculcated at an early age. His father, a Suquamish tribesman, once persuaded other tribes around Puget Sound to join him in building a potlatch house large enough that all the tribes in the area might gather in it to share food, friendship, and peace. Young Seattle grew up in the shadow of the potlatch house which by its sheer size, one thousand feet in length, was an imposing reminder of the indigenous custom of gift-giving; it housed as many as eight thousand Indians under its roof on some occasions. The potlatch festivals helped to forge the social cohesion that kept the peace with the surrounding tribes.

The potlatch house was built along a narrow strip of water separating an offshore island from the mainland. A bank of earth protected the area from the north winds, and the flat and sandy beach made it easily accessible by canoe. Covering almost two acres, the potlatch house served also as a fort for the allied tribes. But it was the experience of working together to build the potlatch house as well as the success of the festivals held in it that helped to bring an end to intertribal wars.

Seattle's father Schweabe took the potlatch tradition a step beyond the practice of gift-giving and feasting to a new dimension of peacemaking and community-building. In doing so, he also imbued young Seattle with the caring instincts that began with a very special compassion for the Suquamish tribes and came to embrace the white settlers as well. The values Seattle later demonstrated were learned from his family during his early childhood. They seemed to have passed through the three "foundation stones" of moral development described by Michael Schulman and Eva Mekler in *Bringing Up a Moral Child*: the internalization of parental standards, the development of empathy, and the formation of personal standards.[5] While the product of a very different moral and political culture, Seattle appears also to have followed this path.

Another factor that shaped and reinforced Seattle's benevolence was his religion. Although he later converted to Christianity, he was first influenced by the religion of his ancestors. In his reply to the government's offer to buy Indian lands, he said, "Your religion was written on tablets of stone by the iron fingers of your God so that you could not forget. Our religion is the traditions of our ancestors—the dreams of our old men, given them in the solid hours of night by the Great Spirit, and the visions of our sachems; and it is written in the hearts of our people."[6] Written in the heart of Seattle was a profile of moral development, blending a healthy dose of the individualism and ego strength needed to be a strong leader with the commitment to community needed to be a compassionate leader.

Kindness and concern for all people was a hallmark of Seattle's behavior, but his moral capacity to think in terms of a larger whole was a trait traditionally associated with all chiefs. According to Jay Miller in *America in 1492*, all Indian communities had leaders, mature members of special families well versed in local lore, sacred history, and a concern for the greater good of everyone. "Unlike other individuals," Miller argued, "these leaders thought in terms of the larger whole, not just their own families and households."[7] Seattle's notion of community, however, went beyond traditional boundaries. In the customary thought of his day, each community was its own world, operating in partial isolation from other groups in its regional networks, except for special threshold moments.[8] The idiom of kinship, mortals and immortals as well, related everything within a community or region to everything else, but the idiom did not necessarily apply to more distant peoples.[9] Seattle's vision, on the other hand, had no such limits.

Leadership in Indian tribes was usually a function of age. The older a leader, the more venerated and respected he was likely to be. But Seattle became leader of the allied tribes at the age of twenty-two. His power was not the power of age or even of reputation as a warrior, gained by winning a strategic military victory; his was the power of persuasion. A tribal leader never ordered anyone to do anything. Leadership was by example and negotiation. Whenever a leader thought that an action was necessary, negotiation was required. Through these negotiations—often extended councils to create consensus—the task would be accomplished, but not until everyone agreed or became resigned to the outcome.[10] As part of the power of persuasion to ensure a desired outcome, the leader who believed something was imperative was likely to present it as having been demanded by the Great Spirit or other immortals. Native Americans of Seattle's time, thus, had their own communal rhythms and social processes reinforced by a sense of connection with a universal spirit. No decision was made without a consideration of its impact on the whole of the created order.

The persuasive powers of Seattle were first evident shortly after he was made chief of the allied tribes. Still a very young man in his early twenties, he learned that the new federation had detractors who were not yet prepared to enter fully into this new union. Instead of using a military strategy like other leaders of his time, including the European settlers, Seattle made a voyage along Lake Washington, holding powwows with the various tribesmen, persuading them that unity was in the best interest of all the tribes. He was thoroughly convinced that mutual understanding and a shared vision was the key to community and harmony. He appreciated and affirmed the meaning and significance of the past, but he was not a prisoner of history. His cosmic clock liberated him for a larger vision of community rather than enslaving him in the older paradigms.

Seattle's view of the world was expanded when he was quite young. The date of his birth was uncertain, but it is assumed to have been sometime around 1786. This means that as a boy he witnessed the arrival in Puget Sound of the British explorer Vancouver and his men in 1792. Even one so young could hardly have missed the furor created by the arrival of the immense ship that the local Indians called a "white-winged bird." Deciding that the vessel was only a huge canoe, Schweabe and his young son who was to become Chief Seattle were among those who paddled out to visit the strange passengers, according to legend. While it is not known for certain whether Seattle was actually a part of the greeting party, he did speak frequently in later years of this visit and Vancouver's friendliness. His first encounter with the white settlers was, thus, an amicable experience that remained with him in memory for the rest of his life.

Seattle had his moments of pathos as well. Long before he was moved to say "the Indian night promises to be dark," he knew the travails of personal misfortune. As he had approached maturity, his father, Schweabe, and his mother, Scholitza, had selected a bride for him. In the spring of 1811, a girl was born who became known as the Princess Angeline. Her mother never fully recovered from the birth and soon died. Seattle was grief-stricken and sought relief in gambling. The gaming sessions were reported to last for a week, with large bets of clothing, fishing gear, furs, and shells.[11] Seattle eventually married again and his life returned to normalcy.

This was also the time that whites began to settle along the Columbia River to the south causing great consternation among neighboring tribal groups. Seattle's interaction with white settlers did not begin until the Hudson Bay Company of Canada established the first white settlement on Puget Sound in 1833. His first experiences with the traders were somewhat disappointing in that they did not possess the civility of manner or the respect for others that were a part of Seattle's nature. He found the missionaries who came later more to his liking. The first missionary he met was a big man called Sampson by the other priests. Seattle respected him and spread the word "to come and hear the big man with the big idea."[12] A man who knew the power of words, Seattle was fascinated with the spellbinding Bible stories that attracted so many Indians to the big man Sampson.

The missionaries opened up a new world of thought and theology to Seattle. Finding parallels to their teachings in his own experience, especially the idea that the Great Spirit meant for all people to love one another, he became a Christian. He helped persuade many of his tribesmen to join him in his new journey of faith, making morning and evening prayers a regular part of tribal life. But while Seattle was preaching his gospel of brotherhood in both the white and Indian communities, clashes between the two groups escalated. Other chiefs were urging their people to war to resist the encroachment of the white settlers. Just as strongly, Seattle urged the tribes of his federation to refrain from violent encounters. His people followed his advice while the other tribes were soundly defeated. But as more land-hungry whites appeared on the landscape, both Seattle's vision and his values were severely tested. Even when whites settled at Alki Point, right across the sound from the potlatch house his father had built, Seattle greeted the newcomers with the same friendly reception that his father had given to the explorer Vancouver. Like Christopher Columbus's encounter three hundred years earlier, the Suquamish under Seattle's leadership shared with the white settlers both the supplies that had been gathered for the use of their families and the knowledge of how to survive in this lonely, rainy place. They taught the Easterners whom they called "Bostons" how to fish the rivers, where to dig for clams, and which plants of the woods and fields to use. They taught them how to split thick cedar logs, and when the settlers' milk supply ran out, the Indian women brought clam juice for the Boston babies.[13]

While Seattle and the Puget Sound tribes trusted the whites, opened their homes and their villages to them, and took delight in treating the strangers as members of their own community, many of the newcomers looked down on the Indians and called them savages. The indigenous people who had demonstrated both superior technical knowledge and moral virtue were regarded as outside the pale of the white settlers' humanity, becoming objects of their scorn rather than subjects of their embrace. Even as the great chief was reaching out his hand and his heart to the whites who needed him, some of their kinsmen were dashing from tribe to tribe, trying to persuade them to sign away their land in treaties.

Was Seattle a naive accommodationist who misunderstood the intentions and underestimated the heartlessness of the white settlers or was he a truly moral man who believed to the very end in the brotherhood of man? After all, it was Seattle who gave flesh and blood to the ideals that the white settlers brought with them. There is no way to know for certain, but his great speech (given in part below), in its original rendering, provided some insight into the measure of this extraordinary man. The times were changing. Seattle's dream of a benevolent community that was Indian and white, human and spirit, the living and the dead reborn, was fast losing its moral potency. Some tribes had tried to drive the whites out of the region. Others had tried the way of Seattle. Meanwhile, the white settlers were making a mockery of the ideals they had proclaimed as universal.

Against this backdrop, Seattle was notified that the Washington Territory's first governor and superintendent of Indian Affairs, Isaac I. Stevens, was planning to visit Puget Sound. Word reached Seattle's bands that he was coming to tell them of plans for a treaty that would place them on reservations. When Stevens arrived, he found the Indians assembled along the beach and a broad-shouldered, impressive man over six feet tall leading them. But while this was to be one of history's great confrontations, it was not a military encounter. It was, instead, the baring of the souls of two men on very different sides of history.

The time and the setting was the winter of January 1855, the beginning of the end of a moral experiment that failed. Stevens spoke first, choosing his words carefully, but there was no easy way to tell a people that their dreams were not to be fulfilled, that those whom they had trusted were about to take away their lands. When Stevens finished, Seattle, the man the *Seattle Sunday Star* of October 29, 1887, described as by far the noblest looking, came forward to speak. It is said that Seattle's trumpet tones rolled over the immense multitude like a reveille. As for Abraham Lincoln at Gettysburg or the Apostle Paul in Athens, this was Seattle's transcendent moment. John Rich, who wrote about Seattle long before he was discovered by the environmentalists and caught the attention of Hollywood, was one of the many who provided the text of the chief's speech. It was like John Adams's sermon on board a ship in Salem Harbor, a vision of community that was to endure. Seattle began, as one might expect, with a reference to the "tears of compassion" of his fathers. And then he continued:

The son of the White Chief says his father sends us greetings of friendship and good will. This is kind of him, for we know he has little need of our friendship in return because his people are many. They are like the grass that covers the vast prairies, while my people are few, they resemble the scattering trees of a storm-swept plain. . . .

There was a time when our people covered the whole land as the waves of a wind-ruffled sea cover its shell-paved floor, but that time has long since passed away with the greatness of tribes now almost forgotten. I will not dwell on nor mourn over our own timely decay, nor reproach my paleface brothers with hastening it, for we, too, may have been somewhat to blame. . . .

Let us hope that the hostilities between the Red Man and his paleface brother may never return. We would have everything to lose and nothing to gain. It is true that revenge by young braves is considered gain, even at the cost of their own lives, but old men who stay at home in times of war, and mothers who have sons to lose, know better. . . .

My people are ebbing away like a fast receding tide that will never flow again. The white man's God cannot love his red children or he would protect them. We seem to be orphans who can look nowhere for help. How, then, can we become brothers? How can your God become our God and renew our prosperity and awaken in us dreams of returning greatness?

Your God seems to us to be partial. He came to the white man. We never saw Him, never heard his voice. He gave the white man laws, but had no word for his red children whose teeming millions once filled this vast continent as the stars fill the firmament. . . .

Your dead cease to love you and the land of their nativity as soon as they pass the portals of the tomb—they wander far away from the stars, are soon forgotten and never return. Our dead never forget this beautiful world that gave them being. They still love its winding rivers, its great mountains and sequestered vales, and they ever yearn in tenderest affection over the lonely-hearted living, and often return to visit, guide and comfort them. . . .

But why should I repine? Why should I murmur at the fate of my people? Tribes are made up of individuals and are no better than they. Men come and go like the waves of the sea. A tear, a tamanamus, a dirge and they are gone from our longing eyes forever. It is the order of nature. Even the white man whose God walked and talked with him as friend to friend, is not exempt from the common destiny. We may be brothers, after all. We will see.[14]

Seattle had much more to say, but these quoted words remind us that his vision of an all-encompassing moral order remained with him right to the very end. His life and his message was a reminder of the close ties that bind together spirit, land, and people. He gave himself completely to both the neighbor and the stranger because his life was without boundaries. In his Native American cosmology, the individual did not stand alone, apart from a network of people, but rather existed as a member of a community with moral obligations and civic duties. Seattle's major contribution may have been his efforts to transform a young nation's emphasis on national community into a new form of earth community in which humanity seeks to live at harmony with itself, with nature, and with the cosmos. His emphasis was not on one environment but three: the natural environment with its meandering streams, flowering trees, and striking wildlife; the social environment in which white settlers and indigenous tribes struggled to find meaning and community; and the moral environment of human values that directed the relationship to each other, to nature, and the world at large.

Seattle lost the territorial battle, but he may have won the theological war. He died on a reservation on June 6, 1866, but his name is now given to a high school, a university, and a great city whose residents repeat that name countless times each day. His vision and his spirit live on, for as he said to Governor Stevens on that memorable day across the river from the potlatch house:

> At night when the streets of your cities and villages are silent and you think them deserted, they will throng with the returning hosts that once filled and still love this beautiful land. The white man will never be alone. Let him be just and deal kindly with my people, for the dead are not powerless. Dead, did I say? There is no death, only a change of worlds.[15]

Chapter Three

Reuben Snake: Walking on the Prayers of Our Grandmothers

At the dawn of the twentieth century, Native American religion, which had been greatly influenced by the messianic and other-worldly features of the Ghost Dance, now gave birth to a religious movement more in harmony with the reality of the Indian as a part of modern society. One of the major exponents and leaders of this movement, now incorporated as the Native American Church, was Reuben Snake, a former chairman of the Winnebago tribe of Nebraska. Snake was also president of the National Congress of American Indians, an organization of one hundred thirty tribes. A lifelong member of the Native American Church, Snake served as a road man for seventeen years. He was also keeper of the Sacred Pipe for six years.

According to its charter, the Native American Church was formed to foster and promote the religious beliefs of the several tribes that engaged in "the practice of the Peyote Sacrament." A second purpose was to teach sobriety, industry, and right living and "to cultivate a spirit of self-respect and brotherly union among the members of the Native Race of Indians."[1] Controversial at its birth in 1918 and a continuing source of curiosity and criticism, so much attention has been focused on the church's sacramental use of peyote that its efforts to foster a new spiritual community have been largely ignored. This commitment to forming "a brotherly union" across tribal lines was one of the first things to catch the attention of the anthropologist James Mooney who wrote in 1918, "The Indian, under the influence of this peyote religion has given up the idea that he and his tribe are for themselves alone, and is recognizing the fact of the brotherhood of the Indian race particularly, and beyond that the brotherhood of mankind."[2]

It would, thus, be a mistake to view the peyote religion as simply a religious community practicing an ancient rite. It has been a major social force as well. Through intertribal visitation, the appeal to some common Indian values and beliefs, and the opportunity to socialize in conjunction with the all-night religious rites, traditional animosities and ancient communal boundaries have been eliminated. Snake points out that if you believe in the connectedness of all living things, you are led to accept all men as brothers—not just Indians, but whites and other races as well. Thus, with the advent of the peyote religion, its adherents moved from being custodians and practitioners of a parochial, tribal religion to becoming advocates of a more universal interpretation of the meaning of human social life.

European epistemology from Heraclitus to pre-Socratic nature philosophers onward built their authority for belief on the world of group-validated experiences. But living as close as they did to nature, Native Americans were motivated to explore a plant world that enhanced subjective experiences. They discovered that peyote, a small, carrot-shaped cactus, could increase the power of introspection and induce a transformation of the mind and spirit. Its ceremonial use goes back to pre-Columbian times when it was first observed among groups in Mexico and the Lipan Apache in what is now New Mexico. Peyote is closely tied to the quest for a deeper and more direct experience of the divine spirit; its most salient physiological characteristic is its ability to induce transcendence. Much like the vision quest of the Plains tribes, the ceremonial and sacramental eating of the peyote provided a transcendental moment in which the individual experienced a sense of oneness with the Great Spirit.

Snake believed that one of the great tragedies of human history occurred when rational thinking replaced intuitiveness as the primary mode of knowledge. In an interview in Santa Fe, New Mexico, he stated flatly, "The Greeks messed up our lives by bringing about the dominance of rational thinking. Greek philosophy and Judean mythology caused the separation of the human community from the rest of the earth. . . . Traditional Christianity has been saddled with the notion that God cursed the earth when Cain killed Abel." Moreover, there is the parallel idea "that God gave man unlimited dominion over the earth." Indians, on the other hand, believe in a higher power who has given them, not dominion over, but intelligence to live in harmony with all of God's creation. Snake's concern with the ravages of rational thought is not anti-intellectual, but it does come close to being antitechnology. He contended that before the coming of the white man and technology, this land was like the garden of Eden, with fifty million buffalo, teeming fish and wildlife, beautiful streams, and natural forests. "If you could go back in time before the advent of technology, this world would be paradise. None of these new developments has brought us closer to God. And that is why so many people are now turning to Indian spirituality for guidance."

The core of Snake's faith and theology is the idea that without spiritual power or access to it, a person is powerless. His objection is not so much to technology or material power as to the idea that material power can function by itself. What the Native American seeks is balance and harmony between the spiritual and the material. The vast majority of Americans believe the world is primarily a physical reality. Snake wanted the importance of spiritual realities to be given more than token acknowledgment. It is this different orientation toward reality, this different assumption about what a person should be like or even what a person is, that points out the critical discontinuities between the two post-Columbus cultures.

The peyote way is, thus, intended to enhance the spiritual connection with the creator, to sharpen the capacity for intuitiveness. The Aztec word for peyote is heart. The peyote medicine is seen as the heart of God. The knowledge received in the peyote sacrament is insight into the way and will of God. The essence of the medicine is God's love. The spiritual oneness one finds with the creator and all created things means that one opens his heart to all creation: whites, blacks, all races, all living things. Snake's vision of community is, thus, all-embracing, open to every one and every thing.

Snake was introduced to the peyote religion at an early age. He was only three months old when he was baptized into the Native American Church on Easter Sunday in 1937. Both his parents and his grandparents were active members. His forebears in the Winnebago Nation first acquired peyote in 1901. Viewed initially by many members of the tribe as an alien religion and a threat to Winnebago customs, peyotism soon adopted some of the features of Christianity. This included the reading of the Bible and the use of peyote songs with a strong Christian flavor. The Winnebago version of the peyote religion which Snake practiced was, thus, a blend of Christian and Winnebago ideas and practices, plus elements drawn from peyote adherents in other tribes.[3] The Christian ideas were primarily those of Protestantism, but when the Peyotists attempted to unite with a local Protestant church they were rebuffed.[4]

The Christianized version of native beliefs and practices has been given increased emphasis in modern times. Reuben Snake's role as a prayer chief or road man was in many ways similar to that of a minister presiding over rituals, songs, prayers, and communion. He leads the group along the Peyote Road (that is, the Peyotist way of life) to salvation. Snake was a strong advocate, spreading the faith, attracting new converts, and participating in recent years in more than three hundred Native American Church services and ceremonies in North America, Australia, and Europe. The services usually began on Saturday night and ended at dawn on Sunday. They were held in a teepee, the open air, or a permanent religious house. Snake's role was to lead the adherents through this all-night vigil, in which through prayer and the eating of peyote they sought a divine revelation. He was assisted by four people: a drum chief who accompanied him when he sang; a fire chief who maintained a ritual fire; a cedar chief who was in charge of cedar incense; and his wife or a female member of the family who brought in, and prayed over, the morning water.

The peyote is used as a sacramental vehicle to facilitate contact with the Holy Spirit in much the same way that the Christian uses bread and wine. The celebrated Commanche chief, Quanah Parker, one of the most effective exponents of the peyote religion, was fond of saying that "the white man goes into his church house and talks about Jesus, but the Indian goes into his teepee and talks to Jesus."[5]

From the very beginning, the peyote groups with a Christian orientation have shown great flexibility, adapting themselves to the beliefs and conditions of their local tribes while retaining their pan-Indian character. Some members of the Native American Church join a Protestant church as well. Peyote leaders include devout Mormons, Methodists, and Mennonites as well as members in other branches of Protestantism and some Catholics. While some frown on such cross-memberships, especially those who feel that peyotism is the last strong link with the aboriginal past, many Indians are not persuaded that membership in a more orthodox branch of Christianity and the peyote religion are mutually exclusive. Hence, peyotism continues to contribute to the sense of community and morale of some Native American groups. Weston La Barre argues in *The Peyote Cult* that despite the apparent and superficial syncretism with Christianity observed in some practices, peyotism is essentially an American religion, operating in terms of fundamental Indian concepts about powers, visions, and native modes of healing.[6] Even those Indians who see the Native American Church as essentially Christian are still likely to maintain that the native version is superior because it blends basic Indian values and beliefs with rites and rituals that are part of the practice of Christianity.

Reuben Snake had to defend the faith as well as proclaim it. Attacks against the sacramental practices of the Native American Church have come from the American judiciary, the U.S. Congress, more orthodox theologians, liquor merchants opposed to the emphasis on sobriety, and even some Indians themselves. But anti-peyote campaigns, rather than discouraging the religion, have strengthened its leaders to develop intertribal solidarity and organizational stability. As opposition grew and increasing numbers of progressive Indians were attracted to it, the peyote religion took on an institutional form that brought a new formality to what had been rather unstructured volunteer practices. While Snake performed his leadership functions as a volunteer, the Native American Church has operated with a very formal structure from the beginning, with elected officers, annual conventions, dues payment, and other such institutionalized arrangements.

Snake's experience as a tribal leader, and even his four years of military service with the Green Berets, taught him much about the demands of modern leadership. When he became chairman of the Winnebago Nation, the tribal organization was $500,000 in debt. When he left his position ten years later, the tribe's enterprises were worth $15,000,000. Through his work in community and economic development, he learned valuable lessons about how the economy functions and how to develop the capital needed to keep private and public institutions functioning. His tenure as legislative assistant to Senator Robert T. Kerrey of Nebraska helped to enhance his skills in making his way through the maze of congressional hearings and lawmaking. He was successful in putting together a coalition to seek a congressional hearing on the First Amendment rights of the Native American Church and was one of the key witnesses when hearings were held in Oregon in 1991.

Snake was very much aware of the tension between traditional leadership values and the social, political, and economic complexities of assuming responsibility today. In the earlier days of Winnebago history, leadership was by consensus. No one gave orders and tasks were not assigned by a central authority. Tribal leadership was collective, with people simply coming forward to meet a need or assume a responsibility as it manifested itself. Traditional leadership was also noncoercive, based on shared responsibility, not control. According to the Inuit leader, Charlie Edwardson, Indian leadership was a process of "eliciting conformity to the unenforceable." The idea, according to Edwardson, was that people were not made to be coerced but are developed to exercise initiative.[7]

Snake and others promoted a model of community in which personal autonomy and collective responsibility are complementary, not mutually exclusive. They emphasized the need to nurture strong, persuasive, even charismatic, leaders, but they want them to use their strength for an Indian common good rather than simply to exercise it as authority or control. Jack Weatherford analyzed a typical powwow in order to demonstrate that elements of the notion of noncoercive, noncontrolling leadership are still present in contemporary Indian practices.

> To an outsider, . . . pow wows often appear chaotic. Even though posted signs promise that the dances will begin at four o'clock, there is still no dancing at five-thirty. Drummers scheduled to play never arrive, and some groups drum without being on the program. Impromptu family ceremonies intertwine with the official scheduled events, and the microphone passes among a score of announcers during the evening. No one is in control.
>
> This seems to be typical of Indian community events: no one is in control. No master of ceremonies tells everyone what to do, and no one orders the dancers to appear. The announcer acts as herald or possibly as facilitator of ceremonies, but no chief rises to demand anything of anyone. The event flows in an orderly fashion like hundreds of pow wows before it, but leaders can only lead by example, by pleas, or by exhortations. . . . The event unfolds as a collective activity of all participants, not as one mandated and controlled from the top. Each participant responds to the collective mentality and mood of the whole group but not to a single, directing voice.

This Indian penchant for respectful individualism and equality seems as strong today in Fargo, North Dakota, as when the first explorers wrote about it five centuries ago.[8]

Many outside observers are confused by the absence of a "single directing voice" when they deal with Native Americans. But it is a style of leadership that worked for tribes across the breadth of North America long before the Europeans arrived.

What is the likely future of the Native American Church as a pan-Indian community? Have Reuben Snake and the other elders passed on the torch to a new generation of leaders? The Snake clan has been involved in the Native American Church from the beginning. Reuben's brother and several other relatives are also road men. Snake liked to point out that among the twelve clans of the Winnebago Nation, the Snake clan is the most populist and the most friendly. It seems that within the Winnebago Nation the Snake clan has traditionally had the responsibility for ceremonies, preparing for them, and even cleaning up after they are over. Children at an early age are socialized into this role, understanding that they are to be outgoing and friendly. This attribute has made members of the clan perfect candidates for leadership within the church and the tribe.

Can the Native American Church retain its adaptive qualities in an information society where one is tied to the majority culture in brand-new ways, and by brand-new technologies? Can the church continue to bridge the gap between cultures and generations? When divergent cultures meet under conditions of dominance and subordination, some people are unable to adapt to either and find themselves caught in an emotional, intellectual, or social no-man's-land. Yet others adjust by excluding much of the incongruent aspect of the offending culture while maintaining as much as possible of their own. The Peyotists have been more successful than any other pan-Indian movement in weaving together traditional beliefs, values, and rituals with elements from the confronting culture. This has provided the basis for a consistent worldview and recognizable identity, but its future depends on how much sanction it is able to achieve, and how much interference it is able to avoid from the dominant culture.

Snake believed that the 1990 Smith decision by the U.S. Supreme Court was a watershed moment for the Native American Church. The Court denied First Amendment protection to the sacramental use of peyote. A religious way of life that had been on this continent long before the arrival of the Europeans was deemed to be a luxury democracy could not afford. The Supreme Court ruling permitted each state to make its own laws regarding the religious practices of the Native American Church. The Court was not persuaded. Historians of religion like Dr. Huston Smith argued that peyote is regarded sacramentally as God's flesh just as Christians regard bread as the body of Christ and wine as his blood. But the Court was not moved. Justice O'Connor, while voting with the majority, expressed concern about the majority opinion, arguing that the purpose of the First Amendment is to withhold religion from the vagaries of the political process. It was Justice Blackmun, however, who made this point most forcefully in his dissenting opinion. But the Native American Church was destined to become entangled in the political process. The United States Congress held hearings and Native Americans used them to urge further protection of religious sites and religious ornaments from desecration. Only twenty-eight states now allow the sacramental use of peyote by bona fide members of the Native American Church.[9] But on October 6, 1994, President Clinton signed into law a bill that essentially overturned the earlier Court decision and created a unique national law protecting the rights of Native Americans to use peyote sacramentally in their religious ceremonies. In the end, national policy came to reflect precisely what Reuben Snake had argued.

The work and contributions of Reuben Snake go beyond the peyote sacrament, court rulings, and the arguments about cosmology and epistemology. He helped put back together the shattered lives of people culturally confused and provided a ready-made answer for those who found themselves deeply conflicted by the tensions of living in two worlds. And in the process, he helped to expand their vision of a "brotherly union" to include those formerly excluded. Snake said that Americans are afraid of the "S" word *spirituality*, but many are, nevertheless, turning to Indian spirituality for guidance.

When asked who are his heroes, Snake pointed first to Tecumseh, who addressed Indian councils from Wisconsin to Mexico, preaching to Indians that "we all belong to one family; we are all children of the Great Spirit; we walk in the same path . . . we must assist each other to bear our burdens."[10] Snake's other heroes were Mahatma Ghandi and Martin Luther King, Jr. Tecumseh is understandable, but how can this man who was a member of the Green Berets at eighteen and who was head of the American Indian Movement during the armed conflict at Wounded Knee in 1972 now confess his admiration for Ghandi and King, apostles of nonviolence? His response to this question was to quote the Hopi man who said, "To be a warrior is great, but to walk the road of peace is even greater." Older and suffering from heart disease just months before his death, he added, "But all of rational thought is not going to save the world, it is God-given intuitive knowledge." His grandmother who taught him to talk to the spirit would have been proud to hear him say that "each of us is walking on the prayers of our grandmothers."

Chapter Four

Zikala-Sa: On the Razor's Edge Between Tradition and Change

Each day on the Dakota Plains of the late nineteenth century, an Indian woman and her daughter took the footpath at the base of an ascending hill to a muddy stream where they gathered water for the family. As they crept through the tall swamp grass that bent over on each side, the woman and the small child often talked as if they were two grown-ups discussing history or theology. Remembering those melancholy days of her youth, Zikala-Sa was to write later that "I was not wholly conscious of myself, but was more keenly alive to the fire within." Of her mother, she wrote, "She taught me no fear."[1]

Born in 1876, the year that the Sioux and Cheyenne annihilated the Seventh Cavalry at Little Big Horn, Zikala-Sa spent much of her life on the razor's edge between tradition and change, struggling with the forces of an accommodating past and an alien present. As a child, she was educated in the cultural history and civic habits of the Sioux. Known on the Yankton Sioux Reservation as Gertrude Simmons, she loved best the evening meals when the old men and women shared stories of a proud and distant past. She ate breakfast of dried meat and unleavened bread with her mother on the grass in the shadow of a wigwam of weather-stained canvas. Lunch was often at her uncle's lodge where those who were passing by stopped to rest and share the hospitality. But it was the evening meal that fired young Gertrude's imagination. She ate her supper in quiet, waiting patiently for the conversation to turn to the exploits of cultural heroes of another era. Often with the distant howling of a pack of wolves in the background, she would pillow her head on her mother's lap and whisper that it was time for the stories. Her mother would then inform her guest that "my little daughter is anxious to hear your stories."

Gertrude's unquenchable appetite for the past was legendary. Mature beyond her years, she wanted perspective in both historic time and ethnic space. Imprisonment in the present was for her the worst of all possible worlds. But her imagination was still that of a child. Content to work with her mother as she made moccasins from trimmed buckskin, Gertrude's life had an easy, natural Indian rhythm. This all began to change one spring when two missionaries came to her village. The rumor spread that they had come to take away Indian boys and girls to the East. Naturally, the village mothers were suspicious of their intent and sought to keep the missionaries away from their children. Gertrude's mother was no exception. She discouraged her daughter's curiosity about the lands beyond the Dakota horizon and warned her of the treacherous acts of the "palefaces" she had known. Finally, the two missionaries came to call on Gertrude and her mother. They talked of the need and value of an education and how the whole family would benefit. Gertrude was excited. Her mother was much less enthusiastic, but after several days of convocation with the Great Spirit, she reluctantly gave her approval. Excited, but still trembling with fear, Gertrude—now eight years old—left her village on the Dakota Plains for a Quaker school in Wabash, Indiana.

This minimally sketched social history provides a backdrop against which to understand the transformation of a young Dakota girl from Gertrude Simmons to Zikala-Sa. Born as Gertrude Simmons on the Yankton Reservation in South Dakota, young Gertrude christened herself Zikala-Sa (Red Bird) as an act of rebellion. Headstrong and independent, she wrote later to her friend Montezuma:

> As I grew I was called by my brother's name Simmons. I bore it a
> long time till my brother's wife—angry with me because I insisted

on getting an education—said I had deserted home and I might give up my brother's name "Simmons" too. Well, you can guess how queer I felt—away from my own people, homeless, penniless—and even without a name! Then I chose to make a name for myself— and I guess I have made "Zikala-Sa" known—for even Italy writes it in her language.

Zikala-Sa's boarding school experience was one of humiliation and mistreatment. Her teachers tried to excise from her all things Indian and to remake her in their own images. After three years, she returned to her mother's house on the Yankton Reservation, remaining there for four years despite the pull she felt to the world of books and writing. She returned to White's Institute in Wabash, Indiana, for three more years, finally achieving her goal and receiving a diploma in 1895. At nineteen, she matriculated at Earlham College in Richmond, Indiana, again traveling the Quaker route. It was there that her amazing ability with the piano, violin, and voice was discovered. With the encouragement of her teachers and schoolmates, she soon demonstrated exceptional ability in writing and oratory as well.

Remembering the pleasant evenings and the stories around her mother's evening meals, she wrote and spoke often of the nobility of Indian life before the arrival of the Europeans. This message played better at Earlham than at White's Institute where the emphasis was on assimilation. A crowning moment in her youth occurred in 1896 when she entered the Indiana collegiate oratorical contest in Indianapolis. In this traditionally all-male, all-white event, Zikala was a curiosity, with some in the audience expressing obvious disapproval of someone of her sex and race on this hallowed platform. Several students from another Indiana college even lifted up a banner with the word "squaw" crudely and cruelly sketched on the canvas. Zikala won second place and left the contest to the cheers of her fellow Earlham students and with increased confidence in her ability to compete successfully in the white world.

Back at Earlham, she published essays and highly formal poems in the school's newspaper and won several debating honors. A few years later, she placed short stories in both *Harper's* and *Atlantic Monthly*, becoming not only the celebrated center of a small literary coterie in Boston, but for many the literary counterpart of the oral storytellers of early Indian life. Her distinguishing quality, however, was the power with which she articulated the experience of Indians living between two worlds—the past with its imperial traditions and the present with its many pressures for assimilation.

Zikala was plagued during her studies at Earlham with assorted illnesses that forced her eventually to leave college before graduating. But her fascination with the arts, culture, and the life of the mind continued. In 1899, she accepted an offer to teach at the most prestigious Indian school of her day, Carlisle, a school in Pennsylvania that produced many of the great Indian leaders of the early twentieth century.

Wherever she went and whatever she did, Zikala attracted rave reviews. An accomplished violinist, she studied at the New England Conservatory of Music and won critical acclaim both as a soloist and an orator. The *New York Musical Courier* hailed her as "charming and graceful." Her recitation of Longfellow's "Hiawatha" was described by the *Brooklyn Times* as a "picture to be remembered." Her creative impulse led her to collaborate in the writing of "Sun Dance," an Indian opera selected by the New York Light Opera Guild as the American opera of the year. Through all of her successes, she continued writing about Indian life and culture. In "Impressions of an Indian Childhood," published in the *Atlantic Monthly* in 1900, she described her early years on the reservation as idyllic:

> I was a little girl of seven. Loosely clad in a slip of brown buckskin, and light footed with a pair of soft moccasins on my feet, I was as free as the wind that blew my hair, and no less spirited than a bound-

ing deer. These were my mother's pride—my wild freedom and overflowing spirit.

In the spring of 1901, Zikala-Sa returned to Yankton. In 1902, she married a Yankton Sioux named Raymond Talefesse Bonnin and gave birth to a son, Raymond Bonnin. Shortly thereafter, her husband took a job as a clerk on the Uintah Reservation in Utah. It was there that the Society of American Indians (SAI) found her when they decided to pursue a broad pan-Indian unity by reaching out to reservation Indians. An important decision of the Lawrence, Kansas, conference of the Society of American Indians in 1915 was to inaugurate a community center movement to establish "social betterment stations" on the reservation. These new centers were to perform services much like those of the settlement houses among the urban poor. And equally as important, they were to provide a vehicle for educated Indians to help those who were less fortunate.

This new movement launched the second career of Zikala-Sa, the pan-Indian activist who wanted most to be a servant of the Indian people, a voice for the voiceless. In 1901, she had divorced herself from what was happening nationally and taken a twelve-year hiatus of silence in Utah. But while her decision to live in the Indian world rather than the white world pleased some of her family and friends, it had left her in an inner turmoil, a state of spiritual unrest and emptiness. She was torn between her duty as a mother and wife and the longing to study, to write, to do more with music, and to be involved in the larger arena of service to the Indian community. The turning point came when she traveled East to place her son in a Benedictine boarding school. She now felt free to be active in pursuits that were far more challenging. Thus, in accepting the invitation to establish the first SAI community center on an Indian reservation, she began her transition back to the role of Indian activist.

Fort Duchesne was not the most likely place for the SAI to start a community center, but no other community had a Zikala-Sa so well prepared for the assignment. Demonstrating her pragmatism, she proved to be a good fundraiser for charitable causes, soliciting and receiving both agency and private funds.

The early activities of the Utah Center were rather uneventful, providing sewing classes for women and serving inexpensive lunches on the days the local Indians gathered to collect their rations. However, Zikala continued to feel deeply that the national policy of acculturation was an assault on Indian culture. The old fire returned and Zikala-Sa, the Yankton Sioux activist, reemerged. In 1916 she was elected secretary of the SAI and persuaded her husband to move to Washington, D.C. Within a few years, she came to personify the new generation of American Indians: articulate and well-respected by even their white peers, but alternating between a controlled rage over the mistreatment of Indians and a desire to help them succeed in the larger society.

How did this very talented and highly successful artist move from the bright lights of arts and culture to a life of social service and social reform? It began with community service in Utah but it eventually led to political engagement in Washington, D.C., where she pressed for improvements in education and health care, the preservation of Indian culture, and the granting of Indian citizenship. An activism that had begun in 1913 with a small focus on ameliorating the consequences of federal inequities was transformed into a full-scale attack on their causes. She used her position as secretary of SAI to press for reform and respect, lecturing and campaigning across the country. Far from a homogeneous group, the members of SAI battled as fiercely with each other over ideology and strategy as they did with the larger society over the treatment and place of the American Indian. In that group, Zikala-Sa was considered something of a radical. She was proud of her Sioux ancestry and insisted that those whom the Europeans called Indians possessed a cultural tradition that was not merely equal but in some ways superior to that of Anglo America. Both as a woman and as an Indian, she sought acceptance on her own terms.

Making full use of her exceptional oratorical and literary skills, Mrs. Bonnin, as she was called during her career of social reform, blossomed into a personality that neither the Congress nor the president could ignore. Even after the SAI dissolved in 1920, she found a forum and a vehicle by which she could continue to serve the Indian community by persuading the General Federation of Women's Clubs to establish an Indian Welfare Committee. From that position, she was successful in forcing investigations into the treatment of Indians and even in influencing President Hoover's appointments to the Bureau of Indian Affairs.

Always the social entrepreneur, Gertrude Bonnin formed her own organization in 1926, the National Council of American Indians. Recognizing both the potential and limits of social benevolence, her altruistic impulses, which had led her to give up a promising career in literature and music for life on the reservation, now led her to work as an independent reformer on behalf of suppressed Indians everywhere. Unlike some of her colleagues in SAI who were eager to find common ground with white America, she remained a staunch advocate of Indian self-determination. Her objective was to find an Indian common ground, to forge an identity larger than the tribe while at the same time protecting the rights of the tribe.

The purpose of the National Council, as proclaimed on its letterhead, was to "Help Indians Help Themselves." The intent was to restore the tradition of self-reliance and caring for each other that had once characterized tribal life. In a newsletter addressed simply to her "Indian Kinsmen," Zikala wrote that "Too many individual Indians ask help for themselves only, and seem to forget the tribe's welfare as a whole." She quoted the assistant commissioner for Indian Affairs who in a speech had lamented the fact that "Indians did not have as much race consciousness as the Negroes, who went back to their own people to give them the benefit of their education."[2]

Zikala's appeal to the educated Indians to give something back to their community did not result in the increased support for her own efforts she had hoped to see. Her tendency to operate independently and increasing concerns about her intimidating personality did not help matters, but she continued to use her skills, contacts, and influence to improve the well-being of the Indian community. Her choice of Washington as the home base of her national organization did not help matters either. It added to the impression that she had left home both physically and psychologically. The Society for American Indians, the professional group that would normally have been her base, was increasingly active alongside a growing group of white reformers, but on a tribal rather than a pan-Indian basis. In truth, the ideas advanced by Zikala with their strong emphasis on maintaining the values, beliefs, and traditions of tribal life were beginning to work in ways she had not originally anticipated. Instead of strengthening the national reform movement, they helped to weaken it by encouraging Indians to work locally. Also, ties among the SAI members themselves were weakening. Many of the older SAI activists had been alumni of the Carlisle School where they had met or learned about each other. This old bond had grown more tenuous as the school was closed and no new generation of alumni followed. All these difficulties did not discourage Zikala, however. With her husband, Raymond Bonnin, now a lawyer, she continued her struggle.

What was it about Zikala-Sa that led her to work for her community rather than accommodate herself to the larger community and accept its accolades? The seeds of her lifelong commitment to the betterment of life for the American Indian population were planted in the early years on the Yankton reservation. She was born shortly after the Yankton band of Indians had been forced to cede approximately eleven million acres of land in southeastern South Dakota in exchange for a forty-thousand-acre reservation farther to the west. A people who were the product of a hunter culture suddenly found themselves forced to take up the plow and to eke out a life in agriculture. Zikala-Sa was too young to understand the full implications of all this, but her mother taught her from the cradle that her people had been greatly wronged by white men and that these men should not be trusted. Writing later about her experience as an Indian child, she quotes her mother as saying "We were once very happy. But the paleface has stolen our lands and driven us hither. Having defrauded us of our land, the paleface forced us away." It appears that Zikala inherited not only her suspicion of the motives of whites from her mother, but her pride in her heritage as well. In *American Indian Stories*, she recalls a scene in which she asked her mother, "Who is this bad paleface?" Her mother responded, "My little daughter, he is a sham—a sickly sham. The bronzed Dakota is the only real man." Though her mother had been married to three different white men and had lived at times off the reservation, she defiantly refused to learn English or to accept any other way of life except that of the Sioux. A strong woman was not an anomaly in the Yankton culture of Zikala's youth. Though the Sioux had been traditionally a patrilineal society, women had now come to dominate tribal life, surrounding young Zikala with strong role models that served her well in the male-dominated world in which she won her way.

The tensions of living in two worlds were to torment her for the rest of her life, however. To those at the Carlisle Indian School where she taught from 1898 to 1899, she was an anathema because she insisted on remaining "Indian," even writing articles that flew in the face of their assimilationist education. But to the traditional Sioux on the reservation, including her mother, she was highly suspect because, in their minds, she had abandoned, even betrayed, the Indian way of life by getting an education in the white man's world. Though she committed her life to working for the rights of Indians, first in her creative writing and later as a pan-Indian activist, she was always on the edge of two worlds, fully understanding but never fully entering either. It was the ambiguity of this twoness that seems to have driven her to take all she could out of one world and to use it for the benefit of the other. A poem she published in the 1916 issue of the *American Indian Magazine* expressed the isolation she seems to have felt even in her finest hour:

> I've lost my long hair; my eagles plumes too.
> From you my own people, I've gone astray.
> A wanderer now, with nowhere to stay.
> The will-o-wisp learning, it brought me rue.
> It brings no admittance. Where I have knocked
> Some evil imps, hearts, have bolted and locked.
> Alone with the night and fearful abyss
> I stand isolated, life gone amiss.[3]

Not much is known about the role of religion in shaping the values and motivating the vision of this strong Indian woman. But her opposition to the peyote religion during her years as director of the Community Center in Utah was made known early in her career. In the same issue of the *American Indian Magazine* in which she published her "Christmas Letter" reporting on the activities of the Center, she wrote that she was "very sad to see that these Utes are beginning to fall victim to that very terrible stuff." As she became more influential in the Society for American Indians, her campaign took on increasing vigor. She spoke out as a junior member even before the society took a formal position on the peyote matter. In later years, she testified before the House Subcommittee on Indian Affairs in support of a bill to suppress the use of peyote among Indians. This was not the first time she found herself opposing the views of some of her colleagues in the SAI. Those defending the peyote religion insisted that it was a genuine Indian religion with many Christian elements, that peyote was useful in curing diseases and was not an addictive drug, and that the religion was morally and socially beneficial to Indians.[4] The anti-Peyotists took the opposite view, arguing that the whole idea of regarding these objectionable practices as a religion was simply a cover for taking drugs and that peyote was harmful physically and degrading morally.

Zikala was very knowledgeable about more traditional Indian religions and appears to have been quite sympathetic to them. Her collaboration in the composition of the opera *Sun Dance* revealed an intimate knowledge of the rituals and ideals of traditional beliefs and practices. The work was so sensitively done that Edward E. Hipsher, in *American Opera and Its Composers*, wrote that this was the reason for its success:

> The opera does not depict the Indian in the dime novel fashion familiar in the stage and screen. It is a sympathetic portrayal of the real Indian in a conscientious attempt to delineate the manners, the customs, the religious ideals—in short, the life of a noble people too little understood.[5]

Very early in her life, Zikala was introduced to the Quakers who fired her imagination and convinced her of the value of education. It was Quaker missionaries who persuaded her to leave home at eight against her mother's wishes and to enroll at White's Institute. It was Earlham, a Quaker college, that sharpened her literary skills and served as an arena for her personal growth and increased self-confidence. Yet, the rebellious spirit that led her to publish a much-discussed article on why she was a pagan seems to have influenced her early attitude toward religion as well. Her notion of deity was conceived in the mysticism of the Dakota tradition "where the voice of the Great Spirit is heard in the twittering of birds, the rippling of mighty waters, and the sweet breathing of flowers." She wrote, "If this is paganism, then at present, at least, I am a pagan." But in later years, she cultivated the relationship with members of the Church of Latter Day Saints that had begun when she lived and worked in Utah. While never converting, she identified with the

Mormons, not because of Christianity but because the Utah Mormons had treated the Indians fairly and, like the Indians, had also suffered persecution. She also liked their emphasis on taking care of each other and on living apart from the rest of the world where they could retain their culture and practice their faith more freely.

An independent and sometimes controversial reformer to the end, she was described by Dexter Fisher who knew and admired her as "a curious blend of civilized romanticism and aggressive individualism." Writing in the Foreword to Zikala's book *American Indian Stories*, Fisher suggested that even her own image of herself eventually evolved into "an admixture of myth and fact." Maligned by corrupt Indian agents and alienated from her own family, even Zikala's critics gave her credit for a lifetime of devotion to the needs of those who had been demoralized by the poverty of their predicament and left with little hope that their voices would ever be heard.

Zikala-Sa stood apart from the traditions and practices of her day, insisting on the validity of old Indian values and the importance of reinventing the notion of "Indianness." She struggled toward a vision of community that included not one but all the tribes, not simply Indians but Anglos as well. Refusing to bend to any constraints imposed on her because of race or gender, she shared her vision of wholeness with a society not yet ready to be made one. Her vision of civic engagement and giving back to one's community was best expressed in a letter to her friend Carlos Montezuma. "Life is not worth living," she wrote, "if it does not demand some little effort on our parts to contrive in it. It is not what we give for nothing but what we inspire others to try or to do—that is the best, most valuable gift we can offer."[6]

In 1938, at the age of sixty-one, Zikala-Sa died and was buried in Arlington cemetery. Her epitaph could easily have been the words she once wrote: "I am free! I am proud! I am chosen!"

African Americans

Chapter Five

The Cosmology of Connectedness

Along a meandering river deep in the heart of Costa Rica, there is a little village where descendants of African slaves share the forest and the waterway with an occasional tourist in search of adventure. On the wall of a one-room school is a poster that reads, "This land belongs to all the people of Costa Rica. Some are living. Others are dead, but most are yet to be born." This cosmology of connectedness and intergenerational obligation characterized the worldview of many in the early African diaspora in North and Central America.

When the Europeans in the Americas thought of human nature, they defined the individual in two ways. The first emphasized the individual as thinker, in the tradition of Descartes and Aquinas. The second emphasized the individual as worker, in the tradition of Marx or Luther. African metaphysics, on the other hand, placed emphasis on three other dimensions of our humanity. The first was the concept of *homo-festivus*, the idea that individuals and communities have both the capacity and the need to celebrate life, even in the midst of tragedy, thus providing insight into the vitality of the African funeral ritual. The second concept was that of *homo-fantasia*, the idea that individuals and communities are visionary mythmakers who imagine different life alternatives and set out to create them. It is this notion of the individual as dreamer that was so ably articulated by Martin Luther King, Jr.

The third concept of human nature stored away in the minds of the early slave was that of *homo-communalis*, the idea that individual identity is communal. This notion of community included both the living and the "living dead." The resources for which individual members were stewards belonged to the community in its varied expressions, not just to those members in immediate proximity. This concept of homo-communalis, the idea that a person cannot be fully understood apart from the community which defines his or her personhood, was fundamental to the African view of moral duty and social obligation. The individual was regarded as part of a network of kin that functioned as an economic, religious, and political unit with its own customs, traditions, and rituals. The members of the larger community were first members of a strong family structure that provided its own norms for orderly functioning. As the core communal unit, the extended family was able to make demands that normally overrode all other duties and obligations.

While the bonds of the extended family were severed by the massive transcontinental displacement that brought Africans to American shores, the spirit of community not only survived but took on new forms and meaning. The beginnings of organized black benevolence can be traced to the early black churches, mutual aid societies, and fraternal lodges. Self-help mutual aid societies and other newly developed voluntary organizations encompassed many of the characteristics of the widely scattered extended family. These groups were used, first, to provide voluntary services and financial resources among free blacks in the North and South, later to ease the transition from slavery to freedom for those who had been slaves, and eventually in efforts to transform an unresponsive government. The earliest of the mutual aid societies were the African Masonic Lodge in Boston and the Free American Society in Philadelphia, both formed in 1787. Both organizations provided economic and social assistance to the black community and paved the way for the formation of other benevolent associations, particularly black churches. By providing aid for the oppressed, educating the young, aiding the aged, and burying the dead, these institutions became centers of black community life.

Whites feared these groups more than they feared the African-American churches and schools that followed. The clandestine meetings with secret signs and passwords appeared to be subversive. Viewing these organizations as a breeding ground for insurrection, some Southern lawmakers prohibited blacks from forming their own institutions or holding meetings anywhere without direct white supervision. While attempts to disband the groups were unsuccessful, only a handful of benevolent societies applied for state charters and most met secretly because of strongly negative white reaction. Their clandestine nature made it difficult to gauge the extent of black membership, but many groups flourished, with some expanding the scope of their benevolence to include the larger community as well. There is a very revealing notation about the scope of black philanthropy in the archives on the great plague of yellow fever in Philadelphia in 1793:

> The elders of the African Society met on September 5 and decided that they must see what the Negro inhabitants could do to help the stricken white citizens. Two by two, they set out on a tour of the city. Absalom Jones and Richard Allen went to a house on Emsley's Alley where they found a mother dead, a father dying, two small children hungry and frightened. They sent for the guardians of the poor and moved on. That day they visited more than twenty white families. Other Negroes did likewise, and afterwards all the elders came together again to tell what they had seen. Next day Jones and Allen called on Mayor Clarkson to ask how the Negroes could be of most use. The Mayor received them gratefully. . . . Most of his Federalist friends had fled, and nearly his entire civil service, but the city was at last producing new and courageous leaders from its humblest people.[1]

When one considers that Richard Allen and Absalom Jones formed the Free African Society after being forcefully removed from a white church for mistakenly sitting in the white section, it is indeed remarkable that they would risk their own health and well-being in order to provide help to the white victims of the plague.

The capacity to express sentiments of generosity for those outside the group, the ability to love the enemy, is an African-American trait that has continued to baffle those who write about civic virtue and communal values. Long before Martin Luther King, Jr., preached nonviolence and led a movement with a remarkable capacity for physical restraint and respect for even the adversary, there were evidences of a universal compassion within the community of Africans in America that embraced both the nearer and distant neighbor. Some scholars would argue that the impulses of Absalom Jones and Richard Allen were simply the learned behavior of those who espoused and practiced Christian charity. After all, both Jones and Allen are celebrated in black history for their role in forming the black church. Those who study cultural and linguistic properties of African origin disagree with this assessment, documenting African survivals in folklore, spirituality, family life, and even the tradition of generosity.[2] Other scholars assert that Africans brought many other elements to the New World that survived slavery and influenced later communal life, including herbology and medicinal practices, divination, metaphysical "first principles," and highly evolved traditions of secret societies with membership linked to specific community responsibilities.[3]

Traditional African societies were highly organized social, political, economic, and cultural entities that operated without regard to the ownership of material things. Land, grain, and livestock were used communally, and the care and nurturing of children and elders was everyone's responsibility. Social and political organization was based on a combination of self-contained but interdependent segments. These segments, generally called secret societies, controlled their members' daily lives.

Three types of secret societies could be found in Africa, many of which existed during the time of the slave trade: mystic and religious societies, democratic and patriotic societies (black benevolent societies closely resembled this group), and subversive and criminal societies. The first two were extensions of traditional authority and set out to achieve the goals established in society. An example is the Poro of Sierra Leone, originating in the fifteenth century, that linked social, political, and economic aspects of its members' lives. The Gbe in Dahomey existed primarily to supply adequate financial aid for burial expenses of a close relative.[4] African secret and mutual aid societies also stressed moral training and good conduct. Hence, it should be no surprise that the free black benevolent associations resembled both the scope of African secret societies and the communal nature of African life, with regard to their tendency toward mutual cooperation and their well-ordered social systems.[5]

Other scholars dismiss the notion of African roots for the benevolent traditions of African Americans, arguing that black voluntary and self-help organizations have been widespread because blacks were excluded from the American mainstream. While the separatist political, social, and economic context clearly contributed to the need for civil society institutions that were black led and black controlled, these were not mirror images or exaggerated forms of the white organizations to which blacks were exposed but denied admission.[6]

The Slave Quarter Community

The tendency to form voluntary, benevolent organizations not only survived the slave experience but was, to a large degree, sharpened by that experience. In *Deep Like the Rivers*, Thomas Webber describes the "quarter community" of the slaves as "the world of the home plantation and the world of their personal experiences."[7] According to Webber, who studied slave narratives extensively, the "tendency of quarter people to view themselves as a familial group, with common lifestyle, common interests and problems, and a common need to stick together is a theme which appears frequently in black source material."[8] Whatever their personal jealousies and animosities or tribal differences and familial networks, as a group the members of the quarter community identified each other as a distinct body of persons tied together by a common historical experience, by a common philosophical and behavioral approach to their world, and by their common struggle against the pressures and demands of slavery. The principal expression of the theme of commonality can be found in the community's unwritten rule never to betray the confidence of a fellow black or to expose secrets of the quarter community. Those who betrayed these rules were treated with scorn and ostracized. Most members of the quarter community understood that it was to their mutual advantage to protect and care for each other and that such solidarity was necessary. Most felt a responsibility, for example, to care for each other's wounds, to warn each other of punishments, and to nurse each other in sickness and old age. One slave narrative reports that "when slaves received whippings their fellow slaves would rub their backs with part of their little allowance of fat meat."[9] Most quarter communities also protected members who were forced to flee to the woods to prevent punishment or sale. "When the slaves would run away out into the woods . . . they would come around and get something to eat and hide out. They would fix something to eat and send it by one of the children. They wouldn't send but one, ''cause the white folks might suspicion.'"[10]

Most blacks under slavery employed the term *family* in much the same way as whites, to mean the blood relationship of father, mother, their common children, and a possible grandparent, aunt, or uncle. Most blacks also believed, however, in a larger pattern of family associations and responsibilities that included not only what is referred to as the extended family but also other persons not necessarily related by blood or marriage. Such individuals might include stepparents, peer group members, community leaders, religious meeting brethren, nursery teachers, doctors, conjurors, special friends, and any other individuals who, for reasons other than kinship by blood, felt a familial responsibility to help nurture, protect, and educate any given black child. It is this larger grouping of persons that was considered to be the quarter child's family under slavery. A blood-related relative, such as a white master, who felt no responsibility for the child was not considered part of the family.

During slavery, the role of mother and father did not have to be played by biological parents. A child was welcomed into another slave family if sold or if his or her parents had been sold or had died. The quarter community also addressed each other with familial titles and accepted the virtue of behaving toward one another as brothers and sisters with quasi-familial reciprocal obligations. Older quarter members accepted the responsibility for the discipline and protection of the quarter children. Younger slaves displayed a respect for their elders and a desire to care for those community members too old to care for themselves. Quarter members also expressed pride in each other's accomplishments.

The themes of communality and family were also expressed beyond the individual community. In many quarters, individual members shared the responsibility of providing extra food and comforts for the community as a whole. Stolen food and animals slaughtered invited occasions for the community to feast. In some quarters the slaves shared the food they grew in their garden patches with slaves of other quarters. Often house building, sewing, basket weaving, and washing were done communally. In addition, most quarter communities acted in concert to protect individual members and the community as a whole from overwork and white abuse. The narratives give evidence of how those in one quarter would take care of neighboring slaves who were treated poorly by their owners. One informant tells of how the folks of his quarters would procure food for the half-starved slaves of a neighboring plantation who "frequently slipped over for something good to eat."[11] Fugitive slaves in need of food, clothing, or shelter were almost always assisted.

Many quarter communities built a network of mutual aid and communication with neighboring quarter communities. Slaves from different plantations came together for both authorized and secret dances, barbecues, funerals, and religious meetings. Often quarters within walking distance of each other shared common leaders. Like the family, the community provided early significant others, numerous and diverse role models, strong negative sanctions and positive rewards, a unique language, and constant reinforcement of family-like obligations and relationships. If a slave was sold, the trauma was cushioned by the entry into a new but familiar quarter community. Though quarters differed in size, organization, and relationship to plantation authorities, most were similar enough to provide a sense of home to those who had grown up within any quarter. A slave could move from quarter to quarter with little discontinuity in the way he or she was expected to understand the world and interact with plantation whites and other slaves. It is in this sense that the members of each quarter community partook in the wider fellowship of the total slave quarter community.[12]

Challenging Social Injustice

African Americans have consistently used their resources to provide manpower and financial resources to initiate and support black political and social movements, including but not limited to the Underground Railroad and the civil rights movement. The Underground Railroad was a systematic effort by blacks and whites to aid slaves in their escape. Its origin dates to 1804 when General Thomas Boude refused to return a fugitive slave and was supported in his action by his community in Columbia, Pennsylvania.[13] The term *Underground Railroad* gained wide usage after 1831. The railroad operated in a very simple way. Fugitive slaves would travel at night, stopping for food and rest at "stations" spaced about twenty miles apart. Four main trunk lines were said to run across the state of New York and several through Ohio and Southern Michigan.

Some estimate that up to two thousand slaves escaped each year from 1830 to 1860 on the route through Ohio.[14]

Harriet Tubman, perhaps one of the most famous conductors of the Underground Railroad, made nineteen trips to the South, emancipating almost three hundred slaves. Rewards for her capture totaled over $40,000. She was always armed with a pistol, which she used to threaten any slave who desired to turn back and thus endanger her entire party.[15]

The Underground Railroad relied on black charitable giving and voluntarism for much of its success. The many acts of benevolence included sponsoring national and international fundraising campaigns, service as volunteers, use of the homes of supporters as railroad stations, and providing escaping slaves with food, clothing, shelter, new identity papers, and money. Many of the black mutual aid societies and fraternal organizations were actively involved in supporting all aspects of the railroad's operation, while Quakers and other groups raised money to keep the movement going. When the operation was low on funds, Harriet Tubman would hire herself out as a domestic and contribute the resources earned to continue the work.

A more recent example of blacks using benevolence to challenge social injustice is in the case of the civil rights movement. It was perhaps the greatest mobilization of charitable activity in American history. Between 1955 and 1968, the various civil rights organizations assembled thousands of individuals into a national protest movement that raised money, collected and disbursed food, and recruited volunteers to participate in boycotts, sit-ins, and marches across the country.

The Black Church

The black church has been involved in mutual aid since its inception. One reason for its benevolent and philanthropic practices is the overriding belief among African Americans that service to God is linked to service to humanity. Thus feeding the hungry, housing the homeless, and providing educational opportunities, social liberation, and economic empowerment are viewed as part of the moral imperative of religious faith. Throughout the South, black life revolved around the church. Free men were baptized, married, and buried in the same church. African-American churches strengthened the family by insisting that marriage be solemnized by religious services. The institution also punished adulterers and occasionally reunited separated couples. The church was a center for education, a provider of social insurance, and a place where blacks might relax and organize community entertainment. Black churches also supported schools and fraternal associations, expressed the community's social conscience by aiding the poor, supported missionary activities, and helped other free black communities establish similar institutions.[16]

Black churches have also been instrumental in the black struggle for full participation in American society. Early black churches served as stations for the Underground Railroad, providing escaping slaves with food, clothing, and financial resources to help them start a new life. During slavery, African-American churches helped slaves purchase freedom. Richmond's First African Church set aside Sunday's collection to liberate Noah Davis, a Baltimore minister; and later it aided other slaves in purchasing their freedom. In addition, these organizations also sponsored pan-African conferences, organized to fight against discrimination, and fought to integrate the armed forces. Moreover, they funded the celebrations of holidays and the independence of black countries. In 1859, for example, St. Louis Masons rented a train to take blacks into the countryside to commemorate the abolition of slavery in Saint-Dominique.[17]

Recently, in addition to voluntarism and giving, black churches have used their resources for economic and social development. Congregations such as Antioch Baptist Church in Chicago have created tax-exempt corporations for the development of low- and moderate-income housing. Voice of Calvary Ministries, in addition to its housing rehabilitation projects, operates a health clinic to serve persons of all income brackets and a company that provides goods to low-income persons at affordable prices.[18] Allen African Methodist Episcopal (AME) Church in Jamaica, New York, has extremely sophisticated social and community economic development programs. It has subsidiary corporations that include a credit union, a housing development corporation, a school, a home care agency, a women's resource center, and a senior citizens' organization.[19]

Black churches are also beginning to adopt some of the more sophisticated techniques of organized giving, with some turning to endowment programs to improve conditions in their communities. The Metropolitan Baptist Church in Memphis, Tennessee, for example, utilizes endowments to establish and provide venture capital to help start black businesses and to provide financial assistance to high school graduates. The African Methodist Episcopal Church uses its endowment to support ten colleges and a number of overseas missions. In addition, the church has established a scholarship trust fund, a credit union, a travel agency, and a revolving loan fund.

In 1986, a Gallup Poll conducted for the Joint Center for Political Studies found that 75 percent of philanthropic dollars in the black community are funneled through religious institutions and that most volunteer activities of blacks are centered around the church. Today, churches deliver food; assist the needy to access local, state, and federal assistance programs; provide free counseling services; offer scholarships; have tutorial programs; and distribute clothing.

Throughout the years, hundreds of black mutual aid societies and organizations with benevolent purposes have been established. African-American popular fraternities and sororities, such as Alpha Kappa Alpha, Delta Sigma Theta, Kappa Alpha Psi, and Alpha Phi Alpha, have as a main goal providing service to the African-

American community. Even the most exclusive African-American organizations such as Links Inc. concentrate on philanthropy and charity toward the black community. Recently, organizations such as the Concerned Black Men and 100 Black Women have been formed with benevolent attitudes and purposes.

Aristocrats of Color

From the very beginning, the benevolence of the black fraternal orders, mutual aid societies, the black church, and the black family was supplemented by a curious cast of aristocrats of color. According to historians John Hope Franklin, Carter G. Woodson, Charles Wesley, and others, individual cases of affluence and philanthropy among free blacks were numerous. The wealthiest black in early America was James Forten, who started out as an errand boy around the docks of Philadelphia, became a sailmaker, and accumulated a sizable fortune. By the time he died in 1832 at the age of sixty-six, he had given away most of his wealth financing the escape of runaway slaves, buying the freedom of others, and contributing to countless causes on behalf of less fortunate blacks. And there were others of significant wealth—like Jehu Jones, a proprietor of one of Charleston, South Carolina's, largest hotels; and Solomon Humphries, a leading grocer in Macon, Georgia.

From their own work and from the efforts of others, free Americans of African descent became large property owners as well. They owned so much property in New Orleans that more than one hundred years ago, they were described by a local newspaper as "a sober, industrious, and moral class, far advanced in education and civilization." As early as 1800, blacks in Philadelphia owned nearly a hundred houses and lots. Aid given by some of these property owners of color contributed greatly to the survival of those in the black diaspora.

Civil society institutions in the African-American community have been critical to preserving the principles and practices of self-help that have sustained the community against the odds of slavery, Jim Crow laws, discrimination, and a pervasive racism. Because of this legacy, black institutions have never had the capital resources of comparable white institutions often funded with public money, but many have survived because of dogged determination and a strong tradition of black philanthropy.

It came as a surprise to many Americans to learn that in 1991 African Americans gave a higher proportion of their household income for charitable purposes (2.7 percent) than did whites (2.2 percent) or Hispanics (2.1) percent.[20] This survey on giving and volunteering in the United States conducted by Independent Sector, a national organization of nonprofit groups, should dispel the myth that (1) African Americans are primarily recipients of charity rather than members of a community with its own tradition of benevolence, and (2) the advocacy of self-help by black conservatives who surfaced in the Reagan administration represented a major break with traditional black leadership.

The truth is that self-help, voluntarism, and philanthropy have long roots in the African-American community. The advocates of these highly celebrated civic virtues are as varied in time, place, and ideology as Booker T. Washington and W.E.B. Du Bois, Malcolm X and Martin Luther King, Jr. Their ranks also include voluntary organizations that have gained national attention as well as groups led by ordinary men and women who never made a newspaper headline or became the subject of a television sound bite.

Even black politicians whom the new breed of conservatives have charged with being preoccupied with the benevolence of government have called for nongovernmental alternatives to the governmental process. In Atlanta, Maynard Jackson, the African American who was mayor of that city during the time of civil disturbances in Los Angeles, boldly defended besieged Korean shop owners and called on black Americans to return to their own tradition of self-help. "We ought to watch what they are doing and do more of it ourselves," Jackson said. "They take care of their own people."[21]

Civil disturbances in America's cities are increasingly reminding us of the need to renew black organizations and civil society institutions. Such a renewal, if it can avoid the specter of separatism, can have both a large multiplier effect and broad social appeal because it emphasizes nongovernmental means, appeals to the pride of those who are searching for ways to address the decline of hope, and makes a contribution to economic and community development. It is as true for African Americans as it was for early European settlers that whenever a person's sense of control over his own life is expanded, whenever he sees himself as contributing to his and the community's well-being, his pride increases, his self-esteem grows, and his capacity for caring is enhanced.

Chapter Six

Thomy Lafon: Black Aristocracy and Benevolent Wealth

Many of the richest, best educated, and most cosmopolitan blacks in the early nineteenth century lived in New Orleans. Their achievements were so notable that even after the Ku Klux Klan had become an intimidating force and Jim Crow practices had become the norm, accounts of their work and wealth remained a part of local folklore. While the written history of the period has relegated many of these individuals to obscure footnotes, it is not too difficult to document and verify their success in business and the professions as well as in the examples they set in philanthropy.

According to historian Robert Reinders, the ratio of skilled to unskilled laborers among free men of color in nineteenth-century New Orleans was "considerably higher than among the Irish and German immigrants."[1] The 1850 census reported that only 9.9 percent of "free Negro males" were unskilled laborers.[2] Some blacks owned cotton and sugar plantations; others were engineers, architects, doctors, writers, artists, real estate brokers, and money lenders. A few were also inventors. As early as 1845, Robert Rillieux had invented the vacuum pan for evaporating syrup in the manufacture of sugar. In addition to their considerable holdings in cash and jewelry, free blacks in New Orleans owned more than $15 million worth of property in 1860. They lived in some of the finest homes in the state and sent their children to France and other European countries for their education.

These aristocrats of color were noted for more than their wealth and social status. Some were prominent humanitarians as well. The most notable was Thomy Lafon, who was born in poverty in 1810 but became one of the richest men in New Orleans. The more money he made, the more he gave away, winning such wide recognition for his humanitarianism that the Louisiana legislature voted in 1893 to honor him by commissioning a bust in his likeness. Long before the Rockefellers, the Kelloggs, and the Packards created the family foundations for which they have become well known, this black man, from whom the city of New Orleans once borrowed money to meet its payroll, distributed his sizable fortune indiscriminately to the needy of every creed and color.

Thomy Lafon was born of a black Haitian mother and a French father. He was deserted by his father very early in his childhood and left destitute. He supported himself and his mother by doing odd jobs and collecting and selling scrap iron. A man of great intellectual capacity, he managed to obtain an education and to become a schoolteacher. In 1850, when he was forty years old, he opened a small dry-goods store on Orleans Street. Those who knew him described him as a tall man of pleasing manners, dignified appearance, and deep compassion who never refused to help anyone in need.

Despite his reputation for giving money away, he managed his assets wisely and began to invest in real estate. A bachelor, he was a frugal man who lived a simple life with his sister in a small cottage. By the time of the Civil War, he had amassed a large fortune and become one of the city's richest men.

Black social life in New Orleans in the time of Thomy Lafon was a mixture of pathos, joy, pain, and suffering. But the free men of color who had been born free or had bought or been granted freedom had accumulated enough wealth to build a life that was not only upper class in status but personally satisfying and professionally admired and respected. New Orleans had been a multiracial community almost from its founding, but under the French a small but critically important group of free blacks began to flourish. There were free blacks elsewhere who amassed significant wealth and acclaim, but more came out of Louisiana than from all the other slaveholding colonies combined.

Thomy Lafon was not a descendant of any of these wealthy forerunners, but his interracial heritage and his fluency in French and Spanish caused him to be identified as a *mulatto*, a term that was often used not only to describe skin color but also to refer to a black Creole elite who were predominantly French in speech and culture. Much has been written about class divisions among blacks and mulattos in New Orleans, but Lafon was unwilling to accept this cultural and social stratification as the defining parameters of either his ambition or his benevolence. Class structure did indeed influence social, economic, and political life, but there is considerable evidence to suggest that the Reconstruction period united most of the black community in New Orleans in a common thought: liberation from social and political bondage.

At a gathering of prominent New Orleans blacks in December 1864, Oscar J. Dunn, a mulatto, opened the meeting by declaring: "We regard all black and colored men as brothers and fellow sufferers."[3] Like Lafon, he and other wealthy, free mulattos rejected the wedge that whites sought to drive between them and their recently freed brothers. They argued that unless the wealthy and educated black aristocrat tried to educate, aid, and counsel the freedmen, the latter group would continue to be oppressed. It was the aristocratic blacks who could move freely in the white community and who organized the Louisiana Equal Rights League and the Bureau of Industry in 1864. The League sent agents to the parishes to check on the conditions of the freedmen, appeal to officials for the redress of their grievances, and call for the establishment of more schools.

In his first monthly report in March 1865, the superintendent of the Bureau of Industry declared that during February the Bureau had obtained rations for 190 of the 192 persons who applied for them, had obtained jobs for 32 of the 37 persons seeking employment, had been instrumental in getting 11 people out of jail, and had given general assistance to 586.[4]

Despairing of changing enough white attitudes to create a more benevolent community, members of the Equal Rights League decided to forge an alliance aimed at breaking the power of the old white planters and helping the freedmen to become self-reliant. On February 27, 1865, they formed the New Orleans Freedman's Aid Association. Its objectives were to rent and lease abandoned plantations for use by the freedmen, to make loans to them, to furnish them with supplies, and to provide them with education and useful information on the cultivation and management of plantations. By August 1865, the association had rented several plantations; made loans to freedmen with a lien on their crops; furnished horses, seeds, and provisions to many laborers; and established prizes "to incite the industry and heighten the zeal of the freed men."[5]

The members of the black upper class in New Orleans were operating from a sense of compassion and civic duty, but they also recognized that their own economic position was fragile and insecure unless there was greater appreciation for the contribution that blacks could make to strengthening an economy that had been severely weakened by the Civil War. Unfortunately, they succeeded so well that white planters, who felt threatened by their efforts to gain a fuller measure of economic power, joined together to bar blacks from renting or buying land. The work of the association was effectively ended when Louisiana joined other Southern states in returning plantations after the war to their "rightful owners."

Black benevolence in Louisiana was far more than simple charity. While described by many as the first "Negro philanthropist" because he gave so much to support the needy, Lafon made large contributions to the abolitionist movement, the American Anti-Slavery Society, and the Underground Railroad as well.

Even among the poor in New Orleans, there was a fierce sense of independence and self-reliance, with the black community rejecting public charity. Most of the paupers in New Orleans during Reconstruction were foreign born. In 1870, 1,178 of the 1,271 paupers in the city were born elsewhere; only 31 were native-born blacks.[6]

Writing about this low rate of public dependency among New

Orleans blacks some years later, John Blasingame attributed it to several factors. First, blacks had an abhorrence of public relief. Whites had contended so vociferously and continuously that the newly freed blacks would not work that most New Orleans blacks shunned pubic relief as a matter of racial pride. Black newspapers tried to discourage their readers from accepting public relief even in times of public disaster.[7] In 1878, Elizabeth Baker, a white resident of New Orleans, wrote, "The Negroes, as a class, dislike the insinuation of applying to charitable institutions . . . many prefer starvation to charity."[8] Another factor that kept blacks off public relief was the activities of the benevolent societies and the myriad forms of self-help groups they formed. Many of these were supported heavily by wealthy blacks like Thomy Lafon who not only gave to a multitude of benevolent associations but built a home for the aged and another for homeless boys as well.

During the 1860s, by the time Lafon had decided to devote his full time to the affairs of the needy, there were more than two hundred registered black societies in New Orleans. These included benevolent associations; racial improvement societies; orphan-aid associations; Masonic, Odd-Fellows, Eastern Star, and Knights Templar lodges; religious societies; social and literary clubs; and rowing clubs and baseball clubs.[9] In addition to their many forms of self-help, these societies were a source of pride and a vehicle for social solidarity. Clad in bright uniforms, members of these groups often paraded through the streets and joined the funeral processions of their members or famous residents. The societies provided a wide variety of recreational outlets as well, with some of the most notable and attractive being group excursions that on occasion included as many as two thousand people. They chartered special trains and steamboats, hired bands, and went to such places as St. Louis and Mobile, and sometimes as far away as Virginia.

This historical nexus between benevolent societies and the disdain for public relief describes only part of the environment in which Thomy Lafon emerged as a preeminent philanthropist. Lafon

was a very religious man in a very religious community. He believed
that one served God by serving his neighbors. As a devout
Catholic, he was a close confidant of the local archbishop and
became one of the major benefactors of Catholic charities. For
many blacks, the church was the most important social institution
in the New Orleans community. But while they left the white
Protestant churches in large numbers during Reconstruction to form
their own separate congregations, most of the black Catholics continued to attend integrated churches throughout the Reconstruction period. The Catholic Church fought consistently against the
idea of requiring blacks to sit in separate pews, a practice that had
become the norm for Protestant churches seeking to retain their
black members. While black Protestants were being relegated to
the balcony, free blacks owned half the pews in St. Augustine's
Catholic Church and attended many other Catholic churches in
New Orleans, encountering no discrimination whatsoever. A
Methodist minister wrote this account of integration in the
Catholic Church: "In her most aristocratic churches in this city, lips
of every shade, by hundreds press with devout kisses the same cru-
cifixes, and fingers of as great variety in color, are dipped in the 'holy
water', to imprint the cross on as varied brows. In the renting of
pews colored families have a chance, and we have seen them sitting as others in every part of the house."[10]

The Catholic Church was not totally immune from the pressures of the Reconstruction period, but the influence of Lafon and
other black benefactors enabled the church to retain its nondis-
criminatory policy. It was thus not surprising that Lafon collabo-
rated so closely with the Catholic Church in his philanthropy. Long
before the establishment of the major foundations in New York and
elsewhere, Lafon used the concept of an endowment in perpetuity
to establish a trust fund, with interest from the endowment to be
used by the Catholic Sisters of the Holy Family on behalf of
orphans and widows. As a continuing reminder of Lafon's many
benefactions, the Sisters placed a tablet in the chapel of their

motherhouse and novitiate in New Orleans on which they inscribed the words: "In memory of Thomy Lafon who died November 22, 1893, aged 82 years, a friend of the orphan and widow."

In 1973, eighty years later, a new generation of Sisters honored Lafon's memory by establishing the Lafon Nursing Home of the Holy Family. The history of their order includes this passage about Lafon:

> He remained to the end unassuming and frugal, freely sharing his fortune with those deserving help without distinction of color or creed. His will . . . attests to the democratic . . . spirit of the man who bequeathed his fortune to the poor, suffering humanity of the Crescent City, for every institution, white or colored, state or private, Catholic or Protestant, received a donation from this noble and generous philanthropist.[11]

It is, indeed, ironic that the roots of community philanthropy in New Orleans, now associated primarily with wealthy whites, extend back to the charitable impulse of a wealthy black man. Long before there was a community foundation in New Orleans, Lafon became the major source of community philanthropy. He understood that philanthropy, like community and caring, rarely happens automatically. It needs a catalyst, a vehicle to activate a latent impulse, to bring community needs and community assets together. So he was often the lead donor, giving generously to the Charity Hospital of New Orleans, New Orleans University, Straight University, and a number of charities of the sort now supported by local community foundations and the United Way.

On Lafon's death, when the Louisiana legislature voted to honor him in memorial for his "broad humanitarianism," the local newspaper reported that this was the first public testimonial by a state to a man of color in recognition of his philanthropy.

Lafon set a pace in both wealth accumulation and wealth distribution that few have been able to match. But he was not the only free man of color to achieve a position of distinction and usefulness in the state of Louisiana. Many others in the state also demonstrated that with equal chance and opportunity they could prosper in a highly competitive economy. In St. Landry Parish, Martin Donato was one of the largest and most prominent landholders. Marie Metoyer of Natchitoches Parish had two thousand acres of land when she died in 1840, and Charles Roques of Iberville Parish left a thousand acres when he died in 1854. Aristide Mary owned a whole block on Canal Street in downtown New Orleans.[12]

Yet, it was not their wealth, but the benevolent uses of wealth that distinguished the black aristocrats in Louisiana. They helped build benevolent associations, churches, and schools that served to knit the community together, create a leadership class, and promote the general welfare.

Thomy Lafon was unique, however, not simply because of his race, but because his philanthropy embraced people of all races. His expansive sense of civic duty was easily understood and exercised during the early nineteenth century when free men of color moved across racial lines with relative ease; but continuing to embrace the larger community in the period following the Civil War was far more complex. The city of New Orleans was an especially confusing place. Integration and segregation existed side by side.

The man who had once been so widely respected and revered that some local banks maintained a special chair for him now found race relations swinging like a crazy pendulum back and forth between what New Orleans was and what the rest of the South was becoming. It was a time of uneasiness, a time when free blacks suddenly found themselves naked and exposed. The white "commoners" who had always resented both the white and black upper classes in New Orleans were increasingly in control. They insisted on a more rigid distinction between blacks and whites.

But there were a number of white establishments that refused to bow to the changing social mores. In June 1874, a local newspaper, the *Louisianan*, applauded "the Catholicity of spirit" in New

Orleans that recognized "the civil and public rights of the colored race more fully than has been the case in any Southern city."[13]

Lafon's New Orleans was clearly changing, however. His benefactions that had enabled the city to survive and grow during threatening times appeared to be losing their appeal. Yet, because of Lafon there continued to be cracks in the New Orleans color line. Perhaps in no other American city did race relations present as complex and as varied a pattern as in New Orleans. Clearly, no city presented as bold and as imaginative a portrait of black idealism and generosity. The contributions of Thomy Lafon, and the respect with which he was regarded, helped increase opportunity for other blacks in the city, both before and after the Civil War. They also contributed to black self-respect, as many identified with the man whose noble deeds had won him an honored place in New Orleans aristocracy.

Memories, however, are short and selective. Very few in twentieth-century New Orleans, black or white, are aware of how much they owe to this black pioneer who gave so much of himself and his resources to building the city that is now Louisiana's largest and one of the nation's finest.

While it would be a great mistake to view all of nineteenth-century New Orleans through the lens of this small black elite, it would be an even greater error to ignore the life and legacy of those who set an example not only in commerce and culture but in humanitarianism as well. Far too little is known of men like Thomy Lafon whose benefactions rivaled those of the white wealthy even though their philanthropy is better known and more widely celebrated. There is indeed a selective national memory, a social divide that morally weakens us all. The whole of the American society can benefit from knowing that in the darkest night of the American soul, when dehumanization was part of the daily drama, a small group of blacks in New Orleans stood against the moral tide, affirming and claiming all of humanity in their embrace.

Chapter Seven

Maggie Walker:
Self-Help and Social Reform

Maggie Walker gave much of her life to enhancing the capacity of African Americans to provide mutual aid and self-help. Her genius was her ability to combine the charitable instinct with hardheaded business acumen. She was born in Richmond, Virginia, in 1867, two years after the Civil War had ended, leaving Richmond in chaos. Vast fortunes in cotton and tobacco had been destroyed by blazing fires. Stately mansions and places of business that once graced the skyline were now simply part of a majestic past. Both white and black residents were consumed with the task of restoring civic functions and bringing back the sanity of civic order.

With the thunder of cannon stilled and the smoke of battle finally cleared, a struggle to capture the minds of the newly freed slaves was now under way. A speech at the Atlanta Exposition by Booker T. Washington drew national acclaim for its views on accommodation and development. With his message of self-help and compromise, Washington developed a pipeline to the White House and access to the purse strings of wealthy philanthropists. A succession of presidents consulted with him on strategies and the educational institution he founded in Tuskegee flourished.

It was not surprising, therefore, that Maggie Walker grew up believing deeply in the Washington philosophy of black self-help, racial pride, and economic empowerment. Yet, like many other blacks of her time, she had her feet in two camps. She became an apostle of self-help at an early age, joining a mutual aid society at fourteen and later becoming the first woman in the United States to be founder and president of a bank. But she also heeded the clarion call of W.E.B. Du Bois, supporting his ideas on political reform as well as the notion of a "talented tenth," a well-educated cadre of black leaders.

Maggie Walker grew up in the period before Social Security and public welfare. Black families lived outside the mainstream economy and government offered them no safety net. They cared for the sick and buried the dead as well as they could. Black children studied from hand-me-down books in hand-me-down buildings. Times were hard, but many vowed never to accept charity.

No one reflected this spirit of self-reliance and independence more than Elizabeth Draper Mitchell, Maggie's mother. Widowed twice at an early age, she kept her family together, supporting them by washing and ironing clothes for the local whites. As a child, Maggie Walker was seen frequently tugging a heavy, loaded wagon, calling for and delivering the laundry. Her work started at dawn— building a fire, filling the tubs, and rubbing homemade lye soap onto the clothes. By the time she left for school, her knuckles were already sore from the rhythmic task of rubbing them up and down on metal washboards.

But instead of being defeated by the many hardships that faced a black child in those years following the Civil War, Walker was determined to persevere, not simply to make a name for herself but to help improve the plight of the black community. She felt the call of civic duty as strongly as she wished for the opportunity to create a better life for herself and her progeny. Experience soon taught her that she had the potential to escape poverty and overcome prejudice if she worked as hard in her studies at school as she did at home with her mother.

Just before graduating from the Armstrong Normal School, Walker learned that she had achieved the highest academic average of the ten students in her class. Her devotion to education was beginning to bring rewards, but the members of the class of 1883 were restless. They felt fortunate to have been exposed to the best education that Richmond offered black students, but they felt a lingering discontent with their second-class status. They decided to challenge the tradition that black and white students should hold separate commencement exercises. Agreeing that it was unfair for their graduation to be held in a black church while the white students held theirs in a public theater, Walker went with her classmates to present the case to the faculty, arguing that their parents also paid taxes. Failing to win concessions, the students decided to strike, going down in history as the organizers of the first school strike of blacks in America. This was a personal risk that Walker was prepared to take for the larger community good. She and the members of her class stood their ground and were eventually presented their diplomas in a school auditorium.

This desire for reform and respect remained with Walker for the rest of her life. She had, after all, heard stories from her mother about the courage of women who stood tall in defense of their convictions. The most notable of these was the story of Miss Van Lew, a white woman in Richmond who became a Union sympathizer and daily risked her life to help Union men escape from the Confederate prison. The Van Lew mansion, located on a hill overlooking Richmond, was Maggie Walker's birthplace. Walker's mother had told her often how the daughter of the mansion's owner had gone away to school in Philadelphia and returned convinced that slavery was wrong. A strong-willed and persuasive young woman, Miss Van Lew persuaded her father to free his fifteen slaves. Among them were William Mitchell and Elizabeth Draper, who, after they were freed, stayed on to work for wages. They eventually married and Walker was their child.

It was at the mansion that Walker first became enchanted with books. She learned to read at an early age and was soon reciting poems with the animation and power that later moved audiences to subscribe to her public values and to support her civic vision. Walker's parents could not have imagined that she would grow up to be one of the great women of her time, but they felt pride in her early accomplishments. Even after Elizabeth Draper's husband died and she was supporting her family as a washerwoman, she continued to see this special quality in her daughter. When delivering the laundry, Walker would pause on Main Street before the house where Edgar Allan Poe had lived with his foster father.[1] As she came to the capitol building a little farther down, she would leave her wagon against the curb for a moment and walk into the capitol rotunda to gaze up at a statue of George Washington.[2] Enriched and enchanted by historical lore, little Maggie Walker delved into her own history with a prospector's fervor, often dazzling her teachers with her knowledge of Africa, the slave trade, and black history.

Time passed and Walker went on to a larger stage. If there was a turning point in her life, it was in 1891 when she joined the Independent Order of Saint Luke, a benevolent society formed in Baltimore in 1867 for the purpose of helping the sick and burying the dead. Like Walker, the organization was fourteen years old with great potential but also much uncertainty about its future. They grew up together as Walker rose through the ranks to become Grand Secretary in 1899. But the society was floundering, its once great potential obscured by bickering among its leaders, a large debt, and a general lack of direction.

Calling on her diplomacy and innate business skills, Maggie Walker set out to turn the organization around, to make it work for the self-development of the black community. She took over the leadership in 1899 of a mutual aid benevolent society with 57 local chapters and three thousand four hundred members. In a few years, it had grown to one thousand five hundred chapters and more than one hundred thousand members. Chartered under the laws of Virginia, the Order was soon operating in twenty-eight states. It provided help in times that could be catastrophic for a black family: sickness, with its need of a physician and a friendly visitor; and death, with its demand for a decent burial.[3] Under Walker's leadership, St. Luke, as the organization was affectionately known, provided both money and a friend.

Always seeking new ways to improve the condition of the black community, Walker became convinced that the next stage in the evolution of St. Luke and the development of the Richmond black community should include a full-service bank. She modestly called it St. Luke's Penny Savings Bank. Her proposal for establishing the bank was approved by her board of directors and the bank was created in 1903. People came from as far away as New York to make deposits in the new bank. The local newspaper reported that on opening day the main office was crowded "with colored people representing all stations of Afro-American society."[4] It was said to be the first bank in the country founded by a woman.

In 1929, St. Luke's Penny Savings Bank merged with two other banks and changed its name to the Consolidated Bank and Trust Company. With Walker as chair of the new board of directors, Consolidated became the most stable bank in Richmond, white or black. This black woman banker, who grew up helping her mother do the laundry of the local elite, lent the city $100,000 in cash to allow continued operation of the schools for both white and black children when the white banks in Richmond were unable to extend further loans to the city. The bank became so widely respected that it was selected to collect city water and sewage fees and eventually became a depository for city taxes.

It was no accident that Richmond became an important center of black business activity. As white banks refused in most Southern communities to provide the black businessman with the necessary capital and credit, Walker had correctly perceived the need for black financial institutions. She knew that black entrepreneurs would invest in their communities out of enlightened self-interest. They lived in the community and realized that in order to operate healthy businesses they needed to operate in healthy communities.

Blacks in Richmond owned and operated restaurants, shoe stores, livery stables, and barber shops. Others found work as blacksmiths, carpenters, brickmasons, and railroad workers. They were a part of the new prosperity that had come to Richmond as the city rebuilt from the devastation of the Civil War. Maggie Walker's belief in the entrepreneurial spirit as the driving engine of change was contagious. Values such as free enterprise, hard work, and industriousness became major weapons for combating the conditions that kept blacks outside the mainstream economy. Even the children of black Richmond formed saving clubs and took more pride in what they were able to save than in what they were able to consume.

Walker possessed a gift that served her well: the ability to sway an audience. She had seen at an early age the respect and admiration the black community accorded the spoken word. Thus, she learned to hold her listeners spellbound with stories of black achievement.[5] Two of her favorites were about the success of a scrubwoman and a one-legged bootblack:

> There is a woman in the office here who came to us 18 years ago. She did odd jobs of cleaning, and we paid her a dollar a week, which she was glad to get. We encouraged her to fit herself for better things. She studied, took a business course at night school, and has worked her way up until now she is our head bookkeeper, with a salary of one hundred-fifty dollars a month. She owns a comfortable home, well-furnished and fully paid for, and has money in the bank.
>
> Then there was that one-legged bootblack at Second and Clay streets. He joined our Order. He had a rented chair out on the sidewalk in the weather. We helped him save, and when he had fifty dollars, we helped him rent a little place with three chairs. That was seven years ago. Now he has a place of his own with twelve chairs. He has bought a home for his mother—paid $1,900 for it—and has it furnished and free of debt. And his bank account never falls below five hundred dollars.[6]

Maggie Walker sought out individuals such as this cleaning woman and the bootblack, encouraging them to acquire additional skills and showing them how to get better jobs. She was deeply concerned about the future of black youth. She had spent a few years as a teacher before enrolling in business and accounting courses and deciding to walk a different path. Her classroom soon became the entire state of Virginia and eventually the nation. She taught thrift, urging her young audiences to save their pennies, vividly describing to them how money, properly invested, could someday work for them. She encouraged the children, whom she recruited to the St. Luke society in large numbers, to sell papers, cut grass, do chores, run errands, and save. Thrift was not an end in itself. Money was important for what it did for one's growth and development. And the most important thing that money could buy was education.

Walker also taught moral values, telling her audiences that the Ten Commandments, the Lord's Prayer, and the Sermon on the Mount contained enough truth to live by. "But do not lock these learned truths into some metal safe; weave them into daily living; they must 'show' in daily acts of kindness," she urged.[7] A religious woman who found time to teach a Sunday school class and to serve as a trustee of the Women's Auxiliary of the National Baptist Convention, Maggie Walker is best remembered, nevertheless, for what she taught about economic values, about putting one's money to work. She impressed on everyone she met the wisdom of saving their money (regardless of how little they earned) while they were young, strong, and healthy. But she reminded them that "part of their duty in becoming independent is getting where they can help others."[8]

Maggie Walker knew tragedy as intimately as triumph. Her brother Johnny died at an early age. Her first husband was mysteriously found dead in the James River, and her second husband was accidentally shot and killed by their son. In 1924, she was confined to a wheelchair. But despite being black, female, and paralyzed, Walker continued her stream of accomplishments. Eleanor Roosevelt wrote her to say: "I cannot imagine anything more satisfying than a life of the kind of accomplishments you have had"; and E. Lee Trinkle, the Governor of Virginia, once said of her: "If the state of Virginia had done no more in fifty years with the funds spent on the education of the Negroes than educate Mrs. Walker, the state would have been amply repaid for its outlay and efforts."[9]

Strong-willed and determined, Maggie Walker was at home with all she met. On the wall of her home were pictures of W.E.B. Du Bois, Booker T. Washington, and Marcus Garvey. An early advocate for black women's rights, she served on the board of trustees of the National Association of Colored Women (NACW) and the Virginia Industrial School for Girls. She organized in Richmond a Council of Women with one thousand four hundred members.[10] They raised money and volunteered time to help young girls improve their status.

Walker recognized the power of the printed as well as the spoken word and established the *Saint Luke Herald*. The newspaper, which had thousands of subscribers, called attention to injustices and provided important information on health, education, home management, and thrift. There was even a children's section that published poems, stories, and articles written by children. The newspaper had an evangelical overtone, constantly reminding readers of their moral duty to "love thy neighbor as thyself." Its editorials were memorable, repeatedly arguing that all the unfair methods used against blacks in civic, political, and commercial life should sooner or later teach them the lesson of racial unity and cooperation. She wanted the community to invest its resources in community enterprise, to recognize the potential of the African-American market. This was all the more significant because throughout the South black businesspeople were losing their white customers. The tiny entrepreneurial class that had grown wealthy during the antebellum period had expanded after the Civil War. By 1930, there were about seventy thousand black business enterprises.[11] But the trades they once dominated were now being preempted by whites. To make matters worse, black customers were taken for granted by white businessmen who heaped upon them all sorts of indignities, assuming this group had no alternatives. Thus, in all phases of community life, economic, cultural, educational, charitable, and religious, Walker stressed the necessity of banding together and building strong black institutions that both provided an alternative and fostered pride. She synthesized the messages of both Du Bois and Washington, urging her generation to get wisdom, but also to get wealth.

A shrewd businesswoman and an apostle of self-help, Walker set an example in charitable endeavors as well. She established a community house and visiting nurse service, raised money for a girl's reform school, and helped to found a tuberculosis sanatorium. She used the wide respect she commanded in the white community to promote civic cohesion and community solidarity, serving on the Virginia Interracial Commission and heading the black section of the Richmond Community Fund Drive.

In 1934, ill health compelled Maggie Walker to discontinue many of her public and private activities. That October she was honored by all the major black national organizations. The month was observed as "Maggie L. Walker Month" and more than one thousand statuettes of her were placed in black schools and businesses.[12] She died the following December, still regarded with awe and honor. The tribute of the *Richmond Times-Dispatch* typified the response of a grateful nation: "The passing of Mrs. L. Walker removes from the scene one of the greatest Negro leaders in America, and probably the foremost member of the colored race ever born in Virginia. . . . Her death leaves a gap in the ranks of American leadership. . . . There is no one at the moment who can replace her."[13]

Alexis de Tocqueville, who journeyed to America in 1831, wrote in his study of this new country that "Americans of all ages, all conditions, and all dispositions constantly form associations. Wherever at the head of some new undertaking you see the government in France, or a man of rank in England, in the United States you will be sure to find an association."[14] De Tocqueville was writing about white America, but had he scrutinized life among blacks as well, he would have found the same tendency to form voluntary associations and benevolent societies. The Pennsylvania Abolition Society conducted censuses in 1837 and 1847 in Philadelphia to refute pro-slavery contentions that free blacks were fit only for almshouses and jails.[15] Edward Needles, who conducted the study, reported that free blacks in the Philadelphia area alone had formed more than eighty benevolent societies for mutual aid and comfort. These voluntary associations drew praise for preventing pauperism and crime, but equally surprising, the study found that when blacks and whites were compared according to the proportion of Philadelphia's population each group represented, a smaller percentage of blacks than whites required public charity.

In developing black associations and voluntary societies at the dawn of the twentieth century, Maggie Walker and other black leaders were not mimicking or reacting to exclusion from white institutions. Quite to the contrary, black voluntary associations not only grew simultaneously with white voluntary institutions, but as Peter Kropotkin concluded in his own work, "mutual aid has been an ingredient in the evolution of mankind."[16] Ralph Ellison, in his critique of the Myrdal study, argued that voluntary associations among blacks were not so much a reaction to their environment as a product of deeper meaning and values. "Men, as Dostoevsky observed," wrote Ellison, "cannot live in revolt. Nor can they live in a state of reacting."[17]

As the propensity for voluntarism among European settlers in America grew out of the need for cooperation during the Revolutionary War and the adjustment to changing patterns of society, so were volunteer societies used to give support, comfort, and status to blacks adjusting to a strange environment. The functions of these black organizations differed because the status of blacks differed. Denied access to the privileges and potential of the governmental sector, blacks created their own voluntary sector out of their own unique values, needs, and aspirations.

Through these voluntary associations, diverse people from widely different tribal cultures were brought together to create a sense of solidarity, cohesion, and community, generating the black church, the convention movement, and other important components of black institutional life. As Margaret Mead and Muriel Brown have observed, "A community is born when people act together."[18] No one understood this sociology of community better than Maggie Walker.

Chapter Eight

Madame C. J. Walker:
Entrepreneurial Philanthropy

Delta, Louisiana, was an unlikely birthplace for Madame C. J. Walker, America's first black, self-made, female millionaire and premier philanthropist of her time. Unlike nineteenth-century New Orleans, an internationally renowned center of culture and commerce, Delta was home to plantations and poverty. This was especially true in 1867 when a former slave, Minerva Breedlove, gave birth to her third child, Sarah, the first member of the family to be born free. Two years earlier the South had surrendered and Delta, like much of the region, lay in ruins, its homes, crops, and livestock destroyed by Union soldiers. Although many of the whites were later to join the Ku Klux Klan, the Knights of the White Camellia, the White Brotherhood, and other white supremacist groups, the Breedlove child was destined to reach heights that not even the wealthiest plantation owners in Delta could have contemplated for either themselves or their progeny.[1]

W.E.B. Du Bois later wrote of her, "It is given to few persons to transform a people in a generation. . . . She made and deserved a fortune and gave much of it away generously." Booker T. Washington, who founded the National Negro Business League and rivaled Du Bois as the foremost black spokesperson of the early twentieth century, hailed her as "one of the most progressive and successful businesswoman of our race." In a headline story in 1917, the *New York Times* noted, "Twelve years ago, she was a washerwoman, glad of a chance to do any one's wash for $1.50 a day. Her friends now say she has a cool million."

The article in the *New York Times* told only a small part of the

109

meteoric rise of the woman who came to be known as Madame C. J. Walker. At the 1912 convention of the National Negro Business League, with Booker T. Washington and a largely male audience generally ignoring the handful of women present, she rose to her feet to say, "I am a woman who came from the cotton fields of the South. I was promoted from there to the washtub. Then I was promoted from the cook kitchen to the business of manufacturing hair goods and preparations. . . . I started in business eight years ago with one dollar and fifty cents. Now I am giving employment to more than a thousand women." In just a few years, the number of women under her employ had reached twenty thousand, including agents not only in the United States, but Central America and the Caribbean as well.

The feature that ultimately distinguished Madame Walker was not so much her business acumen, although it was considerable, as her generosity. The wealthier she became, the more charities and social causes she supported financially. She had great respect for Booker T. Washington and his emphasis on self-help, but she knew that self-help alone was not enough; it needed to be accompanied by individuals and institutions engaged in social protest and promoting social change. Closely allied with William Monroe Trotter, the crusading editor of the *Guardian*, and political activists A. Philip Randolph and Ida B. Wells, her contribution to the anti-lynching campaign of the National Association for the Advancement of Colored People (NAACP) was the largest that organization had ever received.

Madame Walker expanded her activities to helping save the home of the abolitionist Frederick Douglass, supporting the work of the educator Mary McLeod Bethune, and helping to organize the 1917 protest that drew more than ten thousand black participants to New York. Constantly warned by some of her colleagues that mixing business, philanthropy, and politics could spell disaster for her thriving business, Madame Walker was willing to take the risk because her primary commitment was to "uplifting the race." Poor for most of her life, she remembered her roots: born to illiterate sharecroppers, orphaned at the age of seven, married at fourteen, and widowed at twenty.

The seeds of her generosity and social concern were planted in St. Louis, where on her arrival she joined the St. Paul African Methodist Episcopal Church, a congregation whose members were committed to helping the poor. Black women were the backbone of the church and the church was the philanthropic arm of the black community. It was not surprising, therefore, that the women at St. Paul extended a friendly and generous hand to young Sarah Breedlove. She reciprocated as soon as she was able by helping others, collecting and supplying them with clothing, food, and other necessities. The membership of St. Paul included some of the most prosperous and prominent black citizens in St. Louis. Many of the women were well-educated, sophisticated, and stylish. Breedlove was impressed particularly by their self-confidence and ability to accomplish their goals. As a child, she had not had time for an education although her parents had dreamed of sending her to school. Illiterate themselves, they, like many parents of their time, saw education as the way to a better life for their children. Literacy was a symbol of freedom, but in reality, the daughters of sharecroppers in Delta had no time for such luxuries as books and school. They rose early in the morning to help their mothers cook breakfast; they spent the daylight hours planting and harvesting. When night fell, they tended the family livestock or prepared younger siblings for bed. On weekends, they helped their mothers earn whatever extra money they could, usually by doing laundry or cleaning houses for whites.

The washboard was central to the life of young black women in Delta and Vicksburg. But life was different in St. Louis with its electric- and gas-lighted streets giving as much vitality to the night as to the day. Of course, there were gamblers, hustlers, and prostitutes, but there were also entrepreneurs and people with ambition preparing for a better future. The fire of ambition began to burn in

Breedlove's own heart and mind. She believed that she could be like the women she admired. Even as a washerwoman, she had delivered her baskets of neatly folded clothes with dignity. Working long hours, living frugally, and putting aside a little money each week, she had been able to save enough to send her daughter to college.

Breedlove now felt an urgent desire to improve her own condition. She reflected first on her appearance. She was losing her hair; it was broken and patchy even though she was still a young woman. The black women she admired most were both successful and immaculately groomed. Yet Breedlove's problem was not unique. Inadequate diet, stress, poor health, and the use of inappropriate hair products caused countless problems for many black women. Breedlove tried the hair treatments of her day, but none worked. After repeated failure to find one appropriate for her hair, she decided to design her own. It was a decision that was destined to make her the Estee Lauder of her time. Her hair was soon growing faster than it was falling out. Her entrepreneurial drive had finally found an outlet. What worked for her, she reasoned, could also work for other black women.

Once again she packed her bags and went in search of greener pastures, this time as an entrepreneur working for herself and helping other black women. She now had the self-confidence, the daring, and, she hoped, the product. On July 21, 1905, she arrived in Denver, a city with very few blacks, but one where many blacks had started their own businesses.

Breedlove arrived in Denver with $1.50 in savings, found a job as a cook, and began to lay plans for her own enterprise. She tested one formula after another on herself until she finally felt that she had created several products that were marketable. She kept her job as a cook but also launched her new business by selling her product from door to door. With her well-groomed hair, she presented herself as an example of what her product could do. She began advertising in the *Colorado Statesman*, a black newspaper published in Denver, generating mail orders on a larger scale than her personal selling could achieve.

Confident, attractive, and increasingly successful, Breedlove married C. J. Walker, a friend from St. Louis. He was a sales agent for a black newspaper and had provided long-distance advice from time to time; now he moved to Denver where he helped his new wife expand her mail-order business. The former Sarah Breedlove thus became Madame C. J. Walker. Even the choice of the title *Madame* seems to have been calculated to enhance marketing of her products. It conjured up the mystique of France, the undisputed fashion and beauty capital of the time.

Madame C. J. Walker soon became a household word not only in Denver's black community but throughout the United States, the Caribbean, and Latin America. Her small staff of her husband, her daughter, and four cousins could no longer keep up with the orders that were pouring in. She decided to expand her business. She hired women and trained them as agents to demonstrate and take orders for her products in return for a share of the profit. She began dreaming of the possibility of empowering black women across the globe to rise up and shape a new destiny. She was already making more than twice the salary of the average white American male and she envisioned legions of black women doing the same.

After a year and a half traveling as far away as New York and back to Louisiana and Mississippi, Madame Walker decided to move her operation closer to the population centers where she had a larger client base. Impressed by the infrastructure in Pittsburgh, its sophisticated transportation system, its thriving banking and industrial base, and its abundant source of steel for the hair-pressing combs she was now marketing, she relocated her corporate office to that city. She opened a training school for Walker agents and began to fulfill her dream of transforming laundresses, housekeepers, and office cleaners into large wage earners and proud independent black women.

Walker had become one of America's most successful business tycoons. She was sought out by men and women of prominence in education, politics, and the arts; yet she was restless and unfulfilled. While she was building a commercial empire, she had also been satisfying her appetite for knowledge, reading widely, attending lectures, and becoming a patron of the arts. She hired tutors and became a keen observer of the business strategies of American industry. Friends reported that after business hours she could be found "until the small hours of the night studiously perusing her books; as she advanced she provided herself with the master pieces of literature."[2] Her intellectual curiosity, abundant energy, and strong commitment to empowering black women would not let her feel satisfied that she had fulfilled her destiny.

She decided to expand her business again and to move her corporate headquarters to Indianapolis, a city more centrally located for covering a national market. She established her office in the heart of the black community and employed neighborhood women almost exclusively. While she was now recognized as a woman of culture as well as commerce, she remained deeply committed to women who were immobilized in the minimal jobs that she had once performed herself. She commissioned the work of black artists for her home, hosted concerts and poetry readings, and dined with educators, politicians, doctors, and lawyers, but she kept her eyes on the problems of the women who were struggling with society's inequities.

Walker was now learning to make effective use of her success in business to influence social change. A transforming experience occurred one evening when she was confronted with discrimination at an Indianapolis theater. While respected by bankers and warmly welcomed in the city's department stores where her money made whites color-blind, she found herself just another "colored person" when she arrived at the Isis Theater one evening. She went home and sued the theater the next day, charging "unwarranted discrimination because of her color," but she took an even bolder step by building an elegant movie theater as part of the Walker complex that occupied an entire block in downtown Indianapolis. As Madame Walker prospered and her wealth gave her a high public profile, she became more involved with black service and civil rights organizations. She encouraged her employees to follow her example, urging her agents to use their economic clout for civic activism. At an agents' meeting in 1917, Walker employees voted to send a telegram to President Woodrow Wilson regarding the uprising in East St. Louis, Illinois, where mobs murdered thirty-nine blacks, seriously injured hundreds of others, and drove thousands of families from their homes. Addressing the agents, Walker advised them to remain loyal to their home, their country, and their flag, but she also cautioned them "not to let our love of country, our patriotic loyalty cause us to abate one whit in our protest against wrong and injustice."

Walker remained a shrewd businesswoman, however. Long before the advent of cause-related marketing, linking corporate marketing with corporate giving, Madame C. J. Walker understood that publicity about her philanthropy could increase her sales. Every time she donated money to a black institution, she publicly linked the purchase of Walker products with the well-being of black America. But her generosity went far beyond enlightened self-interest. She knew how to multiply the impact of both charitable and business dollars. In constructing a group of homes for Indianapolis blacks in 1916, she made certain that the work was done by black workers. Few blacks in her time understood as well as she did how to use their resources to develop real economic clout. Her lectures to her agents on how to market Walker products could have come out of the best marketing texts used by the best business schools.

At a time when American business was primarily local, the former Sarah Breedlove, who was born of illiterate former slaves in rural Louisiana, envisioned expanding her business overseas. As was now her custom, she spent some time doing research on the matter before she set out to visit Jamaica, Costa Rica, and the Panama Canal Zone. She used the techniques that had made her successful when she first started in the United States, demonstrating personally her Walker Hair Care Method. The results were the same. Women were eager to buy her product and to sign on as agents. The

Walker enterprise went international, providing power and pride to black women wherever they resided. She was selling more than a product. She was selling self-confidence and economic independence. Her ads called it "the Walker System," but it was really the Walker philosophy. The Walker Beauty School textbook asserted that "to be beautiful, does not refer alone to the arrangement of the hair, the perfection of the complexion or to the beauty of the form. . . . To be beautiful, one must combine these qualities with a beautiful mind and soul; a beautiful character."

While Madame Walker was dazzling the world with her business success and her philanthropy, she was also enjoying her wealth and causing a stir among the nation's cultural and social elite, black and white. She bought three lots in Harlem, tore down the old brownstone buildings that occupied them, and built a mansion. The 1917 issue of Funk and Wagnalls' *Literary Digest* called her the "Queen of Gotham's Colored 400."[3] Social functions at her home were attended by nearly every important black in America. Around her dining-room table, black and white leaders discussed the important philosophical ideas of the time and planned economic and political strategies to improve the plight of American blacks. Her biggest social coup came when she bought a strip of land at Irvington-on-the-Hudson near the exclusive residences of some of America's wealthiest families. The black architect Vertner Tandy designed for her a thirty-room Georgian mansion that was furnished with rich tapestries, French Renaissance furniture, enormous oil paintings, a $60,000 pipe organ, a gold-plated piano, deep-piled Persian rugs, and trees imported from Japan at a cost of $10,000.[4] A close friend and early guest, Enrico Caruso, suggested its name: Villa Lewaro.

Madame Walker's life among the rich and famous did not diminish her concern for those who were less fortunate. She increased her contributions to educational institutions, giving especially large amounts to those institutions headed by women, even endowing an academy for women in West Africa. The demands made on her by friends, her business, and the many social needs of her era soon began to take their toll on her health. Despite warnings from her doctors, she continued to speak widely and to involve herself in civic and social causes. Her rags-to-riches story came to an end on May 25, 1919, when at the age of 51 she succumbed to the effects of high blood pressure that had severely damaged her kidneys. Her friend Mary McLeod Bethune summed up her life when she said that Walker's story shall live as an inspiration not only to her race but also to the world.

Madame Walker's generosity was reflected in her death as it was in her life. Her will listed countless organizations as beneficiaries, stipulated that the Walker company was to remain in the control of women, and directed that two thirds of its profits be allotted to charitable organizations. Many years later, both Villa Lewaro and the Walker building in Indianapolis were added to the National Register of Historic Places by Interior Department officials in the Carter administration.

The Walker family wealth did not survive in any substantial way beyond the second generation. Fortunately, her contributions transcended both the times in which she lived and the assets she accumulated. Her legacy lives on in both her philanthropy and her philosophy, with a new generation of black women reaffirming her claim that beauty is deeper than physical traits, encompassing the mind, the soul, and the character.

Many times in her life Madame C. J. Walker could have accepted defeat, blaming her predicament on the circumstances of her birth. Instead, she was driven by the desire to excel. Like many other black Americans of her time, she was motivated rather than beaten by the social boundaries and economic barriers that sought to stifle her ambition and limit her reach. Her life was both a call to arms in the revolt against racism and a guide for those who seek to transform society through nongovernmental means. She was both a successful entrepreneur in business and a pioneer in entrepreneurial philanthropy.

Asian Americans

Chapter Nine

The Bridging of Cultures

Akira Suzuki is one of almost eighty thousand Japanese Americans to receive a check and a belated apology from the United States government as recompense for the government's incarceration of Japanese Americans in concentration camps after Japan's attack on Pearl Harbor in 1941. Suzuki's distinction lies in his decision to donate his redress payment to a community center in Los Angeles that serves a mixed neighborhood of African Americans, Latinos, and Asian Americans. The nonprofit fund was to be used into the next century to finance activities of the All Peoples Christian Center, where Suzuki had been a volunteer for many years. This bridging of cultures, like the charitable act itself, does not fit the image most Americans have of Japanese Americans, who are better known for caring for their own community than for acts of benevolence toward those outside the group.

As Akira Suzuki's story demonstrates, Asians have not had an easy time in America. From the start, they were subjected to harsh discrimination. The earliest arrivals were the Chinese who were lured by gold in California in the nineteenth century but remained to help build railroads and to perform other important tasks. They were followed by the Japanese who came first to Hawaii and later to the west coast in the 1890s. The first generations saw themselves as sojourners who came to this country to improve their fortunes, planning always to return home with the material gains realized from their hard labor.

The next group of Asians to arrive were the Filipinos who were recruited after the Asian Exclusion Act of 1924. Their status as U.S.

nationals was used as a technicality putting them outside the reach of the 1924 law. The first wave of Filipinos were bachelors who came for education, to work in agriculture, or to learn a trade. A few married, but most did not, remaining without family ties and moving from town to town following the harvest and availability of labor contracts. Their ties to agriculture have remained, leading many to help organize the multi-ethnic United Farm Workers' strike against grape growers in the California central valley in 1966.

Unlike the Japanese, the Chinese, and the Filipinos, the Koreans came to the United States because of military involvement in their homeland. Their common tie with the other Asian groups was a cultural background that placed great emphasis on education, a focus that served them well as they struggled to find their way in a new world. Unlike the other Asians, many of the Korean immigrants had strong religious bonds with mainstream American culture. Largely Protestant and highly educated before they arrived, they advanced at an even more rapid pace than the Japanese and the Chinese.

The Vietnamese, the Cambodians, and the Laotians, all Southeast Asians but each subject to different regulations, fit no special pattern. Far from homogeneous, their ranks include former mountain tribesmen and destitute boat people as well as large numbers of the educated former leading families of South Vietnam.

Asian Indians, who are sometimes overlooked when Asian Americans are discussed, brought with them a strong tradition of voluntary associations and organized charity and philanthropy. Asian Indians are the largest group of Asian Americans from South Asia, which comprises Bangladesh, Bhutan, India, Pakistan, Nepal, and Sri Lanka. As early as 1669, the Parsi faithful in India had created an institution known as the *punchayet* that initially meted out justice but evolved into a charitable entity receiving donations from and dispensing relief to Parsi communities.

The Asian-American population in the United States is probably the most heterogeneous of any racial or ethnic group. There are now more than thirty Asian ethnic groups in the American society. In addition to cultural, language, and religious differences, many of these groups have a history of distrust and hostility toward each other, and their stories cannot be reduced to a single theme.

It would be easy to concentrate on the noble stories of individual Asians, to revel in the success of individual groups in education and business, and even to generalize about pan-ethnic cultural traits. But to fully appreciate and understand the civic ethic and communal vision of Asian Americans, we must look at each group separately. To provide a sense of the wide differences as well as similarities in communal vision, it is useful to examine the civic traditions and civic habits of several of the larger groups.

The Chinese Americans

Early Chinese arrivals in America lived in Chinatowns which, because of laws forbidding the entry of spouses and children to this country, were essentially bachelor societies. While a major purpose of the Chinatown communities was to assure protection and security, the fabric of benevolence was woven deeply into their social texture from the very beginning. Most of the meager funds the Chinese were able to accumulate from their labor went to support relatives back home or to their savings, as they planned to return to China to improve the quality of life of their families and kinfolk in the homeland. In the early decades of Chinese settlement, these immigrants, beset with a hostile racist movement opposing their very presence in the United States, built their own community structures.[1] Drawing from life in China, they organized their own benevolent, protective, and governmental bodies, experiencing a measure of isolation and communal self-government far exceeding that of other ethnic communities.

Inside a Chinatown, the merchant class became the ruling elite. They controlled immigrant associations, dispensed jobs and opportunities, settled disputes, and acted as advocates for the Chinese sojourners before the white society. They governed the Chinatown through the complex interrelationships between clans, and through *hui kuan,* multipurpose organizations based on ethnicity, village of origin, or common language.

The clan traces its origins to the lineage communities of southeastern China. Overseas clans assumed a number of the duties traditionally associated with the authority of lineage in China. The surname alone established identity and clan members assumed blood relationships on the basis of a common name. The clan provided the boundary of the incest taboo, reminded the sojourner of his obligations to the village and family in China, and afforded an opportunity for commercial monopoly by confining trade secrets to their members. In place of the village, the overseas clan was organized around a leading merchant's store. The merchants took on the duties that lineage communities had been responsible for in China, providing aid, advice, comfort, and shelter.

Second-, third-, and fourth-generation Chinese Americans form nuclear families and are not inclined to register with their clan associations. Also, the charitable assistance and mutual aid once provided by the clans to aged and indigent members are now confined to occasional recreational activities, such as a clubhouse for elderly members. Furthermore, loans once available informally are now strictly regulated.[2]

In addition to clans, immigrant Chinese established hui kuan organizations. Similar to their counterparts in China, these groups united all those who spoke a common dialect, hailed from the same district of origin, or belonged to the same ethnic group. The hui kuan served as a credit and loan society and employment agency. It also acted in a representative capacity, speaking for its members to other hui kuan and to the white society. In addition it provided arbitration and mediation services for its members. To the individual Chinese, it could also withhold financial aid, order social ostracism, and render a punitive judgment. The hui khan was first

composed of five prominent family associations, but in 1858 it con-
federated several groups into one.

In some settlements where clans and hui kuan failed to form,
secret societies became the sole community organization. These
societies enrolled members according to their interests rather than
by kin or district ties. As in China, they provided the organizational
base and muscle to protect against individual and collective oppres-
sion. In the United States, their energies were directed at the powerful elite in Chinatown where they provided a check on clan and
hui kuan exploitation and control over immigrants. Nineteenth-
century immigrants from Kwangtung included many members of
the Triad Society, China's most famous clandestine association.

The charitable and fraternal activities of the secret societies
were confined to their own members. As the societies prospered,
they erected elaborate halls that reflected their affluence and were
used for fraternal and charitable purposes. An example was the Chinese Society of Free Masons, a euphemism for the Triad Society.
When its members opened a new building in San Francisco in
1907, one of the floors was designated for housing destitute widows
and orphans.[3]

Similar to the hui kuan, the societies provided sickness and
death benefits, housing, mediation and arbitration, and commercial regulation. However, stringent rules governed the allocation of
aid and charity. For example, should a poor man become solvent,
he was obligated to repay the money that had been advanced
to him.

It is not possible to understand Chinese civic and cultural traditions without understanding the influence of Confucianism.
Robert Lee, who published a guide to Chinese-American philanthropy, attributed the primary impetus for Chinese benevolence to
certain tenets of Confucianism.[4] Confucianism is tied to morality,
humanism, and the pursuit of knowledge and sageness, interpreted
as a commitment to public service. Other features are respect for

others, a sense of responsibility in social relationships, an emphasis on equity, and a regard for the inherent goodness in each person.

An important aspect of the Confucian ethic is the concept of *Jen*, transformed by Confucius into a universal virtue. Jen is frequently used to refer to love and to the highest perfection of goodness, which can only be obtained after the attainment of a state of being that includes wisdom and service. Jen is manifested by the practice of goodness, love, compassion, altruism, kindheartedness, and concern for others. The seminal idea of Jen involves benevolence.[5]

Chinese benevolence is generally directed toward the elderly, an aim that is consistent with the high regard accorded the elderly and the extended family. Benevolence in Chinese culture is also evident in Chinese traditions. For example, it is customary in connection with weddings, birthdays, funerals, and other special occasions for the family to make a contribution to the family association, the Chinese hospital, or to a favorite charity. These gifts are symbols of one's good fortune. *Lei see*, or little red envelopes with money enclosed, are given by the guests to the honoree on these occasions.[6]

The Japanese Americans

Coming to the United States later than the Chinese, the Japanese had a different experience. While the Chinese immigrants had to leave their wives in China, the Japanese brought or imported brides who bore them children and provided a family life far different from that of the lonely Chinese bachelor.

Japanese Americans are deeply bound by traditional obligations of gratitude, loyalty, and deference; principles such as charity and brotherhood are relative latecomers to their lexicon of civic virtues. The focus is on the group; their willingness to sacrifice for the good of the group is stronger than that of most Americans, but the Japanese are generally less likely to sacrifice for those outside the group.

While the religious beliefs and moral behavior that have influenced Japanese Americans are changing as they come into contact with other value systems in this country, their civic habits and social institutions have been shaped largely by personal loyalties rather than more generalized civic values. There has been no civic imperative dictating compassion or charity for those outside their primary network of obligations. Native Americans have a long history of standing up against overwhelming odds; African Americans also have traditionally rebelled against officially constituted authority. But Japanese Americans, and many other Asian Americans, are likely to accept what is—and to adjust accordingly. Because they are of a culture that honors authority rather than transcendent principles, they are more likely to use voluntary activity for social welfare rather than social reform.

The Issei, the first generation of Japanese immigrants, were excluded legally and socially from American life; to compensate, they formed organizations to satisfy virtually every social need. The Issei viewed their community as the primary group and an extension of their kinship system. When serious problems such as illness arose, help came from the extended family or professionals within the community. Harry Kitano, in *The Japanese in the United States: An Evolution of a Subculture*, notes that the Issei found employment mainly as agricultural laborers or in small businesses, either working for other Japanese or establishing small shops of their own.

The children of the Issei, known as Nisei, were generally born between 1910 and 1940. This group, influenced by their parents' attitude toward education, availed themselves fully of American educational opportunities and were encouraged by their Issei parents to become totally "Americanized." However, opportunities for this group were restricted by prejudice and hostility, especially through the World War II years. Unfortunately, that prejudice persists, but for the most part the Sansei, or third generation, born since the second world war, is intricately involved in the many institutions of mainstream America. Nevertheless, as the Sansei have matured, a renewed interest in their Japanese heritage has emerged for themselves, their children, and their grandchildren.

The traditional Japanese family was characterized by strong solidarity, mutual helpfulness, and a patriarchal structure. Family themes included filial piety, respect for age and seniority, and a preference for male children.[7] After immigration to the United States, the early families continued the traditional Japanese pattern of interdependency. They usually lived in rooming houses operated and populated by the same *ken*, residents from the same geographical subunit of the Japanese state. The welcoming and socialization of immigrants began with other Issei. New immigrants were provided food and lodging, assisted in locating employment, and invited to share recreational and religious activities.[8]

An example of how people from the same ken of a Japanese state cooperated in various ways is demonstrated by the case of barbers in Seattle. "After the first barber from Yamaguchi-ken became established, he helped his friends from the same ken with training and money, so that eventually most of the Japanese barbers in Seattle were from Yamaguchi-ken."[9] Eventually ken became a very important factor in differentiating occupation, experiences, and even acculturation.

The Japanese Association was the most important Issei group and could usually be found in every community with a Japanese population. Many of these associations were founded within a few years after Issei immigration; therefore they date back to the start of the century. The Japanese Association had five areas of concern—finance, social welfare, commerce, education, and young people's welfare.[10] It also served as an informal arm of the Japanese consular offices, which were not equipped to handle the relations between Japan and the widely scattered Japanese nationals. Although a principal function of the Japanese Association was protective, a major portion of its activities was devoted to mutual aid and intracommunity affairs. The Japanese Associations established and maintained cemeteries, provided translators, placed people in contact with legal and other necessary services, and policed their communities' activities. They also sponsored picnics and supported youth groups and youth services. Contacts with the majority community were limited to formal business or ritualistic occasions and involved only the leaders of the association. The associations also played a conservative role in acculturation and were important in keeping the ethnic community Japanese.

The Japanese American Citizens League (JACL) can be thought of as the second-generation counterpart of the Japanese Associations. It, too, developed in response to the special problems and interests of the community, but primarily to those of the American-born Nisei. The JACL was a civic and patriotic organization concerned with the well-being and political and economic progress of American citizens of Japanese ancestry; it was established in the 1920s by young Nisei who felt that the Japanese Associations were not serving their interests. Its initial function was protective, but it also sought to accelerate acculturation. The JACL was the only national Japanese-American organization operating during World War II. Therefore, when the JACL decided to cooperate with the government order for Japanese Americans to evacuate from their west coast homes, most Japanese Americans followed its lead.

In contrast to the Chinese, the Japanese are known for their rapid acculturation. A measure of this difference is the absence from the language of a designation of *Japantown*, analogous to *Chinatown*. The Japanese refused to be tied to Little Tokyos, and Japanese-owned businesses were not organized on the basis of guilds, as were the Chinese. Moreover, the earliest associations among the Japanese emphasized defense against prejudice and support for the larger society's customs and laws. Finally, the Japanese emigrated from a place that was already a nation and comprised states where village life had long ceased to be circumscribed by kinship.[11]

With regard to values in Japanese culture, group needs are given priority over individual needs. Important values are conformity, a high regard for conventional behavior, and obedience to rules.

Compromise and yielding are also highly respected. Codified norms of the Japanese are *on* (ascribed obligation), *giri* (contractual obligation), *chu* (loyalty to one's superior), *ninjo* (humane sensibility), and *enryo* (modesty in the presence of one's superior).[12]

In *Japanese Corporate Philanthropy*, Nancy London writes: "Japanese define the community to which they are responsible and to which they owe a social obligation differently from the way that most Westerners do. The relevant community is not the undifferentiated mass of society but, rather, that contained group of people with whom one has some relationship."[13] For example, "most Japanese routinely and voluntarily contribute to defray the funeral costs of a member of a friend's or a colleague's family, but these same people would be nonplused to be asked to contribute to a funeral society for the benefit of the general public."[14]

London also views Buddhism as an integral part of the complex features that shaped Japanese benevolence. The Buddhist view is that the individual acting alone can accomplish nothing and therefore individuals tend to organize themselves and make decisions in groups. The group is held together "by a series of functional relationships, and the most obvious manifestation of such functional relationships today is the company or groups of companies."[15] Hence, an individual Japanese is always a part of the company community and the neighborhood is merely the place where one happens to sleep.

The Koreans, Vietnamese, and Other Asian Americans

Until 1965, a quota system in the United States restricted Korean immigration to one hundred persons per year. The years immediately following the abolition of the quota saw Koreans coming to the United States at such a rate that even the Census Bureau had difficulty keeping track of them. In a very short time, they transformed produce stores, dry cleaning establishments, restaurants, and stationery shops in New York and Los Angeles into Korean commercial havens. In other metropolitan areas, like Washington, D.C., they have established an economic presence far out of proportion to the size of their population. They have been described as "resourceful free-market entrepreneurs who provide whatever customers want—from groceries to gospel, from southern-cooked greens and ribs to black pride paraphernalia."[16]

Korean clashes with African Americans in central cities have made the headlines in the 1990s, but hostility and indignities toward Korean Americans had their genesis in white American attitudes that predated the more recent years when blacks found themselves sharing their economic turf with Korean merchants.

The molding of Koreans into merchants is itself a story of communal self-help and sociocultural solidarity. Among what other groups can you find people with doctorates running dry cleaning businesses and neighborhood delicatessens, working long hours seven days a week? Unlike the mercantile Asian Indians and the overseas Chinese, Koreans have little history as merchants. Moreover, in the Confucian hierarchy, merchants were ranked far below scholars and farmers. But finding the professions closed to them when they arrived in the United States, they found a back door into entrepreneurship.

Korean business success is aided by an ancient Korean tradition of thrift called *keh*. Operating somewhat like a credit union, Korean families pool their resources with a group of other families, usually from ten to twenty, and form a keh. If necessary, they work several jobs and sacrifice most of the comforts of life to contribute to the group. In succeeding months, each family in turn is given the funds collected, which can total $20,000 or more. The profits from businesses started with such savings often are plowed back into the keh to accumulate funds for future business opportunities. Once they enter the business world, most Korean merchants view each business as a stepping stone to the next. While the many who are well educated would prefer to be doing something else, they are sacrificing to provide opportunities for the next generation to enjoy the upward mobility they have been denied. Their children reflect the parental emphasis with a discipline and dedication to education unknown in most American households.

For Korean Americans, moral behavior is still very much influenced by Confucian beliefs. Although many are Protestant Christians, their respect for elders is of such paramount importance that a child thinks nothing of sacrificing personal satisfaction in order to uphold filial duty.[17] Moral virtue is the fulfillment of a prescribed role in which parents and children, brothers and sisters, husbands and wives all know what is expected of them and act accordingly. Personal happiness resides not so much in individual success as in the fulfillment of the obligations to the family. Although the sense of family obligation is lessening for successor generations, the cultural traditions of the parents still dominate group life.

Korean-American churches are central vehicles for socialization. The relationship between Koreans and American churches dates back to the nineteenth century when Christian missionaries in Korea habitually sent their students to the United States to "get a Christian education." More recently, the immigrants have seen Christian congregations act as a broker for them in their relationship to the larger society. Korean-American churches provide social services and help immigrants find work and housing.

With another group of Asian Americans, the Vietnamese, the most important factor in their culture is the family. The family is at the center of the individual's life and the basic institution developed to perpetuate society and provide protection to the individual. The immediate family includes not only the husband and wife and their unmarried children but also the husband's parents and the sons' wives and children. The extended family consists of the immediate family and close relatives sharing the family name and ancestors who live in the same community. As with members of the immediate family, members of the extended family are bound together by a strong sense of collective responsibility and mutual obligation. They are expected to give one another mutual moral and material assistance, especially in times of stress. "By virtue of the principle of collective and mutual responsibility, each individual will strive to be a pride of his family."[18] Other values of importance to the Vietnamese are the concept of a "good name," respect and admiration, and love of learning.

Tet, the Vietnamese New Year Festival, is celebrated to welcome the new year, which is hoped to bring a new and happy chapter in the lives of everyone. It is also a celebration of the return of spring—considered the time of rebirth of nature, gathering of the family, and celebration of birthdays—for everyone becomes one year older on New Year's Day. Tet is also an occasion for giving and receiving gifts. A week before Tet, presents will be offered to those to whom one feels a debt of gratitude for help during the year. Wealthy people offer presents to their relatives who are less fortunate. Gifts are also presented to in-laws and in-laws-to-be.[19]

The first Vietnamese refugees to enter the United States were those who came in the years just before the fall of Saigon. They included students, wives of U.S. servicemen who had been stationed in South Vietnam, some officials of the South Vietnamese government, and friends of U.S. service and government personnel who traveled to America for personal reasons and stayed on as residents. The collapse of Saigon in 1975 brought the first major wave of refugees. Many of these people had been members of the South Vietnamese government and military forces or had worked in some capacity in the war effort against the North. These refugees were better educated and wealthier than those who came in the following years. They also were able to escape in large multigenerational, extended family groups.

Sponsorship by churches and American families was prevalent throughout the phase of immigration marked by an influx of boat people, who exited Vietnam in vessels largely inadequate for the rough waters they traveled. However, in many areas, such as in Oklahoma, the largest group of sponsors came directly from the Vietnamese immigrants' families and relatives. Following the arrival of the first Vietnamese in 1975, many boat people used the family network as a strategy for entering and settling in the United States. Vietnamese organizations, primarily the Vietnamese American Association (VAA), also sponsored refugees.[20] Others were sponsored by friends whom they had known in Vietnam or someone they had recently met in a refugee camp.

Government assistance in the form of food stamps, Medicaid, and even loans was provided to the refugees. Assistance was also provided by the Vietnamese-American associations (including the Vietnamese Buddhist Association, the Vietnamese Society for Culture, the Vietnamese Students Association), which were formed when people began to settle in local communities. These organizations were established to help refugees adjust to life in America and at the same time preserve many aspects of their old culture. The associations provided English classes, job counseling, housing assistance, driving lessons, and coordination for the Tet celebration. They also sponsored refugees and served as centers of information for locating Vietnamese in the United States and reuniting families.[21]

The Vietnamese American Association traces its origins back to the refugee camp at Fort Chaffee, Arkansas, where Vietnamese who were later to become VAA members first organized to teach English classes. The association was registered as a nonprofit corporation in Oklahoma on April 19, 1978; its purpose was to promote mutual understanding and friendship between Vietnamese and Americans and to assist Vietnamese refugees in adapting to a new way of life. The Vietnamese American Association is the product of a limited core of elites within the Vietnamese groups, who occupy leadership positions in the existing Vietnamese organizations.[22]

The traditional Vietnamese pattern of large family systems has not been transplanted to the United States, and in many areas, such as in Oklahoma City, the majority of Vietnamese live in nuclear households. However, the boat people continue to assist their families in Vietnam by sending home packages and supplies.

The rapid growth of the Asian- and Pacific-American population in the United States poses enormous challenges and presents extraordinary opportunity for building a truly multicultural society. Although Americans of Asian descent made up only 2.9 percent of the total U.S. population in 1990, the group increased in size by 95 percent from 1980 to 1990; it is expected to reach ten million by the year 2000 and twenty million by 2020.[23] This growing population remains ethnically diverse, but they share many common concerns related to political empowerment, economic advancement, education, race relations, civil rights, and community. It would be a great loss to all Americans if in shaping a new America with a new national and civic culture, the needs, concerns, and traditions of Asian Americans were ignored.

Chapter Ten

Le Ly Hayslip: When Heaven and Earth Changed Places

No example of benevolence, no message of forgiveness, reconciliation, or community is more powerful in modern America than the life story of Le Ly Hayslip. Born a peasant girl in a small village near Da Nang in Central Vietnam, she made her way to the United States and, after early years of struggle, became wealthy enough to establish a foundation to "heal the wounds of war." Along the way, she was raped and sentenced to death by the Vietcong, tortured by South Vietnamese interrogators, and abused by American soldiers who beat her, molested her, and exploited her.[1]

For her to have given in to self-pity or vengeance would have been easy, but Le Ly Hayslip survived physically and grew spiritually to become a one-woman peace movement. The mission she has chosen is to bear witness to the tragedy of war and to bring healing and wholeness to a badly fractured world. In a personal interview granted during a visit to New York, she attributed her ability to endure and her capacity for compassion to the Buddhist vision taught to her by her father in the rice paddies of Ky La. "He taught me," she said with pride, "to love god, my family, our traditions and the people we could not see: our ancestors." While she was raised to feel a special bond with those who shared her history and beliefs, she also knew what many Americans "did not know or understand," the many different forces tearing apart the fabric of Vietnamese society.

For most Americans, there were two Vietnamese communities: the North and the South, the communists and those who spoke the language of democracy. But the citizens of Le Ly Hayslip's village

137

knew little of democracy and even less about communism. Their fiercest battle may have been over religious ideals, the Buddhists fighting the Catholics. Behind the religious war, according to Hayslip, was the battle between city people and country people, the rich against the poor—a war fought by those who wanted to change Vietnam and those who wanted to leave it as it had been for a thousand years. Beneath that there were vendettas between native Vietnamese immigrants, mostly Chinese and Khmer, who had fought for centuries over the land. And then, of course, there were the American outsiders who had replaced the French outsiders in seeking to keep the land divided, "telling some people to go South and others to go North." In Hayslip's village, people argued that "a nation cannot have two governments anymore than a family can have two fathers." They wondered why so many people were seeking to save their country by trying to destroy it.

How could one develop a vision of community, a notion of benevolence, that included the stranger, when so many forces were converging to emphasize differences? For Hayslip's father, there was a deeper bond, what his daughter described as the Buddhist vision. It was rooted in a special relationship to the ancestors, but it also included the notion that Buddhahood is innate in each individual, that regardless of station, status, race, or religion, all people inherently possess a life of great goodness and are, therefore, deserving of respect. So as Hayslip grew in faith and experience, she came to identify with the Buddhist idea that "our nationality, race and sexual orientation are not our true self, but rather a transient appearance of this life alone."[2] According to the Buddhist, "these are mythologies that have been created, but fundamentally we are exactly the same. There is no distinction. We are like pieces of wood. There is dark mahogany and there is pine, but all is wood."[3]

This is not the assertion of the naive who believe that the answer to racial discord lies in color blindness. The central tenet of the Buddhist vision of community is clear: while it is only natural to search out our ethnic and cultural roots and to be proud of them, a person who stops there denies an essential part of human whole-ness. We need, argues the Buddhist, to look more deeply into our lives and remember, "Yes, I have an ethnic and cultural heritage. I feel proud of that and that is a sense of who I am in this lifetime and I can enjoy that, but let me never forget the deeper message— I am fundamentally a human being and no different from anybody else. All human beings, no matter how different they look or what language they speak, are exactly as precious, and I have to respect them for that."[4]

Le Ly Hayslip's ability to resolve the conflict between unity and diversity, to embrace former adversaries, and to enlarge her sense of community, had its roots in the Buddhist principle of *itai doshin*, which means many bodies with one mind. This principle has two aspects. The first is *itai*, or many bodies. Buddhism respects, encour-ages, and understands the importance of maintaining and respecting our diversity. At the same time, to resolve the conflicts and misun-derstanding that can arise from this diversity, the Buddhist seeks to unite with the same mind, or *doshin*. In the Buddhist vision of com-munity, it is thus possible, despite our differences, to share the same goal of peace and harmony, or *kosen-rufu*.

The peasants in Hayslip's village knew all this intuitively, but they were forced to take sides, sometimes alternating between the Vietcong and the South Vietnamese in the same day. Hayslip was born in 1949, the year of the water buffalo in the Chinese astro-logical system and, as she put it, was "destined to be a servant of mankind." Life in Ky La, now called Xa Hoa Qui, was as difficult at that time as in any place in Vietnam. Villagers literally lived in the mud. Heavy rains, strong winds, and perilous monsoons thrashed the countryside with regularity. The youngest of six children, Hayslip weighed two pounds at birth and was believed to have very little chance of survival. The midwife who delivered Hayslip advised her mother to suffocate her. Nurtured to normalcy, she still faced the hardships of life in central Vietnam where the struggle for survival was a daily occurrence.

But there was another side to Ky La, the side that shaped Hayslip's view of the world and her vision of community. Ky La's vitality and beauty was not in its rice paddies, the tropical forests, or the family huts, but in the temples, the pagodas, and the shrines. When American soldiers leveled the village years later to provide a killing zone to defend the area, the villagers were devastated. Houses could be rebuilt and damaged dikes repaired, but the loss of the temples and the shrines could mean the death of the village culture itself. To destroy the artifacts of the people's religion was not simply to destroy the rituals of worship but to cut the umbilical cord to the ancestors, the very root of four thousand years of social bonding. The rhythms of life had become tied to the agricultural cycles, the phases of the moon, and the spirits that inhabited the land. The soil, the sun, and the moon were all sacred. Even growing rice was considered a sacramental act.

The erosion of the religious grounding was accompanied by another hard and bitter reality. Hayslip grew up in an age of war in which even her family was divided. The men went North to fight with the Communists while the women allied themselves (by day at least) with the South Vietnamese. But before the war was over, Hayslip had spent time on both sides. She worked for the Vietcong as a sentinel until she was arrested by the South Vietnamese. Demonstrating the audacity that was to serve her so well in later years, she bribed her way out of prison. But the Vietcong were suspicious about the circumstances of her escape from their bitter adversaries, so they in turn arrested her and condemned her to death. Even after being forced to dig her own grave, she escaped to Saigon.

These were the years of her adolescence. Her brother was killed on the Ho Chi Minh Trail and her father killed himself by drinking acid. She went to work as a maid in a Saigon household where she was seduced by her employer and became pregnant. He responded by firing her for the misstep of having his baby. She went back to Da Nang where she eked out a living as a hospital orderly, a black marketer, and a bar girl; in at least one instance, she added an act of prostitution to her list of survival techniques. Only once, she says, did she sell herself to a soldier, but the $400 she received was enough to feed her family for a year. She struggled mightily to find the balance between her own integrity and her struggle to stay alive. And while the scale sometimes tipped on the side of survival, she was usually able to maintain her sense of dignity and to return to strengths and virtues she learned from her mother.

Despite her many ordeals, Hayslip has a warmth, attractiveness, and personal appeal that conceals both the horrors of her early years and the enormous cultural adjustment she has had to make in the United States. Now in her forties, she arrived in California as a newlywed of twenty, with a fifty-five-year-old husband whom she had met while he was a civilian contractor in Vietnam. She brought with her a three-year-old son and a second son just two months old. The peasant girl who grew up in the rice paddies of the tiny village of Ky La spent her honeymoon in Las Vegas.

Her first husband died in 1973 and a second husband with whom she had a third son died twelve years later. She worked as a maid for $2.75 an hour, then secured a job as an electronic parts assembler, rising quickly to become a supervisor. As she developed an understanding of how the United States worked, she took business courses in her spare time, bought a restaurant, and succeeded handsomely in real estate. But she still felt lonely and unfulfilled. "I was a millionaire," she said, "but the more I got, the emptier I became." Her second husband had been a Baptist who didn't subscribe to his wife's Buddhist views, so he had discouraged her from practicing her religion in the home. On his death, she set up a Buddhist shrine in her living room and sought to fill a void in her life through the practices and traditions of her ancestors. Free now to examine her life more fully and to explore the resources of the spirit, she started visiting the American equivalent of the Vietnamese *thay dong*, seers who can communicate with the dead. But the American mediums, psychics, and fortune-tellers could not satisfy her yearning for something more to life. It was not until she returned to Vietnam in 1986 that she found her calling.

Back home again in touch with the soil and soul of her ancestors, Hayslip was struck to see the land beyond the rice paddies of her childhood that used to be potato fields now filled with graves. Everywhere she went she was greeted by suffering: children wandering homeless, once-prosperous farmers now living near starvation outside the mainstream economy, peasants maimed by mines still buried in the fields. She was seized again by the Buddhist vision of her father, the urge to help, the need to embrace all those who were suffering as members of a community to whom she was tied not only spiritually and culturally but by a common humanity.

While benevolence was a part of the Vietnamese family tradition of caring for each other, rich Vietnamese did not normally choose to give their money to strangers, those outside the network of family. But this is precisely what Hayslip set out to do. She sold her two homes and consolidated other assets to form the East Meets West Foundation, a nonprofit charitable organization that raises money for rural clinics in impoverished areas of Vietnam. Since the establishment of the foundation in 1988, ten delegations of American teachers, doctors, and other volunteers have gone to Vietnam to provide assistance to hospitals, schools, and orphanages. Medical supplies have been shipped to China Beach and two hospitals receive ongoing support. In 1988, the foundation built the Mother's Love Health Clinic and Medical Facility on China Beach near Da Nang. Hayslip's most ambitious project is a Peace Village in Da Nang that is to include a medical facility, an orphanage, a cultural center, a physical rehabilitation center, and educational units. She would like to reach out as far as she can to "take care of the poor, educate the children, put limbs on the disabled, and provide charity to the homeless." In a 1992 newsletter from the East Meets West Foundation, she put her goals in perspective: "East and West are opposites just like heaven and earth. . . . You are working with Huu hinh, I'm working with Vo hinh, the 'tangible world' and the 'non-material world.' Both are the same. The only difference is that the non-material world puts more emphasis on humanity, virtue, morals, pure honesty and compassion."

In 1989, Hayslip published her memoir *When Heaven and Earth Changed Places*. She has donated the proceeds from the book to the foundation. But she continues to dream big dreams. Her life story caught the attention of the movie producer Oliver Stone who was one of the first to contribute to the Mother's Love Health Clinic. He has now applied his skills as a filmmaker to Hayslip's cause, enabling her to tell her story to a larger audience. But her philanthropy, like her life, has now been caught in the maelstrom of politics. Some of her fellow Vietnamese have questioned her story and voiced concern about her involvement with the current Vietnamese government. While she has taken careful note of assassinations and other acts of reprisals against those in the American-Vietnamese community who have spoken out for reconciliation and normalization, she insists that the only politics that interest her are the politics of reconciliation and healing.

The little Vietnamese girl who worked knee-deep in mud in the rice fields of Ky La has brought new meaning to the Vietnamese tradition of public philanthropy, transforming it from royal patronage to private giving based on emotions of the heart. Yet she sees her philanthropic activities as neither alien nor revolutionary, but rather as a natural outgrowth of the Buddhist vision taught to her by her father.

In the epilogue of *When Heaven and Earth Changed Places*, Le Ly Hayslip makes this universal appeal:

> Most of you who read this book have not lived my kind of life. By the grace of destiny or luck or god, you do not know how hard it is to survive; although you now have some idea. Do not feel sorry for me—I made it; I am okay. Right now, though, there are millions of other poor people around the world—girls, boys, men and women—who live their lives the way I did in order to survive. Like me, they

did not ask for the wars that swallowed them. They ask only for peace—the freedom to love and live a full life—and nothing more. I ask only that you open your heart and mind to them, as you have opened it to me.

The message of the book, despite its tales of torture and terror, is one of forgiveness and hope, of an enormous capacity for compassion and community. It teaches us about both giving and forgiving, reminding us that how you do it matters as much as what you do. In the prologue, Hayslip wrote this to the Vietnam veteran, "I invite you to read this book and to look into the heart of one you once called your enemy. . . . I will try to tell you why almost everyone in the country you tried to help resented, feared and misunderstood you."

Hayslip has always liked to sing. Her book, like her life, is punctuated with songs. It is not surprising that she begins her book by quoting songs she memorized as a little girl and concludes with this Buddhist song of enlightenment, a song, she says, that the spirit of each of us has been singing since the moment of our birth:

> Late afternoon—
> Hear the bell—
> The bell wakes up
> My soul—
> We must hurry to become
> Enlightened—
> We must kneel beneath the tree of
> Buddha—
> We look into the face of god and
> Forget the past—
> To forgive our brother is to forgive
> Ourselves—
> We abandon our revenge;

Our lives have seen suffering enough.
We are tired and worn out with
Ourselves—
If I take revenge, it will be the cause;
The effect will follow me into my next life.
Look into the mirror, see the compassion in your
Heart.

Chapter Eleven

Patrick Okura: In Quest of Justice

On the day in 1963 when more than 250,000 Americans gathered in Washington, D.C., to demonstrate their support for the civil rights movement, the focus was on Martin Luther King, Jr., and the other civil rights leaders whose courage and conviction had touched the conscience of the American people. But in the crowd was a small contingent of Japanese Americans who, much to the consternation of some in their community, had decided to align themselves with the civil rights movement. Their leader was Patrick Okura, national president of the Japanese American Citizens League (JACL).[1]

Some within the JACL objected strongly to this participation. A number of older Nisei who were fairly well established in business did not want to challenge the mainstream ideas. As Okura explained some years later, "It was the feeling of a great majority of our chapter leaders that what the blacks did was their business, their problem, and that we shouldn't get involved in the civil rights movement. I was convinced that after the way we had been discriminated against we should take a leadership position in the whole area of civil rights."[2] Many JACL members disagreed. They felt that the war and the internment issues should be their priorities. Others among them shared the concern, and even the outrage, that many Americans felt during the turbulent sixties. But the notion of a coalition with other minority groups was not popular, even though the JACL had been one of the founding members in 1948 of the National Leadership Conference on Civil Rights.

The small group of Nisei who founded the JACL on the west

coast in 1918 had been among those Japanese banished to the segregated "Oriental" school. They had grown up in a period of persecution when they had seen their fathers beaten for no reason other
than being Japanese, their family businesses picketed and boycotted,
and the windows of their homes smashed while police officers
looked the other way.[3] Known originally as the American Loyalty
League, the JACL was founded by a group of recent college graduates who were determined to claim their rights as citizens and to let
others know that they were Americans. The JACL remained in the
forefront of the civil rights activities of Japanese Americans, but
many of its members feared that joining in a coalition with other
groups would dilute their own efforts. It is this legacy of isolation
that faced Okura when he decided the time had come to embrace
and work with the larger civil rights community.

In 1963, the JACL had thirty-two thousand members and more
than one hundred chapters. Okura had risen through the ranks of
the organization, serving as third vice president, second vice president, and first vice president before becoming national president.
When the idea of the march on Washington surfaced, he was just
completing the first year of a two-year term. JACL's Washington
representative visited Okura in Omaha to discuss the next annual
board meeting scheduled for San Francisco, but he found the new
president preoccupied with the proposed march, convinced that the
JACL had to take a stand. Okura was concerned that a discussion
of this issue in San Francisco, where there were so many members,
would invite controversy, so he decided to hold the national board
meeting in Omaha. The board deliberated for three days, hammer-
ing out a statement on civil rights and agreeing to participate in the
historic march. Most of the five hundred members of the Washington, D.C. chapter worked for the federal government; they
opposed Okura's proposal not on philosophical grounds but by
claiming that participation would probably be a violation of the
Hatch Act, the law that prohibits federal employees from participating in politics.

Nonetheless, Okura was able to persuade fifty Japanese Americans to march with him in Washington under the JACL banner. There was even a seat reserved for him on the platform. While the press of the crowd prevented him from joining Martin Luther King, Jr., and the other leaders in a place of honor, his presence did not go unnoticed. He had persuaded the JACL board to issue a strong statement on civil rights and to authorize formal participation by its leaders. So when criticism came later, he replied that "what we did was the only action we could take as Americans."[4]

Patrick Okura was not the most likely champion of American ideals and national community. After the Japanese attack on Pearl Harbor, he had been investigated by the Los Angeles Police Department, and the mayor, Fletcher Bowron, had described him as "one of the most dangerous Japanese Americans in the country."[5] Yet, while incarcerated, he worked so closely with the camp administration to improve the plight of those held behind barbed wire that he was accused by some evacuees of being on the federal payroll. "I was quite bitter when I went into the Santa Anita Assembly Center and had decided to simply sit out the war and not lift a finger," he says.

It was a time of bitterness throughout the country. Even in Congress legislators were debating a resolution to declare the presence of all persons of Japanese lineage, aliens and citizens alike, a threat to the safety of the United States. White supremacists, in particular, found it easy to shift their contempt and hatred of African Americans to the Japanese. Senator Tom Stewart of Tennessee argued that the Japanese were "cowardly and immoral . . . different from Americans in every conceivable way, and should have no right to claim American citizenship." At the suggestion that Japanese Americans be simply required to take an oath, he replied that "taking the oath of allegiance to this country would not help. They [the Japanese] do not believe in God and have no respect for an oath."[6] Congressman John Rankin of Mississippi was even more adamant, contending that "This is a race war. . . . The white man's civilization has come into conflict with Japanese bar-barism. . . . It is of vital importance that we get rid of every Japanese whether in Hawaii or on the mainland."[7] This was strong language for many nonwestern members of Congress who had shown no pre-vious interest in what westerners were calling "the Japanese prob-lem." Many simply acquiesced to the western members who felt that all Japanese Americans should be evacuated from the strategic areas of the west coast.

After his first week at the temporary camp at Santa Anita, Okura recognized that he had to rise above the national rancor and his personal bitterness and help eliminate, at least, the chaos and confusion that reigned. "I could not sit back any longer," he said. "I took it upon myself to talk to a number of my friends and got their support to suggest a self-government program to help the Caucasian administrators."

Throughout his life, Okura has fought for justice and the well-being of Japanese Americans. He joined the JACL in 1937 hoping to be able to reduce discrimination. At that time, more than fifty thousand Japanese Americans were living in the city of Los Ange-les, but none of the twenty thousand public employees in that city was Japanese. Okura decided to take the Civil Service Examination and to try breaking the race barrier. He passed the exam and was hired by the Los Angeles Civil Service Department.

When the war broke out, Okura received a call from the mayor's office and was told that the deputy mayor wanted to see him. On his arrival, he was met by one of the mayor's assistants who asked for his resignation. It was December 1942, the early part of the war, and allegations of disloyalty were being made against any Japanese American who appeared to have a following. The local newspaper charged on the front page that "there's a Japanese Amer-ican working for the city of Los Angeles who has infiltrated the civil service by disguising himself as an Irishman and using the name K. Patrick Okura. He has made a specialty of the Water and Power Department and plans to blow up the city when Japan attacks the West Coast." Okura's crime was that he had encouraged Japanese

engineers and other professionals working in fruit markets and gro-
cery stores to take the national examination and to seek employment through the Civil Service System. As a result, when the war
broke out fifty Americans of Japanese descent were working for the
city. The mayor's office "encouraged" Okura to resign "along with
his henchmen." When he refused, Okura got a notice of evacua-
tion to a relocation camp along with one hundred twenty thousand
other Japanese Americans. Defiant to the end, he signed instead a
leave of absence with the city for the duration of the war.

The ten relocation centers spread across the country were not
ready yet, so Okura was sent with nineteen thousand other Japanese Americans to the race track in Santa Anita where he and his
wife lived in a stable for nine months. His father, who was one of
the two thousand men picked up the night of Pearl Harbor, was
labeled an "internee of war," evacuees who were to be sent to
Japan in exchange for American prisoners there. The younger
Okura was eventually offered a job with Father Flanagan in Boys
Town, Nebraska. Once in Omaha, Okura started a JACL chapter
and relocated his father who had been sent to Santa Fe, New
Mexico.

After seventeen years at Boys Town, Okura took a job as Chief
Probation Officer for the city of Omaha. Once again, he cam-
paigned to improve the quality of life for a group of American citizens. This time it was the large black population in North Omaha
whose children were disproportionately represented among juve-
niles held in the county jail. Working with church women and
other groups he was able to mobilize, Okura made more than three
hundred speeches urging the establishment of a separate juvenile
court, hoping to change some of the practices of the justice system.

Why did Patrick Okura, a prominent leader of the JACL,
choose to identify with the problems of non-Japanese? "I was able
to see, I think, a bigger picture than those who lived exclusively
within the Japanese community," he replies. "With my work in psychology, with my work in juvenile court, with my outlook and work
at Boys Town, that kind of set the stage," he adds. Okura grew up

in Los Angeles. His father worked at the creamery while his mother operated a rooming house and small hotel. He went with his sisters to a nursery school at a Japanese Christian church, and while he knew that Japanese Americans lived in segregated areas, he was insulated from the discrimination he encountered later.

When his mother became ill, the Okuras moved to the small town of Wilmington, California, where there were only two Japanese-American families. It was here that he first learned "that if you weren't white, you were excluded. . . . The first time I felt really discriminated against and really learned that I was different, and that people were treated differently," he says, was when he pledged along with his white friends to join the junior organization of the Masons. Accompanying his friends to join the group, he was told that "this was only for white children." Remembering that experience with a touch of sadness, he said, "We were fairly well-known. We ran this store. I had a lot of friends, my parents had friends, I was elected the American Legion Most Successful Student and all of that in high school." Okura was also an outstanding athlete who played basketball, baseball, and football. Despite his size, he was elected both the outstanding athlete and the outstanding student when he graduated from high school in 1928.

It was at graduation that he experienced the second jolt from discrimination. "I was the valedictorian and a Mexican girl was number two in a class of thirty-three," he said. He was scheduled to sit in the front row, but he was told, "we can't have two minorities sitting in the front row—a Japanese American and a Mexican American, so one of you will have to sit in the second or back row." Polite and wanting to fit in, Okura decided that he should sit in the back and let the Mexican girl sit in the front. It is an experience he never forgot even when he went on to the University of California at Los Angeles (UCLA). He admits feeling resentful at the time, but he simply thought to himself, "I guess I have to be better than anyone else and show them that I am just as good." His baseball coach, a UCLA graduate, encouraged him to enroll at his alma mater saying, "You'll get a fair chance at UCLA, you're a pretty good baseball player, and I think you have the ability to make the team."

After playing semiprofessional ball with a local team that summer, Okura enrolled in UCLA where he learned rather quickly that he could not belong to any organization on campus—no fraternity, no sorority, no university groups at all. There were about twenty Japanese students at UCLA at the time. Several organized a Japanese Bruin Club, so Okura joined only to discover that they could not live at Westwood Village, "the very elite, upper-middle-class area," where the new university was located. "I was told," says Okura "that no blacks, no Japanese Americans/Asians (in those days we were called Orientals) were allowed to live here, so we had to go eight miles away to a little town in what is now called West Los Angeles. Eight of us got together, rented a house, and hitchhiked the eight miles to school."

This treatment did not discourage young Okura. He went out for basketball but was told he was too short, so he gave baseball a try. He made the team as a second baseman and played for two years despite the worse forms of discrimination. This was a few years before Jackie Robinson, the outstanding black athlete who had demolished all sorts of records at UCLA, broke the color barrier in the major leagues. The baseball coach was very fair, telling Okura and his teammates that he would play the best nine players on his first team. "A Jewish boy and myself, we made the first team, but on the road we always had to room together," reported Okura. "And when I look back, I wonder and think to myself, why did I stick it out, why did I play the two years being discriminated in that fashion, because every night it was, 'we gotta get rid of that Jap and that Jew, we gotta make this an all white team.'"

During those years at UCLA Okura says he found out that things were not equal, that despite their abilities, he and other minorities were never recognized. Yet, he persevered, graduating in 1935 with a master's degree in psychology. What was it that enabled him to endure the indignities of the time without allowing them to destroy either his self-esteem or his ambition? Was it religion? Only in the sense that it was sports that led him to become a Presbyterian although his father was a practicing Buddhist. "They were the only church in town that had an indoor basketball court. Even our high school did not have an indoor court," Okura said with a twist of irony. "The minister was an All-American from Princeton who stood 6'6" tall," he continued. In order to play basketball, Okura not only had to become a Presbyterian, but he had to go to "church in the morning, Christian Endeavor in the evening, and three times on Sunday." The Presbyterian connection stuck, however. "Despite all the struggles we had being Japanese Americans," he says, "when it came time to get married we had a Presbyterian wedding in a Buddhist church because as the oldest son I wanted to follow my father's wishes."

From his father Okura learned the values that led him to acts of compassion and openness to others whose humanity he shared. The older Okura seemed sometimes to young Patrick "more willing to do things for others than his own family. . . . My father," he says, was "out three to four nights a week, attending meetings, being active in the Chamber of Commerce, the Japanese Association and the Kin Societies." With obvious respect and admiration, he added, "My father used to go to more funerals—when people got sick he would always visit them, handle all the funeral arrangements, and that sort of thing. . . . People have asked me," he continued, "Why are you at your age, especially now after you have retired, still actively involved in community affairs, and all these civil rights groups, and mental health, and all that?" His answer, "Well, I guess it's to some degree the upbringing and example that was set in my life by my father."

Prodded to be more explicit, Okura replied, "So much of the value system of the first generation of Japanese in this country [was] pretty much akin to the value system of this country, in terms of honesty, in terms of hard work, in terms of respect for parents, in terms of minding your parents, etc. All of these values taught to us again and again were basic Japanese values." Of his father, Okura said, "I remember him always saying that whatever you do reflects not only on your brother or your sister, but the whole family—and it goes back even further—it reflects on your ancestors." It was family honor and family respect that provided the moral underpinnings of Okura's urge to reach out and help others. "It was prodded into us," he added, "that if you don't do anything wrong or if you don't do anything bad, the Japanese family is more prone not to lose face, to be respected by the community."

"As far as values in terms of how to get along with other people and other cultures," Okura cautions that "you are likely to have a better outlook when you are outside your group than you do if you are too closely identified with your own ethnic group." Okura is saddened by the present state of intergroup relations in the United States.

> I think personally that we have gone backward. In the 1960s and 1970s right after the Martin Luther King march, on the campuses and other places, people took on a different attitude about race relations and people were getting along much better. But now we see all of this tension and racial hatred on the campuses, and I'm not sure whether it's the mood of the country or whether it was the leaders and politics of the 1980s.

Reminiscing about the 1960s and 1970s, he went on:

> I remember going on campuses and talking to groups and so on, even going to the naval and military academies and talking about race relations and how minorities have been treated in this country and explaining this to the students; it was well received and I thought things were getting better. But now you go on these campuses and they're completely separated. Each group is interested in their own and they're fighting even among themselves.

I asked Okura, as a psychologist and social activist who has long fought for human rights, what he would do to bring reconciliation to badly fractured communities:

> I think we need to get back to the basics in education, in terms of teaching the culture of other groups and that we are equal, although we look at things differently. If we are going to make our life here in America, then we are all going to have to be seen and treated as Americans and recognize that Americans can be of different shades, colors, and cultures. Let's not forget that people of color are going to be the majority. From a world standpoint, people of color are the majority.

How did Okura go through the bitter experience of relocation, deal with a daily diet of racism and exclusion, and not remain bitter?

> I think again the experience at Boys Town got rid of a lot of that bitterness. I was mad. I was bitter, I said, "This shouldn't happen." But at the time it happened I said, "This can't happen to us." It might happen to our parents, they're aliens ineligible for citizenship, for after all we are at war with the country of their birth. So something could happen to them. But as citizens, nothing will happen to us. We may have to subject ourselves to a curfew, I thought. But I never believed that we would be picked up bodily and placed into these camps. Now that was a tremendous disappointment.

Now eighty-three years old and still seeking to bring about reconciliation and community, Okura is busy with the work of the Okura Mental Health Leadership Foundation. One of the ironies of the American experience is that both he and his wife, Lily, have donated the redress money they received from the American government for their detention, as well as substantial annual personal contributions, to support new and promising young Asian-

American leaders to continue Okura's work. The man who could be bitter, and who refuses to retire, still believes that his dream of one America, pluralistic but unified, is still possible. Within the Japanese community and within the larger society, Patrick Okura has spent much of his life healing old wounds, righting old wrongs, and warning Americans that the gravest problems our nation faces revolve around the continued denial of full equality and justice to large segments of our population.

Chapter Twelve

An Wang: Humanity Without Benevolence Invites Destruction

In 1860, the California superintendent of education defined the Chinese as one of the "inferior races" and barred Asians from attending the same schools as whites.[1] In 1993, the Wangs of Massachusetts, an American-Chinese family, made a gift of $4 million to the Boston Metropolitan Center, rescuing one of the city's preeminent cultural institutions from near bankruptcy. A grateful community, thankful for the unprecedented gift, renamed the Metropolitan Center the Wang Center for the Performing Arts.

The road from public outcast to public benefactor, from public insult to public praise, was full of bumpy detours, but the Wang family was only one of many Chinese families who traveled it successfully. When asked what prompted the generous gift, Fred Wang, executive vice president of Wang Laboratories, replied that it reflected his family's belief that a product of doing well is that you have a responsibility to help create a better life for your community.

The origin of the Wang family's view of civic responsibility is to be found in the public philosophy of An Wang derived from his Confucian upbringing, then fused with American ideals and business realities. In his autobiography, he wrote, "As an individual, I have a direct responsibility to return to the institutions and communities that nurtured and educated me a portion of the benefits I have derived from them. For this reason, in both my corporate and individual activities, I have taken pain to pay the greatest attention to the concerns and needs of those closest to home, which in my case is Boston and its surrounding towns."[2]

Wang's idea of community—as those with whom one is in proximity—had grown from an early identification with Chinese Americans to include the company community of his employees and now "Boston and the surrounding towns." As his sense of community expanded, so did the scope of his philanthropy. He was especially generous to people and institutions that had helped him along the way. An earlier gift to Harvard had led him to write, "I benefited greatly from my years at Harvard, but that does not mean I was entitled to these benefits. Even had I not succeeded financially to the degree that I have, I would still owe a debt to Harvard."

An Wang was born in China in the middle of what has been called the age of confusion, the struggle for the soul of China after centuries of medieval rule. According to Wang, "The bloodshed of this struggle, and later the Japanese invasion of my household, disrupted every aspect of my childhood. It was a time of complete uncertainty, not just for me and my family, but for the institutions and ideas that previously defined China." Some years later, as a wealthy entrepreneur in the United States, Wang was awarded the Medal of Liberty during the relighting of the Statue of Liberty. He was one of twelve Americans born abroad who were honored for having made their mark in the United States. Included in the group were Elie Wiesel, a survivor of the Holocaust; Irving Berlin, the composer; and I. M. Pei, the architect.

This was a long way from the China of feuding warlords and Japanese brutality that Wang had known as a young boy in the 1920s and 1930s. During these upheavals he lost both his parents and a sister. Yet, it was this experience, the necessity of negotiating his way in unfamiliar territory, that gave him the confidence not only to migrate to the United States but to compete successfully in the marketplace of computer technology. His success was even more noteworthy because of the high standards he set for himself and his company. He refused to compete in markets where corruption and bribery were considered a normal part of doing business, and he severed connections with South Africa because he felt that country would never change unless people like him made strong statements.

As Wang Laboratories prospered, so did Wang. The spirit and principles of the company, like its founder, were reflected in the company's motto, "Find a need and fill it." Contained within the idea is the notion of individual initiative: "Don't ask whether something can be done; find a way to do it." The company motto also characterized the Wang approach to philanthropy. But like many other Chinese Americans, he could not explain his cultural roots, his business philosophy, or his many acts of benevolence without coming to terms with the influence of Confucianism—which he described as a combination of the golden rule and the notion of moderation and balance. "Just as many of the attributes or principles that I feel are important to success in business—such as moderation, patience, balance and simplicity," he wrote, "so is my belief that a sense of satisfaction comes from service to one's community."

Confucian scholar and dean of the Graduate Theological Union at Berkeley, Judith Berlin has noted that "all Chinese are Confucian—simply to be Chinese is to be Confucian at some level."[3] Robert Lee in his *Guide to Chinese American Philanthropy* argues that it should come as no surprise that Chinese Americans consciously or subconsciously turn to the Confucian legacy. Traditionally, Confucianism had no "membership" in the Western sense. As a diffuse religion that permeated its culture, it was simply embedded in the institutions and practices of society. Hence, there was little social cleavage or separation between religion and society as is customary in the West.[4]

Wang believed that humanity without benevolence invites its own destruction. Confucianism has always emphasized good conduct and wisdom, but Wang reflected a neo-Confucian spirit that places even more emphasis on good conduct as service to others. To be truly wise is thus to possess a sense of responsibility in social relationships.

In 1951, only six years after setting foot in the United States, An Wang founded Wang Laboratories. His Chinese friends were sensitive to discrimination against Asians and did not think it was wise to start a business in an area still perceived to be the province of the establishment. This was a legitimate concern. While the Chinese were no longer treated as they had been in the nineteenth century when they were attacked by lynch mobs, many more subtle forms of discrimination persisted. On one occasion, An Wang and his wife, Lorraine, sought to rent an advertised apartment only to be told, when the superintendent saw them, that it was not available. "When I encountered this type of discrimination," said Wang years later, "my response was to take it as an unpleasant fact of life and then to redouble my efforts to succeed."

Wang's strong sense of pride and self-confidence had early roots. The strength of Confucian virtues, the stability of his family life–six generations in the same town—and the depth of his knowledge of Chinese culture served him well. No act of private discrimination or public humiliation was about to shake his confidence in his abilities or diminish his pride in his heritage. It was this unshakable grounding that allowed him to assimilate new ideas without necessarily discarding old ones. "I was determined to show that the Chinese could succeed at something other than running laundries and restaurants," he observed later.

Wang looked for the similarities between cultures while others were preoccupied with the differences. It is not that he ignored or undervalued differences; he refused to see them as permanent barriers. "I am never able to convince people that I did not suffer culture shock when I arrived in the United States," he was fond of pointing out. "People insist that I must have been overwhelmed by the things that make America different from China—the wealth, the people, the food. But this is simply not true."[5]

He was surely not overwhelmed, securing a master's and a Ph.D. from Harvard in three years, using his $600 savings to start a company that grew into a $3 billion enterprise, and becoming the holder of forty patents on computer technology. This rags-to-riches story was a direct result of Wang's refusal to entertain the notion that there were some things he could or should not do. He never considered success as part of his birthright, as did some of the wealthy sons of Harvard he met in Harvard yard; but he was quick to admit that while his accomplishments were earned, they placed on him an obligation that remained forever in his consciousness.

It would be a mistake to dismiss either the Wang vision or the Wang generosity as the isolated values of an exceptional man who transcended his culture or the traditions of his group. There are many other Chinese who have shown a spirit of compassion and generosity as they have accumulated wealth. Moon Yuen could only get a job cleaning latrines after he left Angel Island. He eventually found better employment, but he left to form his own engineering company when he hit the glass ceiling that restricted the mobility of Chinese executives and reminded them that they had advanced as far as the corporate culture allowed. In a few years, his company was competing for, and winning, large-scale power contracts—in competition with his old company. Like Wang, Yuen acquired a reputation for his generosity in support of community needs.

The perceived frugality of the Chinese has perhaps led to the conclusion that "they are mercenary takers, not givers," according to Robert Lee.[6] Although much of Chinese giving is in their own community, the Chinese also respond to the needs and concerns of the larger community. During the devastating earthquake in Mexico City in 1985, the Salvation Army in San Francisco's Chinatown raised $160,000 for victim relief.[7] When the Salvation Army did a follow-up study to determine who the givers were, it found that much of the money came not from the affluent merchants but from the ordinary Chinatown people, "the elderly on fixed incomes and what may be regarded as the poorer element in the community."[8]

The affluent Chinese are benevolent as well. With the increase in wealth has come an increase in the number of Chinese families creating family foundations. These foundations are truly private and make few grants outside the Chinese community. But the May/June 1990 issue of *Foundation News* magazine reported a preliminary compilation in 1989 of 103 Chinese foundations.[9] Add to this the more than one thousand Chinese social services organizations listed in the San Francisco Bay Area alone, and the high level of commitment to philanthropy among Chinese Americans is clearly demonstrated.[10]

There is great wealth in the Chinese community, but there is a privacy about money matters that borders on secrecy. Since humility is a highly regarded virtue, to flaunt one's wealth and philanthropy in public would be considered unbecoming.[11] As head of a large public company, An Wang found his life and assets an open book. Keeping a low profile about financial matters was not an option. His philanthropy won him more attention than even his professional success. While he is best known for saving Boston's Metropolitan Center, a run-down theater that was resuscitated by his $4 million gift, he first started to attract attention when he moved the headquarters of Wang Laboratories from Tewksbury, Massachusetts, to Lowell in 1976. He caught the attention of many in and outside Massachusetts for his quick turnaround of a textile ghost town with 15 percent unemployment to a reasonably affluent community with an unemployment rate less than one fifth of what it had been.

Three years after his arrival in Lowell, Wang established a postgraduate institute for computer sciences and subsequently added a Chinese Studies Program. Concerned about how little Americans knew or understood the culture and traditions of the Chinese, he also donated money to Harvard's Fairbanks Institute for Chinese studies.

What Wang called his "compass of values" began within him, with his strong sense of civic obligation, but it was reinforced by the abuses he had seen in the interior of China during World War II when people had no sense of social responsibility. Although he prefers to talk in direct, straightforward language and concepts, shying away from the idea of a philosophical system, Wang has bridged Eastern and Western thought with Eastern and Western experience. As a boy in Kun San, thirty miles from Shanghai, he was as much inclined to play as to study. His father was an English teacher and his high school used English textbooks to teach mathematics, geography, and history, providing a grounding in English that served him well for the remainder of his life. After high school, Wang attended the so-called MIT of China, Chia Tung University in Shanghai. As an electrical engineering student with some command of English, he assisted his colleagues by occasionally translating into Chinese articles from *Popular Mechanics* or *Popular Science*. It was no surprise that when he graduated in 1940 he was offered a job as a teaching assistant at the university.

In August of 1937, while at Chia Tung, Wang had experienced the Japanese invasion, so he was eager to leave Shanghai. He and eight classmates escaped to Kweilin in China's interior. No day passed that did not remind him of the war; not only the bombing raids but the tyranny inflicted on the peasants by the local Chinese generals burned in his memory for years to come. China was at war so he expected the inhumanity of the Japanese adversary, but it was debilitating to see the treatment of the local Chinese by their own troops who were supposed to protect them. The area around Kweilin was already poor, but with corrupt military men and provincial officials squeezing people to the point of starvation, he wondered what had happened to the values he had believed to be embedded in Chinese culture.

While he was in Kweilin he received news of a program enabling Chinese engineers to visit the United States. Sponsored by the Nationalist government and supported partly by American money, the purpose of the program was to prepare Chinese engineers for the reconstruction of their country. Wang applied and, after a competitive exam, was selected. Getting into the program was easy compared to the trip to the United States. The time of his departure was April 1945, and the Japanese were still active in the area. There were stories of planes mysteriously losing parts of wings and parts of tails, causing considerable anxiety for anyone anticipating a flight; however, except for the discomfort of flying in a plane that was not pressurized, the completion of the first leg of his journey to India was uneventful. Traveling from Calcutta by American transport vessel through the Suez Canal produced even more tension than Wang had experienced on the DC-3 flight from China. The German surrender had occurred only a few weeks earlier, and Wang's ship was the first to travel through the canal after it had been cleared. There were still fears of hitting an undetected obstacle or mine.

After traveling for a month across the Indian Ocean, up the Red Sea, across the Mediterranean, and then across the Atlantic, Wang finally arrived in Newport News, Virginia, in June 1945. Most people having endured such an ordeal and knowing the rumors of discrimination against the Chinese would have been filled with fear or anxiety. Wang, however, felt no insecurities and was eager to improve his technical skills. Finding an apprenticeship proved to be difficult, but undaunted by this change in his fortunes, he decided to apply to Harvard instead.

He was accepted and excelled as a student. But China was still on his mind. He continued to feel an obligation to return home to help build his country, but by then a civil war was going on between the Communists and the Nationalists. While he was apolitical, Wang had seen the abuses of the Nationalist leaders and doubted their ability to maintain the trust of the Chinese people. "While I did not want the Communists to win," he said, "I thought that some form of coalition government was best for China."[12] He continued to think of returning until mid 1947 when it became increasingly likely that the Nationalists were going to lose. His parents had long since passed away and his brothers and sisters were under the care of other members of the family. He felt that there was little to return to. He wrote in his autobiography, "I also knew myself well enough to know that I could not thrive under a totalitarian system. I had long been independent, and I wanted to continue to make my own decisions about my life." He remained to become the consummate entrepreneur and to demonstrate extraordinary values.

Michael Dukakis, former governor of the Commonwealth of Massachusetts, worked with Wang and described him as an enterprising innovator whose dedicated idealism has gone beyond the boardroom. On the jacket of Wang's autobiography, a *Wall Street Journal* quote describes him as "an industry phenomenon who combines the charity of a Rockefeller . . . with the public relations savvy of an Iacocca." Through all his success and fame, An Wang remained committed to the Confucian idea that humanity without benevolence invites its own destruction.

Latinos

Chapter Thirteen

The Primacy of Family and Church

For most Hispanic Americans, the principle of self-help and mutual assistance is closely linked to the idea of community. As early as 1598, Mexicans in the Southwest organized *mutualistas* (mutual aid groups) for their security and survival. These were both a response to the social conditions of the time and a reflection of a communal ethic that emphasized self-sufficiency, cooperation, and generosity. According to Jose A. Hernandez, who made a special effort to identify the philosophical vision of mutual aid groups among Mexican Americans, the mutualistas contained vestiges of Indian and Spanish thought, Christian doctrine, an altruism paralleling the ideals of Herbert Spencer and Leon Bourgeois, elements of nineteenth-century liberalism, and the power of positivism built into the philosophy of August Comte.[1] There is no tradition of the poor or needy Mexican American turning to government for help because, as an American sociologist observed in a 1934 study, "He received a great deal of assistance in a communal spirit from his kin, friends and societies."[2] Hernandez quotes another observer as reporting that "the Mexicans are awfully kind to each other. Even with a house full of children, they will take in another family."[3]

This spirit of generosity and social solidarity can be found among other Hispanic groups as well. While there are wide differences among the various subgroups, they tend to share some core values and civic habits that transcend family and nationality, shape behavior patterns, and draw them together in a functional community.

The most basic of Latino values is the primacy of the familial

171

relationship. Grandparents, parents' siblings, and the latter's children, termed *primos hermanos*, are all considered close relatives; and indeed, there seems to be a great deal of social interaction with such persons throughout life.[4] Studies of Mexican Americans in south Texas and New Mexico show that the extended family is the most important unit in such areas as economic cooperation and recreation. It is also the primary agent of socialization and control. While the status roles within the family are changing, with the younger generation exercising more independence, the family is still a highly visible and functional unit. And there is still the tendency for individual family members to take care of a large circle of poor relatives. In ways unparalleled in some European groups, the Hispanic community is a "kin-based" society and the most lasting, deepest ties are between "kin-related" members. The function of socialization and social control is to an increasing extent being taken over by other bonding units, but even in these areas the role of the family has not been superseded completely.[5]

A second social unit creating an important bond with special obligation is defined territorially. In the past, this was often a village, but it is now more likely to be a neighborhood—a Chicano *barrio*, for example. The individual identification with some aboriginal territorial locale is made more difficult by the large number of immigrants now settling in the United States with limited opportunity to relate to the community that spawned them. In these instances, different patterns of identification have developed. In the large cities of the Southwest, for example, one finds cliques of people who once lived together in a village. They seek each other out and the social unit becomes a part of the system of courtship and marriage, and even political patronage.

A third dimension of social solidarity is described as *la raza*, a term that is literally translated as "the race." But la raza is increasingly ambiguous, with brown skin color, Spanish language, or other characteristics that transcend nationality no longer having the strong social bond that was once assumed. There is still a group of people, however, for whom la raza has a kind of mystical bond that cuts across other forms of social or familial units. But this group is in no way a cohesive corporate unit. Differences include a mixed racial makeup that is often glossed over by those who emphasize the European component exclusively; national origins that cause many Hispanics to identify themselves as Cubans, Mexican Americans, or Puerto Ricans rather than as Latinos, Spanish-Speaking, Latin Americans, or any of the other more general terms of reference; and divergent cultural and political values that are so deeply held by some Hispanics that they become the primary source of social cohesion or group solidarity.

La raza may be a unifying concept or principle, but it has not proven to be sufficiently strong to override some of these other interests and commitments. The same is true of the constellation of values that is often attributed to la raza. Scholars disagree about what these values are, but there seems to be a general consensus that the Latin-American tradition inculcates certain ideals of social behavior based on honor and dignity, on the integral value of a person that puts more value on one's spiritual makeup than on one's economic status, on personal confidence in certain persons, and on self-help.[6] There has been considerable discussion of Latino authoritarianism, present-time orientation, and fatalism. Some even simplify so-called Latino values to pro-family, pro-God, and pro-country. But some of the values attributed to Hispanics as a group mistakenly contrast agricultural values with industrial values and confuse class characteristics with ethnic characteristics.[7]

Social class also plays a role in Hispanic solidarity. There are often profound antagonisms among classes based on either present circumstances or historical memory. The upper class is more likely to be of European heritage. In early America, they were the noblemen and officials appointed by the crown and later by Mexico to conquer and hold the land, search for wealth, and maintain order among the citizens.[8] There was also a group of farmers of both Spanish and Spanish-Indian descent who were successful enough to be granted a union card in the social system of the upper class. The lower class was distinguishable by the darker complexion of most of its members, by a lack of formal education, and by a low income and poor standard of living. Even the more recent immigrants have come from a rigidly stratified social system where race has played a major role in shaping the social personality, values, and attitudes that are reflected in interclass relations today.

The middle classes tend to be the most "anglicized." Members of this group are the most likely to speak only English in their homes, reside in middle-class neighborhoods, send their children to dancing schools and to summer camp, sometimes become Protestants, change their dietary patterns, and increase their participation in Anglo voluntary associations.[9] Since the members of this class are still not secure, either financially or socially, they are likely to suffer the psychological stress of a confused identity and they are likely to be especially unaccepting of the behavior of other Hispanics who do not emulate the middle-class norms they have adopted.

Religion is another source of bonding in the Latino community. But despite the common stereotype that Hispanic equals Catholic, there has always been a minority of Hispanics who were not raised in the Catholic tradition. In the United States, Protestant ties among Hispanics are increasing rapidly. In 1980, Hispanics were 15 percent Protestant. By 1988, the number had grown to 20 percent.[10] Much of that growth has been among the Pentecostal evangelical churches that are more likely to have Hispanic clergy and more likely to be perceived as a resource broker between the immigrants and mainstream society. According to Father Allen Figueroa Deck of the Academy of Catholic Hispanic Theologians, there are 300 Hispanics enrolled in Catholic seminaries and theological schools and 938 Hispanics in Protestant seminaries and theological schools.[11]

Historically, Hispanic benevolence has been church centered

as well as familial, but the church has been more of an intermediary than a broker. Unlike the Europeans whose clergy emigrated with the people, the clergy serving Hispanic Catholics are frequently from other groups in the American society. As a result, they tend to be much more concerned with ritual, theology, and worship than with how the considerable resources of the Catholic Church can be used to provide basic services to meet basic human needs.[12] Whether this will be different with the evangelical Pentecostal churches is problematic, but there are likely to be increasing efforts to utilize the religious dimension of community life to support community development and to integrate the spiritual and the material. The more Hispanics come together to develop a common social agenda, the more they are likely to integrate religion and culture, theology, and economics.

To gain a better understanding of benevolent traditions and paradigms of community among Latinos, we should look at several of the subgroups that exist as independent cultural units.

Mexican Americans

Unlike many other immigrant groups who came to this country, for Mexican Americans in the Southwest the country came to them. Their territory was annexed and many were reduced to positions of servitude. The infiltration of Anglo Americans into Mexican territory began in 1820 when Anglo-American settlers petitioned the Spanish government for permission to settle in Texas. Territorial conquest and forcible acquisition of land by the settlers were accompanied by exclusion of the Mexicans living in that area from participation in the political process, by economic exploitation of them, and by the denial of even social self-determination. In order to combat the oppressive conditions, the Mexicans organized mutual aid groups and societies.[13]

Within the United States, Mexican immigrants organized hundreds of mutualistas in their barrios and *colonias* (rural areas with primarily Mexican population) to meet their need for sickness and death benefits, and in a broader context to recreate their social networks in a new environment. Some Chicano mutual aid societies were similar to the Chinese *hui kuan* benevolent fraternal orders in America, which acted as unofficial governments. They not only stressed benevolence but also provided services in the form of credit associations, employment agencies, and representation for their constituencies in dealing with other organizations and white officials. These societies were in no way a substitute for the family unit; rather, they were an extension of the kinship system.

Jose A. Hernandez, a professor of Chicano Studies and Urban Affairs, made an extensive study of Hispanic benevolent organizations and published his findings in *Mutual Aid for Survival*. He points out that the earliest mutual aid and benefit societies founded almost immediately after the Spanish arrived in New Mexico were the *cofradias* or *confraternidades* (lay brotherhoods), out of which evolved fraternal orders, health cooperatives, and other specific purpose organizations. Initially, these groups were fraternal orders with a religious orientation, emphasizing church-related activities. They conducted worship services, cared for the sick and needy, supervised burials, and rendered other resources of charity and assistance.

According to Hernandez, the oldest known voluntary association in what is now the United States is the Confraternity of Brothers of Our Father Jesus of Nazareth, commonly known as Los Penitentes. This organization, founded around 1598, constituted the basic institution around which early American life in New Mexico and Colorado was organized. The Penitents were members of a religious cult combining both Meso-American and European folkways in their practice of the Catholic religion.[14] They cared for each member in the society and their families in times of sickness or distress. They also made funeral arrangements, buried the deceased, and cared for widows. There is considerable evidence to suggest that these earlier associations were native to New Mexico and not transplanted by the Spaniards.[15] Eventually, these types of associations grew into powerful political machines as Mexican Americans were forced to seek new ways to protect their economic and political position.

The Alianza Hispano Americana founded in Tucson in 1894 by a group of distinguished Mexican-American families served as a force to fight for material and economic rights, and to protect the Mexicans from exploitation by their employers. It first functioned as a local society, but in 1897 it was incorporated as a mutual aid society under the regulations governing fraternal associations in territorial Arizona. The organization dealt principally with the various problems of the working class. It sought to improve health and domestic conditions and was a pioneer in the Mexican-American labor movement. As the organization evolved, it also played a key role in the civil rights movement. For example, it acted as a legal aid society by providing defense funds for individuals who were victims of injustice. By 1910 the Alianza had almost three thousand members.

The founders and early organizers of the organization were men of wealth and education in high standing while the majority of its members were persons of humble means. The first president of the organization, Carlos I. Velasco, was born in Hermosillo, Sonora, Mexico. He acquired a legal education and served in various key positions in the Mexican government before he moved to the territory of Arizona. In 1878, he began the first Spanish-language newspaper in Tucson.

Another type of Mexican-American mutual aid society is demonstrated by the Sociedad Progresista Mexicana (Mexican Progressive Society) founded in 1911. The formation of this society was based on a need to protect its members from paupers' funerals. Each member contributed one dollar when a fraternal member died. Benefits depended on the contributions of the active membership. In its first decade the organization cooperated with other California fringe benefit associations by providing services and relief to the needy families of the barrios. This mutual burial society is still in existence.[16]

The mutual aid associations also took the lead in organizing Mexican-American workers into unions. "For example, in 1927 a federation of mutual aid societies from throughout southern California gathered in Los Angeles and formed the first Mexican-American labor union in 1928, La Confederacion de Uniones Oberas Mexicanas."[17]

The mutualistas, or mutual aid societies, were first concerned with survival and security. By the end of the 1930s the mutualistas took a different turn as conditions in the general society changed. When Mexican Americans began to share in the economic, political, and social benefits of American society, the political role of mutual aid and benefit societies in the Chicano community began to decline and the benefit associations became a convenient tool for individual awards.

When Cesar Chavez, an American-born farm worker, began to organize farm laborers in 1963, he ushered in a new era of Mexican-American organizations, groups organized for advocacy and social reform. The sixties proved to be a significant turning point. Chavez was soon followed by Reies Lopez Tijerina, who startled many Americans by forming La Alianza Federal de Mercedes to demand that the lands of northern New Mexico be returned to the Mexican-American people. In 1968, both the National Council of La Raza and the Mexican American Legal Defense Fund were founded. The role of these nonprofit, voluntary organizations went far beyond mutual aid and social services. Their strategies included advocacy through legislation, lawsuits, administrative reform, research, and education. They tackled problems varying from educational opportunity to employment practices, residency, language, and voting rights. The Mexican-American community led the way in taking the case of Hispanics to American foundations, national church bodies, government, and the public at large.

Mexican-American voluntary organizations have enjoyed a high degree of member participation, with much coming from the working class and individuals of low socioeconomic status.

Puerto Rican Americans

Puerto Ricans have come to the United States as citizens since 1917 and have had an established right of free entry since 1904. There are more than two million Puerto Ricans presently living on the mainland and another three million residing in the Commonwealth of Puerto Rico. Like the Mexican Americans, they developed their own benevolent organizations to help them adapt to and survive within the American society. According to Virginia E. Sanchez Korrol in *From Colonia to Community: The History of Puerto Ricans in New York City, 1917–1948*, Puerto Rican associations were formed to acclimate incoming immigrants to their new environment, provide an avenue for them to participate in group activities based on common interests, and to represent the colonias before the host society. Between 1917 and 1948, three types of associations were predominant. The first, the mutual aid societies of the early decades, patterned themselves after those on the island, addressing migrant needs as they had served the community on the island. Eventually, these societies began organizing the working-class colonia into trade unions, affiliating them with those on the island and on the mainland. By the mid twenties another type of organization emerged, focusing on representing Puerto Ricans before the non-Hispanic community. These groups, exemplified by the Puerto Rican Brotherhood of America, embodied similar characteristics of the earlier mutual aid groups but also emphasized cultural values and tradition and responded to more immediate concerns. In the thirties, special-interest or single-interest organizations emerged, such as the Post Office Workers' Organization.

The working class from Puerto Rico brought with it the concept of self-help organizations. On the island, *gremios*, patterned

after the Spanish guild system, limited competition, regulated arti-
san markets, controlled conditions of employment, and provided
fairs for the exchange of merchandise. *Cofradias* and *hermandades*
provided medical care and hospital aid, raised dowries or ransoms,
and supplied burial, social, and religious services for their members.

The earliest groups in the New York colonia, or settlement,
were the mutual aid societies established by pioneer migrant
tobacco workers in Manhattan's Lower East Side and Chelsea district. Tobacco workers' associations, mutual aid groups, and trade
unions were the first groups to emerge in the colonias because for
the first decades of the century, tobacco workers and their families
predominated among the Puerto Rican working class.

The growth of the settlements produced such social units as the
hometown or regional clubs, which responded to more basic needs,
providing both social and recreational activities for the new immigrant. These groups soon offered job-related information, visited
the sick, provided monetary aid, and resolved problems. Finances
came from dues, collections, and activities from members. The
hometown clubs also supported the island, continental political per-
suasions, Latino cultural societies, and civic-oriented associations.

Founded in 1923, the Puerto Rican Brotherhood of America
was a very prominent mutual aid association. It was established to
promote unity, brotherhood, and mutual aid among Puerto Ricans
according to the consent of its members. Among other activities,
it organized social gatherings, promoted cultural identity, and
defended the rights of other Puerto Ricans. The women's auxiliary
generated publicity, directed the youth groups, supervised fundraising, and performed charitable works.

The Brotherhood was instrumental in establishing La Liga Puer-
torriquena e Hispana, an organization formed to represent the Hispanic community before the larger society. Its goals were to unite
all Hispanics without national distinctions, to represent the community before the authorities, to be a benevolent society, to pro-

vide an education and information center, to encourage voting while refraining from partisan politics, and to work toward the economic, political, and social betterment of Puerto Ricans and Puerto Rico.[18]

Cuban Americans

Although they represent a much smaller population than either Mexican Americans or Puerto Ricans, Cuban Americans are easily the most affluent. They are concentrated in a metropolitan area, Greater Miami, and they have a large role and stake in its development. Their perspective on their role in the larger community is that of mainstream insiders rather than marginalized outsiders. However, they tend to think of themselves as an exile group and direct more of their attention toward their homeland than other Hispanics.

According to Lisandro Perez in "Philanthropy Among Cuban Americans," organized philanthropy among Cubans is mostly political in nature and finds its most evident manifestation in the work of the Cuban American National Foundation (CANF). Founded in 1981, the CANF is anti-Castro in focus and uses strategies similar to those of most interest groups in America. "CANF members are all successful businessmen who annually give thousands of dollars in dues and contributions, to further the organization's work."[19] Deviating from their usual anti-Castro preoccupation, the CANF has recently organized support and resources to help with the migration of hundreds of Cubans in third countries to the United States.

Perez reports that in the Cuban community there are also insular philanthropic efforts—that is, efforts that are confined to benefiting the Cuban community. The Cintas Foundation is an example of this type of philanthropy as is La Liga Contra el Cancer, an organization transplanted from Cuba that has a large annual telethon to raise money for cancer research.

The most notable philanthropic initiative in Cuba was the founding in 1793 of the Sociedad Economica de Amigos del Pais by the sugarocracy, which sought to bring Cuba into the age of enlightenment by creating an intellectual, cultural, and scientific institution that would promote agriculture and commerce. There were also philanthropic initiatives that centered on education and health.

In the 1960s, which were the early years of Cuban exiles in America, the Catholic Church played an important role in the relief and adjustment of the newly arrived refugees and helped form the basis of the few voluntary associations. However, the church does not have the same importance among Cuban Americans as it does among other Hispanics in America.[20]

Among younger Cuban Americans, local initiatives are now apparent. One example is the Dade County Cuban American Bar Association composed of Cubans trained in the United States who have joined with their black colleagues in fundraising efforts to rebuild buildings and programs damaged by the recent riots in predominantly black neighborhoods in Miami.[21]

The majority of Cuban-American immigrants have been disproportionately possessed of a complex of skills, aspirations, and experiences that have provided them a relative advantage in the process of economic adjustment.[22] The socioeconomic selectivity of Cuban immigration and the high family income to which this has led have distanced Cuban interests from those of the many Hispanics who are on the margins of the economy. There were sizable communities of Cubans in New Orleans and Key West before the 1959 Cuban revolution, but the greatest contemporary Cuban presence is a direct result of the revolution that put Fidel Castro in power in Cuba and it reflects post-revolution values.

A shift from the political exile mind-set to that of Cuban Americans is already occurring in the new generation. The immigrant entrepreneurs who created the Cuban-American community we know today are not reproducing themselves. Many of their well-educated children are joining the professional and civic institutions of the larger community. As their stake in the larger community increases, so will their sense of belonging and their feeling of obligation. This will undoubtedly alter their relationship to other Americans and expand their vision of community.

Paul Ylvisaker, who was a driving force in encouraging American foundations to join hands with Hispanics in developing Hispanic voluntary organizations, once wrote that "it is no accident or wonder that the host of different groups that we now label as Hispanics would take recourse to voluntary action as a means to achieve their common and more often divergent purposes. They found themselves in a society where they were too outnumbered to count on the support of government or the majority that by definition controls the government."[23] Looking toward the future, Ylvisaker predicted that to the degree that tension and discrimination ease, a shift from advocacy to service may well take place. But for the moment, advocacy is expected to remain a central part of the mission of Hispanic volunteer groups.

As for individual giving, the approach of many of the Hispanic groups was summed up by a Mexican-American woman who told researchers at the University of San Francisco:

Mexicans see it as sharing, not giving. I have this and someone else needs it, so it is automatic that I give it to them. You share of yourself no matter what your economic level. . . . The Mexican kids at junior high school; if someone forgets their lunch money, they will pull out the change from their pants and give it to them, or they will tell me and see if I can help. They've lived it and they know what it's like, they have empathy. One little girl, a recent arrival, was coming to school with a thin little sweater and it was cold. One of the kids pointed this out to me. They said they had asked Maria if she was cold and she said no, but she was always shivering. . . . The next day the kid who told me brought in a bag of clothes for Maria that his sister had outgrown, meanwhile he and his family are wearing secondhand clothing, and he gave it to me to give to Maria. . . . You don't give directly in such a situation. . . . You like to use sharing, not giving. People get offended. We are careful not to offend anyone.[24]

Chapter Fourteen

Patrick Flores: The Mariachi Bishop

The roots of benevolence among Americans of Mexican descent are closely tied to the history and hope of the Catholic Church. Patrick Flores, the archbishop of San Antonio, is a vigorous example of these historic ties. As a boy, he and his family followed the migrant trails north in search of work. As a young priest, he supported the economic claims of the farm workers who followed Cesar Chavez. And as bishop, he identified the church with the moral claims of liberation theologians who taught that justice for the poor required not simply charity but active political engagement.[1]

Born in Ganada, Texas, in 1929, the sixth of nine children, Patrick Flores shined the shoes of his classmates in seminary to earn money for his incidental needs. As a twelve-year-old in Pearland, Texas, he helped organize his school and his neighbors to oppose school segregation. Strongly identified with the needs and aspirations of the poor and disinherited all his life, he once raffled off his episcopal ring for $2,200 to pay for the defense of a twenty-one-year-old man charged with a murder he did not commit.

Bishop Flores's vision of community is much broader than his ecclesiastical jurisdiction. His parish is the world. He went to Ecuador to show his solidarity with the local bishop and was kidnapped at machine gunpoint by government troops. Undaunted by the controversy, he has also gone to Cuba to discuss personally with Fidel Castro the state of the Cuban church and the release of political prisoners. His influence and popularity do not stop at the boundaries of the Catholic Church. When he was installed as archbishop in 1979, spokesmen for many Protestant denominations greeted his appointment with enthusiasm. A San Antonio rabbi said, "Flores is exceedingly sensitive to human needs . . . he does not shut off consideration of others because they are of a different faith."

When he vigorously defends the rights of the dispossessed, wherever and whoever they are, Patrick Flores is driven by his acute awareness and sensitivity to the generations of neglect that have afflicted Mexican Americans. San Antonio has Hispanic roots that go back nearly four hundred years. Until the appointment of Flores in 1970, however, there were no Mexican Americans among 285 Catholic bishops in the United States. This omission was especially remarkable in the Southwest, a region where people of Mexican descent constitute the largest minority and where, generations ago, Spanish-speaking priests established missions that are still a treasured inheritance.

Two observations are helpful in explaining why Bishop Flores's appointment was so important to Mexican Americans and how his public theology and civic values have been shaped by his experience as a Hispanic. First, as Joseph Fitzpatrick points out in his study of the Hispanic church in the United States, being religious in Latin America is not perceived, as it is in the United States, primarily in terms of adherence to the organized church.[2] To be Catholic in the United States means to be affiliated with the church, to belong to its associations, and to be identified with its structures. In Latin America, the religious practice is marked by the quality of *personalismo,* the pattern of close intimate personal relationships that is characteristic of Spanish cultures everywhere.[3] Individuals perceive their religious life as a network of personal relationships with the saints, the Blessed Virgin, or various manifestations of the church made flesh and blood. They pray to the saints, light candles to them, carry their images in procession, build shrines to them in the home, make promises to them, and expect them to deliver the favors, help, or protection that is characteristic of *compadres*, close friends. But this personal relationship with the saints takes place outside the organized structure of the church.[4]

Second, because institutions in the United States tend to be more formal and bureaucratic, they often appear to Hispanics to be cold, impersonal, and void of personalismo. Part of Bishop Flores's attraction as a pastor came from his effort to put feeling and spirit into the church. Because of his unusual church services, he was at one time known as the "Mariachi Priest." His services included music with mariachi bands and sometimes, afterward, a fiesta and dancing.

It was not surprising that the *Cursillo* religious movement played an important role in the life and work of Patrick Flores. The movement began in Texas as a program of renewal and spiritual discipline, combining music and group dynamic techniques with an emphasis on sacrifice and compassion. Many of the Hispanic leaders of the 1970s owed their social conscience to the Cursillo, including Cesar Chavez and many of the farm workers in his union.[5] During his early years as a young priest in Houston, Flores was forbidden to speak Spanish to Mexican parishioners, even when they addressed him in that language. He found himself facing a similar situation in regard to the Cursillo. In 1962, his bishop banned the movement in his diocese, but reversed himself a year later when he saw how effective it was in renewing the faith of Hispanics. Through his "mariachi masses," filled with charismatic preaching, Flores generated a new sense of hope and pride for Hispanics.

When Flores was appointed bishop, there were fiestas and celebrations throughout the Mexican-American community. But some Anglo Catholics worried that he would be a Mexican-American bishop first, a Catholic one second. In an interview in the *Houston Chronicle* on June 28, 1970, the new Bishop was asked: "How do you see your function as the first Mexican American Bishop in a predominantly Mexican American city and diocese? What do you expect to do in San Antonio?" Flores responded: "I hope simply to be a servant to everyone to whatever extent I am able. My doors will not be closed to anyone. Although I am not coming to San Antonio to minister exclusively to the needs of the Mexican American people, I will probably spend much of my time with their problems because their needs are the greatest and they comprise the majority of Catholics in the diocese."

The rituals celebrating Flores's promotion to bishop—from his consecration on a Mexican national holiday to the controversial participants he invited—all demonstrated dramatically that he not only acknowledged his Mexican-American roots but also proudly proclaimed them. He wanted everyone to know just where he stood by including leaders that gave Hispanics a new sense of hope and pride in their cultural identity. One of the controversial participants in the consecration mass was Cesar Chavez, head of the California Farm Workers Union, who read one of the scriptures. He and Flores were long-term friends, having worked together in the 1950s and 1960s on the Bishop's Committee for the Spanish Speaking. The presence of Chavez was more than a symbolic announcement of the bishop's abiding commitment to the poor.

The public identification with the plight of farm workers was not new to Flores, nor was he daunted by criticism of his friendship with Chavez. On December 4, 1970, California Supreme Court Judge Gordon Campbell in Salinas, California, ordered Cesar Chavez jailed until he called off a boycott of lettuce produced by growers who did not have contracts with his United Farm Workers Union. Bishop Flores flew to California to visit him in jail, causing a storm of protest in the San Antonio media. Some local citizens demanded to know why a Catholic bishop would visit such a radical in jail. Flores held a press conference to point out that "visiting prisoners is a work of mercy stressed by Jesus Christ." He reminded his critics that more than three hundred Catholic bishops in the United States were supporting Chavez's stand. Flores further explained that Chavez was the only hope for the migrant farm workers and that he was a symbol of nonviolence. By prohibiting

their picketing and boycotting rights, the California court was invit-
ing violence.

The hate mail, the phone calls, and the newspaper attacks continued. But two years after flying to California to visit Chavez in
jail and to identify publicly with the plight of Chicano farm workers, the bishop marched in a protest line in front of a local super-
market, asking the people of San Antonio to avoid buying grapes
and lettuce without the United Farm Workers' Black Eagle
Trademark.

Primarily a pastor, Flores believed that his ecclesiastical calling
required more of him than simply comforting the poor and ameliorating social injury. He felt a call to raise his voice in opposition to
injustice and exploitation as well. He had been one of the founders
of PADRES, an acronym for Padres Associados para Derechos Reli-
giosas, Educativos y Sociales (Priests Associated for Religious, Educational, and Social Rights), and had brought to it a strong effective
voice, a sense of balance and maturity that won him respect from
even his severest critics.

But a growing debate was emerging about the separation of
church and state. Even Henry Cisneros, a young city councilman
who was to become mayor of San Antonio and later secretary of
the federal Department of Housing and Urban Development,
entered the controversy. He wrote in the *Express News* religion col-
umn of March 30, 1980, "Every clergyman has to realize that when
he steps onto the turf of the secular world, he is engaging in a dia-
logue which is fair game. No particular mantle of sacredness extends
to a clergyman's comments on secular matters. I would think that
a clergyman would think twice before making himself vulnerable
in that respect." Cisneros also warned that there was "a very real
skepticism among all peoples about mixing religion and politics."
The bishop's response to this, and other similar comments, was that
"the good of the community is my business. It is the business of
every citizen and as a citizen I have a right to express my opinion."

Flores never knew or acknowledged boundaries to his ministry.

He could not accept the neat distinctions between the religious and the secular that would have him remain silent on the great issues affecting the poor and the marginalized. A moderate man whose theology was by most measures traditional, he was also a moral man who saw himself called to wear the activist mantle of the prophet as well as the sacramental mantle of the priest. He often quoted Pope John Paul who had said in Mexico that "if Jesus was identified with the poor, the dispossessed and the disinherited of the earth so must we identify with them." Flores's outrage with the suggestion that the church should be silent on matters of justice and equity had long roots. As a boy, he had once been scolded by his mother for criticizing a visiting priest who had spoken eloquently about Jesus being born in a cold stable, implying that his poverty had been a blessing. Young Flores saw it as an insult, suggesting that Mexican-American families were somehow lucky to be able to imitate Christ's poverty. So irked was he by the priest's poverty theme that in the middle of a devout discussion among friends and relatives after the mass, he blurted out, "I wish Christ hadn't been born in a stable so that we wouldn't have to imitate him."

Flores had little patience with those who wanted the church to be a vehicle for communion and confession among the poor rather than a source of empowerment. He was a founder of the Mexican American Cultural Center (MACC) whose mission was to serve as a multipurpose center to help Latino Catholics realize the value of their own cultural identity and prepare them for community and professional leadership as they became part of a predominantly North American culture. The bishop also hoped that the center would help others understand the culture and tradition of Chicanos and other Latinos. MACC was founded on principles used by similar centers in Cuernavaca, Mexico, and Quito, Ecuador. It would be the first educational center in the United States "to emphasize that the Gospel can not be spread without a deep consideration of a people's culture."

In addition to teaching at the center, Flores surprised everyone in 1974 when, as a fundraising technique, he recorded an album of ten songs titled "The Singing Bishop." Five of these songs were religious hymns and the others traditional Mexican ranch songs, reminiscent of his youthful days when he and his sister sang and danced in the cantinas. Flores once again received a barrage of criticism, not for his singing but, as some Texas Catholics put it, because he was "too liberal, too racially divisive, too militant and even too leftist."

The humanitarian side of the Chicano bishop's character took on a new sophistication as he began to use the techniques of organized philanthropy to match his own charitable impulses. He founded the National Hispanic Scholarship Fund in 1975 because he felt that education could help break the cycle of poverty and he remembered how the lack of funds had nearly stopped him from becoming a priest. The fund awards yearly scholarships totaling $1.2 million to Latinos.

In 1986, Flores accepted a $1 million contribution to the National Hispanic Scholarship Fund from August Busch of the Anheuser Busch Brewery. The bishop was flown to a baseball game in St. Louis to accept the gift from Busch who was also president of the St. Louis professional baseball team.

The more successful he became, the more Flores remembered his roots. He had vivid memories of working from dawn to dust in the fields, the barns, and the sheds on the migrant trails; lacking electric lights to read by; twice dropping out of school; suffering discrimination and racial slurs.

During these years, Patrick's father, Pete Flores had taken a job with a trucking company in an effort to help his family escape the migrant farm life. When his children asked him how he was able to find his way to places outside of Texas since he could not read, he explained that often he had to drive out of his way fifty to a hundred miles before he found someone to give him precise directions.

But Pete Flores developed a kidney problem and became too ill to work, so young Patrick Flores did what so many other Chicanos did. He dropped out of school.

Writing about this period in the 1985 issue of *Today's Catholic*, he summed up his state of mind at that moment in his life:

> Listen to me as I tell you about a little boy who toddled behind his father following the harvest north, the young son of a Mexican American laborer. He lived in sheds—sometimes with water and sometimes without—he knew the dull state of hunger. He saw family-learned prejudice grow in the eyes of his classmates. By the tenth grade, this little boy was defeated, and like 40 percent of all Mexican American children, he dropped out of school.

Flores was defiant rather than defeated. He used his bout with bigotry to keep his eyes on what needed to be done. He once said of his critics, "They are afraid I will lead people in a revolution. I only want to lead people to the Lord. I'm simply a Christian in the process of self-conversion."

Chapter Fifteen

Sister Isolina: The Mother Teresa of Puerto Rico

Ponce is Puerto Rico's second-largest city, with a population of 210,000. Visitors revel in its charm. Some stroll around the Plaza Las Delicias, with its perfectly pruned ficus trees, graceful fountains, gardens, and park benches. Others visit the Ponce Museum of Arts or walk down Calles Isabel and Cristina to see turn-of-the-century wooden houses with wrought-iron balconies. At the museum, one is reminded of the benefaction of Luis Ferre, the third elected governor of Puerto Rico, who has had a distinguished career as a businessman, philanthropist, sponsor of the arts, and political leader.

Across town in a waterfront community far away from the romance of Puerto Rican heritage and culture is the Sister Isolina Ferre Center, where the youngest daughter of the Ferre family works among the urban and rural poor. Sister Isolina, the nun whom some call "the Mother Teresa of Puerto Rico," grew up in a family of privilege and power, the closest approximation Puerto Rico has to nobility. As a child, she had all the advantages of life, but she chose to work with those who knew only the disadvantages. Instead of following her father into business or her brother into politics, she felt the call to service of a different kind.[1]

Sitting in her office on the Playa de Ponce, she spoke softly, but forcefully, about more than fifty years of transforming communities and sowing the seeds of hope; of challenging people to change behavior; of cultivating and strengthening the values and customs that allow people to take control of their lives.

Even if Sister Isolina did not have such a finely tuned empathy for those who are oppressed or abandoned, it would be hard for her not to feel the pain or share the misery of those in society who are rejected or marginalized. Her work rests on the fundamental principle that "the glory of God is man and woman fully alive."

In a few months, she will turn eighty, but she is still vigorous, committed, and challenged. Looking into her animated eyes, watching her expressive hands, and listening to her youthful voice, one senses that he is in the presence of a deeply spiritual person. So the conversation naturally turns to religion—its role in her own life and that of the Puerto Rican people. With her large blue eyes sparkling, she acknowledges her desire to connect with others at the deepest level. "Inside a Puerto Rican," she says, "is a religious feeling that's often unacknowledged in a formal religious way. So a lot of poor or marginal people with whom I work turn to superstition. They want to approach God quickly, so they go to the supernatural. There is a lot of spiritism even in our young people." Adding that she is a Catholic nun and her orientation, of course, is Catholic, she acknowledges a special affinity, a shared religious feeling that creates a special bond with Puerto Ricans of all faiths and religious beliefs.

Sister Isolina first began to think of becoming a nun at age fourteen; she wanted to join an order when she was seventeen, but actually joined the Missionary Servants of the Most Blessed Trinity at twenty-one. She was greatly influenced by her mother who taught her "that all people are equal in the sight of God" and encouraged her to "have compassion for those less fortunate." Her mother died during Sister Isolina's first year in college. Returning home to help take care of her brothers, the young Miss Ferre was confronted with the misery she had seen in her early childhood only during rides with the family chauffeur. She now took long walks along the playa where she saw the needs of the children and decided to do something about them. "I used to get them together, talk to them," she said. "Sometimes," she added, "I would give them catechism and bring them to church. . . . Other times I would have parties for them. I converted my house in town into a place where the children would come from different sections, many from very poor sections. I would bring them home and I would call a few friends to help me do all this."

But her calling to a more focused vocation, her urge to join a religious order, was still strong. Her mother had taught her that "when you give, you don't just give a little, you give everything." One of her brothers wanted her to stay home and become a social worker for the industries he ran, arguing that there was no need to become a nun, to take vows of poverty, in order to help others. Another brother encouraged her to follow her calling. He persuaded her father that as her brothers had gone off to Harvard and elsewhere for an education, Sister Isolina could continue her education by studying to be a nun. Her father finally accepted that notion and gave his blessing.

But why not a social worker instead? "My mother gave me a very solid Christian foundation," she said. "I became convinced that if I really loved this idea of serving, loving God and serving my fellows, I had to do it the right way," which meant giving everything. "I had to cut my cord from my family, from everything and serve as best I could." She went on, "I was trained by the madams of the Sacred Heart, who were teachers of rich girls. I said no, I don't want that; other people can do that. I want to enter a community that works for the marginal, the abandoned."

Understanding her earliest experience with poverty helps explain the depth of her commitment. She tells this story:

> When I was a little girl, my father's chauffeur used to come in the afternoons to pick me up and to take me around for a little ride, and he used to take me to his girlfriends all over town.
>
> I began to notice as a little girl that the houses were quite different from my house. There were little houses and wooden houses, for example, and inside there was often only one little chair, maybe a broken chair and a little table. But they were very nice people always and they would give the chauffeur some black coffee and I

would get some little candy. The people were nice and so good to me, but the houses were so different. So I began to wonder why there were big houses and why there were small houses. Why can't everybody have the same things?

In this youthful, innocent mind the seeds of a lifelong commitment began to germinate. Later, she went to school and was astounded by what she learned about the plight of poor people in other nations. She considered doing missionary work abroad, but she met a priest named Father Judge, the founder of an American Catholic order serving Puerto Ricans. He asked her why she was thinking of the missions in India and China and other places when so many people in Puerto Rico needed to be helped. A woman of universal compassion and at home in any culture, Sister Isolina nonetheless remembered her early childhood experiences with her father's chauffeur and decided to do her work on Puerto Rican soil.

Even so, there were to be many years and many experiences elsewhere before Sister Isolina's work took root in Puerto Rico. In 1935, she entered the religious order of the Missionary Servants of the Blessed Trinity in Philadelphia, Pennsylvania. Her first assignment after completing her training was in the Appalachian coal mining region of West Virginia. She later worked with Portuguese immigrants from the Cape Verde Islands in Cape Cod before distinguishing herself in New York for her work with Puerto Rican gangs on Long Island. She was awarded the key to the city of New York by Mayor John Lindsay and the John D. Rockefeller Award for Public Service and Community Revitalization. Her efforts to rebuild badly fractured urban communities soon brought her national and international attention. She was selected a United States delegate to the World Conference of the Mid-Decade for Women held in Copenhagen, Denmark, in 1980 and was declared Woman of the Year at the National Conference of Puerto Rican Women in 1983.

Sister Isolina's approach to community revitalization begins and ends with community. Most of her life she has targeted the young. "I also realized from the beginning," she says, "that you have to work with families and communities. They are the people surrounding the young." In New York, she chose the most difficult of the young, hardened, often violent, street gangs. The young people with whom she worked joined gangs because they were seeking community, a social bonding that was missing in their lives. As she put it,

> I used to ask the Puerto Rican gang member, "Why are you in a gang?" And he would answer, "Well, it gives you a kind of power, Sister. It gives you a sense of belonging to something . . . and we don't belong to anything." And so I said, "But it doesn't help, hurting each other, to give you power." And he said, "No, but it gives you a kick."

With a trace of sadness in her voice, Sister Isolina added that violence for them was just a question of getting people to notice them. It wasn't violence for the sake of violence. They did not really want to hurt people; they just wanted to be noticed. Sister Isolina noticed. While at the Doctor White Community Center in Brooklyn, she began working as an intercessor, mediating between African-American and Puerto Rican gangs and the juvenile justice system, fighting to keep the young people out of trouble and helping them to build a future.

It was hard enough to see these young people destroying their own lives and destroying each other at the same time, but when the juvenile justice system intervened, it simply finished the process. What alarmed Sister Isolina was that the authorities "picked them up and took them to jail with no conviction and they were forgotten in there for months and months. These were fifteen-year-olds with no schooling, not older young people like the gangs are today." She walked the streets getting to know the young people, their families, their community. At first she was looked on as a sort of curiosity, but then she became a trusted friend, attracting large numbers to the Doctor White Community Center in the middle of Brooklyn, at the entrance to the Brooklyn Bridge. With obvious pride, she said,

> I had 150 black kids, young men and women, in a Drum and Bugle band; they were great. When they walked all over and marched everywhere I was with them. Then, we had another group, the Puerto Ricans playing in the Steel Band. We took them to all sorts of places. Soon they began to work together. I learned a lot about them, about groups and about families and communities.

Sister Isolina became known for helping people to help themselves, organizing the poor to find their own solutions. She intervenes in their lives where she finds them, but what she seeks ultimately is social justice rather than simply an improved quality of life. "What's the use of just fixing them up at that moment if they go back to the old life once that moment is over?" she asks rhetorically. "It seems to me," she adds, "you cannot just work with an individual and train and help them without being concerned about what happens next. So you have to work with the whole community to improve the quality of life as well as to have the community concerned with its own."

Sister Isolina defines her strategy as (1) awakening a sense of personal worth, (2) creating a vision expressed in community, and (3) participating in a revitalization process. "We believe in God," she says, "and we believe every person has a wonderful thing which is his own personal worth. Before you work with anybody, you have to show the respect and dignity due that person." You cannot maltreat or show disrespect for a person or his community and expect to establish the relationship needed to change him or transform his community. Sister Isolina's approach is to say to a person, "Your father and my father is God. That makes you and me brothers and sisters, and I respect you because you are a child of God and you

have to respect me in turn. . . . And I say to them, you are a marvelous person, a marvelous people, you are a wonder, a wonderful
person." She meets many who feel they are worth nothing. "You
should see some of them when they come," she exclaims. "They
even cringe when they come to talk to you. They are afraid."

But believing in oneself requires more than a changed way of
thinking; it often requires a changed way of being. Sister Isolina
likes to tell the story about a boy she met who was visibly depressed,
despondent, and angry. She asked him, "Do you ever smile?" He
responded, "Why should I smile, I am no good, I have nothing to
do—I am hungry—I have no work." Startled, she replied, "Let's get
you some work." And she did, at a coffee plantation. When she saw
him next, he had changed. He saw the world in a different way, but
she insists that it was not just the work. "It was also the way we
treated him that made him say later, 'I am somebody. They are pay-
ing attention to me. I belong.'" And for Sister Isolina, that's the
secret. "Self-worth is a part of everybody, but many people have not
been given hope." She finds the abandoned person and tells him,
"You are worth it. You are a wonder. You can be more and we can
work together."

Restoring a sense of self-worth, building dignity, and developing self-respect are not easy. Sister Isolina tells another story about
the early days of the center in Ponce.

The treatment of the handicapped was awful. They were thrown
aside, nobody cared for them. We met a little girl when we went out
to visit a family. Actually, we asked her parents how many children
were in the family, but when they answered it was obvious that one
had not been counted. There was this little girl sitting in the corner,
and I asked, "What about her?" and they said "Oh, she doesn't
count, she's deaf, dumb and blind, she doesn't count." And I said,
"That's a little child of God too." So we began to work with her, to
get her out. She wasn't dumb, she had no eyes. But once we began
to work with her, not only did we find that she was intelligent, but

she had a great love for music. We used music to bring her out and she even graduated from the ninth grade.

This breakthrough made believers and supporters of not only that family but also much of the community. As Sister Isolina was to observe later, "We taught them about possibility. We gave them a vision that these children were not just anything, that they were worth something. And we began to work within the whole community to tell them how much they could do about this problem." Once their consciousness was raised, parents began to look at the whole picture. Sister Isolina urged them to go to a hearing about the handicapped. "And they responded by helping to change a law," she beamed. The community came alive through its advocacy for those who were once neglected.

It began with a vision, giving them hope, but it ended with a political strategy as people all over came to realize what could be done. "We don't give people welfare. We are not a welfare agency," Sister Isolina cautions. Referring to her center in Ponce, she says with pride:

We are an institution that develops people's sense of self-worth and prepares them to do something. Not only did many of the children with whom we work not know how to read and write, but they did not want to go to school. So we prepared our teachers to teach children with little or no hope. We are preparing them [the children] for jobs and teaching them how to get them. So now they trust in us. They share the vision.

There has been quite a change in the attitude of the people on the waterfront. "They had no idea they could be what they are today," says Sister Isolina. "When you see them walking around, you say, Oh, my gosh, are these the same kids that we had before? Some are teachers; one is a doctor, another is a lawyer, and there are social workers.'" It is obvious that the woman some call the

Mother Teresa of Puerto Rico has done more than transform under-prepared young people into competitive and independent adults. She has cultivated a spirit of caring and compassion as well. She says with obvious pride, "They don't forget. They come back. We get them involved in the community."

One of the important aspects of developing and maintaining the social bond of community is celebration. "We believe in celebration, we are continually celebrating," Sister Isolina says. "We celebrate all sorts of things with the people doing the organizing and the planning." Why this emphasis on celebrating? "Because it brings people together. We are trying to bring back the idea of community. Celebrations get you together and you talk to this person, you talk to that person. You cannot hate each other when you are singing together." Sister Isolina cites an example:

In May, we have what we call the "Fiesta de Cruz" which are parties in which we sing to the Cross. It's a two hundred-year-old tradition that we observe in the open air. And the people come. The whole family comes, father, mother, children, grandparents, everybody. And they are there singing to the Cross; no fear. Nobody hurts anybody.

She modestly proclaims that there is power in celebrating. "In La Playa, we don't have violence and vandalism." People around the world who are trying to combat violence, build community, and promote civil society are taking notice, wondering what Sister Isolina's secret is, how she is able to change people in such a way that they take the responsibility for changing their communities.

The project that Sister Isolina founded at La Playa de Ponce community has extended to the communities of El Tuque in Ponce, Caimito in San Juan, and Puerto de Jobos in Guayama. Despite the growth in scope and services, the centers remain true to the vision of their founder and driving force. They help people to find their own solutions and encourage them to become masters of their own lives. The centers foster change, not from the outside but from within. Believing that without self-commitment, men and women cannot fulfill themselves, they rely on the inner resources of the people they serve, each of whom must make a personal commitment to become a complete, well-rounded individual. The philosophy of the centers is summarized in the message to each person, "You shall become what you choose to become."

For Sister Isolina, the urge, the need for social bonding cannot be avoided. "A child is born into a community of parents, siblings, relatives, and friends. We become the heirs of the social network into which we are born and in which we are socialized." A community, however, can suffer circumstances in which it loses its vision, becomes inert, and slips into a feeling of helplessness, hopelessness, and loss of esteem. That was the situation to which Sister Isolina returned in 1968 after a sojourn on the turbulent streets of Brooklyn. Twenty-five years later, helplessness has been replaced by hope. Violence is controlled by a sense of community solidarity, a sense of belonging, a feeling of obligation to, and respect for, each other. Moreover, there is the omnipresent vision of a community fully alive. Each individual is seen as a child of God—a person whose dignity must be affirmed, retained, and/or rescued, without distinction of race or creed. What matters is cooperation and mutual help among neighbors, and attention to the needs of children, young people, and adults. The entire community is an advocate for all its members.

Chapter Sixteen

Cesar Chavez: Apostle of Nonviolence

The ferment of the 1960s that led to the rise of the civil rights, anti-war, and black power movements also fueled a new social activism in Latino communities. Inspired partly by the events of the time but also drawing from earlier struggles, a new group of social reformers burst onto the national scene. The group included Reies Lopez Tijerina in New Mexico, Corky Gonzalez in Colorado, Jose Angel Gutierrez in Texas, and Dolores Huerta and Cesar Chavez in California. Along with others who were not as well-known, they energized a mobilization, primarily of Chicanos, seeking new political power, economic advancement, cultural self-expression, and services and programs for their communities.

At the forefront of the group, and often compared to Martin Luther King, Jr., was Cesar Chavez, the Latino apostle of nonviolence. Praised by Senator Robert Kennedy in 1968 as one of the heroic figures of our time, Chavez drew national attention to the working conditions of migrant farm workers. Others had created interest and developed sympathy for the plight of migrants before Chavez, but neither John Steinbeck's writings nor Edward R. Murrow's television documentary had succeeded in actually empowering farm workers. Chavez emerged as a national spokesman when his fledgling union launched a consumer boycott of grapes, winning him a reputation as a defender of the downtrodden. He was a very modest man, small in stature and quiet in manner, but at a time when growers were reacting violently to organizing attempts, he demonstrated an iron-willed commitment to strikes, boycotts, and other strategies used by union organizers.[1]

Chavez came by his compassion and concern for farm workers naturally. He delivered a eulogy for his mother, Juana Chavez, in December 1991, recalling his early life as a very young child when he watched her challenge the oppressive conditions of farm workers in California's Imperial Valley. "We were the strikingest family in all of farm labor," he said. "Whenever we were working where there was a strike or when the workers got fed up and walked off the job, she'd be the first one to back up our dad's decision to join the strike." Juana Chavez also insisted that her children learn to share and to avoid an obsession with money. Chavez had no trouble identifying the source of his strength, courage, and staying power. "We were," he insisted, "constantly fighting against things that most people would probably accept because they didn't have the kind of life we had in the beginning, that strong family life and family ties which we would not let anyone break." When confronted by an injustice, "there was no question. Our dignity meant more than money."[2]

Cesar Chavez was an unlikely leader. He attended thirty to forty different schools, following his family from farm to farm, and dropping out of school in the eighth grade. Yet when he spoke to workers, his words were not of his failed past but of the possibility of a very different future. His listeners were mesmerized by his sincerity and magnetism. They wanted to share his strength and emulate his courage.

Writing about Latino values, leadership, and diversity, Margarita Melville identified three types of leaders: "brokers, advocates and token leaders."[3] Broker-leaders are individuals whose main goal is to prepare and promote the acceptance of minority group members in the larger society. They often serve as unofficial representatives of the community and form organizations to further the community's goals.[4] Advocate-leaders are individuals who recognize the unequal distribution of service, wealth, or power and create movements designed to seek redress. They attempt to secure for their community those things that mainstream society has put beyond their reach, without sacrificing emphasis on ethnic identity.[5] Token-leaders are individuals selected as minority leaders, not by their peers but by others from the larger society. They can, given their visibility and influence in the majority community, divert resources toward their minority communities and enhance the understanding and acceptance of their group by the majority society, thereby becoming broker-leaders. But according to Melville, broker-leaders often struggles with the tension of two loyalties. "One loyalty," she argues, "is toward those who selected them to serve as token leaders to assuage the demands of Latinos for representation or to serve as translators of the behavior, desires, and needs of the Latino communities. The other loyalty is to their communities of origin which did not actually select them to be its representatives."[6]

Like other minority groups before them, Latino communities have had their share of all three types of leaders. But in the life and legacy of Cesar Chavez, only the first two of the three foregoing attributes, the broker-leader and the advocate-leader, are manifested. He was a man of the people, one who understood that farm workers would cease to be victims only when they discovered the means to take control of their own lives. He had experienced the virulent racial attitudes that tended to define not just Chicanos but all persons of color as unequal. But he also understood that while considerations of race and ethnicity compounded the plight of farm workers, their mistreatment was also rooted in the economics of industrialized agriculture.

In 1965, waving the red flag of his union with a black eagle in the center, he called for a national boycott of grapes to reinforce La Huelga—the strike—and organized a three-hundred-mile march from Delano, California, to the state capitol building in Sacramento. In 1973, he called a strike, organizing mass protests that resulted in three thousand five hundred arrests for violating court-ordered limits on picketing at ranches. A member of his union was shot to death on the picket line, but farm workers continued to follow his leadership.

Born March 31, 1927, near Yuma, Arizona, the second child of Librado and Juana Chavez, Cesar Chavez grew up fully aware of the plight of migrant workers. He spent the first ten years of his life on a farm that belonged to his grandparents. But the Depression smashed his family's dreams as the family farm was taken for non-payment of taxes. Penniless, the family moved to California where they initially found work in the Imperial Valley tying carrots for a dollar a day. They went from there to the vegetable fields of Oxnard, and then to the grape vineyards near Fresno, where they worked for weeks on the promise of pay—only to have the contractor disappear one day, leaving the family destitute.[7] Chavez said later that the worst work in those days was thinning crops in the field with short-handled hoes—bent over all day—for eight to twelve cents an hour. Winters were especially difficult for the family. "The winter of 1938," he reported, "I had to walk to school barefoot through the mud, we were so poor." After school, Chavez would fish in the canals and cut wild mustard greens to help his family survive.[8]

The migrant lifestyle brought with it the experience of prejudice and rejection. Discrimination against migrant farm workers also carried over into the schools. Describing the poor treatment of migrant children, Chavez recalled: "The schools treated you like you didn't exist. Their indifference was incredible." The attitudes he encountered on the farms and in the schools were present in every other aspect of his life as well. In 1943, at the age of sixteen, he went to a segregated movie theater in Delano and sat in the "whites only" section. When the police came, they had to pry his hands off the seat and drag him to the police station.[9] The humiliation and powerlessness of the experience left an indelible imprint.

It was not until he returned from service in the U.S. Navy in World War II that Chavez began to channel his frustration into active rebellion against the conditions facing migrant farm workers. He met Fred Ross, who had been sent to California by Saul Alinsky, the director of the Industrial Areas Foundation in Chicago, to organize the poor into grassroots, self-help groups. Ross had set in motion the Community Service Organization (CSO) when he heard about Cesar Chavez who was working in the apricot orchards around San Jose. At nineteen, Chavez had joined an abortive attempt to organize farm workers through a union that soon failed. Chavez's father had also joined one of these short-lived groups, and although he had been unable to make a direct impact on the conditions of farm workers, his son was now determined to succeed.

Chavez became an organizer as a CSO volunteer, working first to register Chicano voters. In two months he registered over four thousand in the first voter registration drive ever conducted among Mexican Americans. He worked next to help Mexican immigrants to secure their citizenship papers. When he was laid off from his regular job, Ross placed him on the CSO staff. He traveled across the San Joaquin Valley organizing new CSO chapters.

During this period Chavez, the eighth-grade dropout, began a rigidly disciplined program of self-education. He borrowed whatever books he could from the public library and developed a special interest in biographies and books on Mexican-American history, the theology of St. Thomas Aquinas and the Apostle Paul, and the teachings of Gandhi. Chavez's biographer, Winthrop Yinger, described him as "a combination of the thinking of Ghandi, Alinsky and his rich Mexican culture—plus, of course, his own unique personhood."

A major influence on Chavez was his religious faith and theology. He seemed to live in the shadow of the Virgin of Guadalupe whose symbol was present at nearly every farm-worker meeting and carried in every procession or march. Chavez often slipped into churches to pray or to receive communion, and he punctuated the farm-worker movement with such traditional religious practices as pilgrimages, fasting, retreats, public prayers, worship services, and special observances. He was particularly close to Father McDonnell, the pastor of the mission church in Sal Si Puedes. He once said, "My education started when I met Father Donald McDonnell. We had long talks about farm workers. I knew a lot about the work, but I didn't know anything about economics, and I learned quite a bit from him."[10] The social gospel espoused by Father McDonnell not only caught Chavez's attention but opened up a new world of ideas on which he began to build his own personal philosophy.

The religious support Chavez attracted was ecumenical. In addition to the priests assigned to the Delano farm workers from the Franciscan religious order, the Reverend Chris Hartmire, director of the California Migrant Ministry, and the Reverend James Drake of the California Council of Churches were close allies. In the concluding paragraph of an essay on the role of the church, Chavez wrote:

> What do we want the church to do? We don't ask for more cathedrals. We don't ask for bigger churches or fine gifts. We ask for its presence with us, beside us, as Christ among us. We ask the church to sacrifice with the people for social change, for justice, and for love of brother. We don't ask for words. We ask for deeds. We don't ask for paternalism. We ask for servanthood.

Chavez often used religious language to explain the meaning of a march, a strike, or a fast. This was most evident in a letter dated March 1966 describing the meaning of the historic three-hundred-mile, four-week pilgrimage to Sacramento. Of it he wrote:

> Throughout the Spanish-speaking world there is another tradition that touches the present march, that of the Lenten penitential processions, where the penitents would march through the streets, often in sack cloth and ashes, some even carrying crosses, as a sign of penance for their sins, and as a plea for the mercy of God. The penitential procession is also in the blood of the Mexican American, and the Delano march will therefore be one of penance—public penance for the sins of the strikers, their own personal sins as well as their yielding perhaps to feelings of hatred and revenge in the strike itself. They hope by the march to set themselves at peace with the Lord, so that the justice of their cause will be purified of all lesser motivation.

Yinger points to Chavez's practice of fasting as the most vivid demonstration of his religious fervor. His longest fast, and the most costly physically, was during the summer of 1988. Fasting to protest the use of pesticides, which he argued were dangerous to consumers, farm workers, and the environment, he did not eat for thirty-six days. When he finally broke the fast, he was so weak that many feared for his life, but those who came to his support included Jesse Jackson and actors Edward James Olmos, Robert Blake, and Martin Sheen. Like her husband twenty years earlier, Ethel Kennedy, the widow of Senator Robert Kennedy, was there to hand him a small piece of bread.

Suffering personally for the benefit of others was one of Chavez's key strategies. But personal sacrifice went far beyond the dramatic threats to his health. The *New York Times* wrote in 1969 that Chavez "still lives on the $5.00 a week all union workers receive and he invariably dresses in the same gray work pants and plaid wool shirt."

Chavez's simplicity of manner, his slight build, his soft voice, and his unassuming appearance belied the inner toughness that led one aide to say of him, "His hero is Ghandi, but he's capable of being quite Machiavellian." Another observer wrote:

Chavez has an Indian bow nose and dark black hair, with sad eyes and an open smile that is both shy and friendly. He is five feet seven inches tall, and since his 25-day fast in the winter of 1968 has weighed no more than a hundred and fifty pounds. Yet, the word "slight" does not properly describe him. There is an effect of being centered on himself so that no energy is wasted, and at the same time he walks lightly.

Sometimes observers overlooked the universality of Chavez's embrace of the poor, his concern about not only Latino immigrants and farm workers but for the neglected and marginalized every-where. The incident that launched him as the leader of migrant farm workers involved not Latino but Filipino grape pickers. In the spring of 1965, south of Delano, California, Filipino workers who were members of the Agricultural Workers Organizing Committee went out on strike for higher pay. When the workers and the strike came north to Delano, Cesar Chavez and his United Farm Workers of America (UFWA) voted to join the strike. The two groups later merged under Chavez's leadership into the United Farm Workers (UFW).

Chavez enjoyed his greatest success through his work as a labor leader. One of the most memorable moments in his long struggle to empower farm workers occurred on May 5, 1975, in a telephone call from Jerry Brown, the new governor of California. Brown called to ask Chavez to repeat by telephone, for the benefit of farm employers present in Brown's Sacramento office, his acceptance of a labor bill to which the farm workers had already assented. Crowded into Brown's office and anxiously awaiting the words of this former migrant worker were representatives of the most powerful agricultural interest group in California history. The strange element of that meeting, according to a report by Cletus E. Daniel, was that the state's leading farm employers should have derived such apparent relief and satisfaction from hearing the president of the UFW agree to a legislative proposal designed to afford farm workers an opportunity to escape their historic powerlessness through unionism and collective bargaining.[11]

For the state's agribusiness, which had once ruled the fields and orchards of California with uncontested authority, acceptance of this bill was a remarkable concession. For the farm workers, it represented a long journey from the fields in 1965 where Chavez had led his small following into a bitter struggle against grape growers in Delano. But even at the height of his success, Chavez still had an aura of ambivalence. He had built a union that was not only flexing its economic muscle but also stood as an extension of his own values, experience, and personality. Yet, there was an enduring tension: was he building a trade union or a social movement?

There were elements of both in the UFW. Chavez himself reflected this ambiguity in saying of the human journey, "God writes in exceedingly crooked lines."

From the beginning, Chavez was the subject of scathing public attacks. His early association with the lieutenants of Saul Alinsky and the timing of his efforts to organize the poor in the heyday of McCarthyism led naturally to the charge that he was a communist. His critics targeted the more cautious members of the Chicano community first. Some, Chavez said, "wouldn't talk to me. They were afraid. The newspaper had lots of influence during those McCarthy days. Any one who organized or worked for civil rights was called a communist."[12] The farm workers' adulation of Chavez and the public support he received from so many who made his cause their own led to another kind of criticism, the charge that he had a messianic complex. In later years, some critics described him as autocratic, saying that he was unwilling to acknowledge other leadership in the farm workers' movement.[13]

The accuracy of these criticisms is a matter of continuing debate. Undeniable, however, is that this man, whose lifestyle was created out of the difficult years of migrant wandering, self-education, fierce determination, and a strong religious faith, taught many that justice is won, and continually won again, by men and women who are free to win it for themselves. Dolores Huerta, vice president of the United Farm Workers of California, spoke to this point in an address on the capitol steps following the Sacramento march:

> Cesar Chavez began . . . as a pilgrim inspiring the workers to organize; giving the confidence they needed through inspiration and hard work and educating them through the months to realize that no one was going to win their battle for them, that their condition could only be changed by one group—themselves.[14]

Conclusion:
A New American Paradigm

While formidable, the task of remaking America can still be a uni-fying national experience. The blueprint for national community was described eloquently and forcefully by John Winthrop when he spoke of a city on a hill in which we delight in each other, seek to make others' condition our own, rejoice together, and labor and suf-fer together, viewing all in our community as members of the same body. But as we have seen in the preceding chapters, there is also much to be learned from Native Americans about living in har-mony with nature; from the neo-Confucians in the Chinese com-munity who argue that a humanity without benevolence invites its own destruction; from those in the Vietnamese community who follow the Buddhist vision and seek reconciliation rather than har-boring hatred or hostility; from African Americans in the central cities who are once again forming institutions of self-help and infus-ing our civic culture with a new vitality; from Latino priests who, in embracing liberation theology, remind us of the early Christian emphasis on the poor and the needy; and from the many other cul-tural heroes and forces that constitute our national identity.

If we are to respect our various component communities and at the same time avoid balkanization, we will need to formulate the intellectual and moral grounds of community in ways that draw on the cultural traditions and noble ideals of all our citizens. And when we do, we are likely to find that the key principles from the tradi-tions of racial minorities are most often in agreement with the ideals affirmed, but not always practiced, by the majority.

The time has come for a new paradigm of community. Neither

the hierarchical pluralism of the assimilationist vision nor the egalitarian pluralism that gives equal validity to myriad traditions will do. While the latter vision has much to recommend it, Orlando Patterson, a professor of sociology at Harvard and author of *Freedom in the Making of Western Culture*, has identified the key problem. He notes that some cultures hold deep convictions about women, about races, about children, about authority, about lawlessness, about the sick, the weak, the poor, and the rich that we must absolutely reject.[1] He argues that where a plurality of cultures exists, we need an overarching set of values cherished by all. The idea of a salad bowl of cultures equally precious, equally valid in their moral claims, is potentially as dangerous as the melting pot vision it seeks to supplant. The new paradigm must focus on both the contribution of each group to the national culture and the uniqueness and vitality of each culture in its own way. It must identify, affirm, and define the shared values that are essential to a national culture and an American identity without suggesting that every belief and every practice has equal moral claim or civic legitimacy. Each cultural tradition has ways of thinking about the common community, and the shared civic culture has to be built out of these traditions, but it cannot give legitimacy or allegiance to any belief or practice that might do harm to a fellow human being or deny access to "life, liberty and the pursuit of happiness."

Shared Values

While some Americans feel threatened by the notion of a new paradigm of national community, even the most conservative among us can take heart in knowing that this paradigm is based on shared values. When we look beyond the neat little boxes that divide us into "we" and "they" groups, we find that most Americans tend to share a common vision. This is the idea, the widely accepted notion, that all men and women are created equal, with the inalienable right to life, liberty, and the pursuit of happiness.

Of course, these rights have not always applied to everyone. And even today, there are men and women who would still restrict the privileges of America to their own kind. Others who have been wronged want retribution or reparation. They remind us that the West was won over the dead bodies of the Native Americans whose aboriginal rights were violated, that the rapid development of the nation came with the labor of slaves. These are only a few of the different stories told and different paths taken to the American dream. We still find common cause and purpose in the noble ideals and bold ideas that endeared the practices of democracy by the Iroquois to Benjamin Franklin, William Penn, and Thomas Jefferson. It is still true, as Ralph Bunche, the noted African American who worked with Gunnar Myrdal on *American Dilemma,* reported some years ago, that among people of all colors there is a strong commitment to the idea of America as the "land of the free" and the "cradle of liberty." Ideals such as these led African Americans to demand their rights and Martin Luther King, Jr., to protest the deferral of the dream.

Why, then, do these shared ideals no longer seem to provide the common ground needed for coherence and community? One answer may be that we have treated them as if they belonged exclusively to the descendants of Europe, showing very little appreciation or respect for the myriad traditions that honor liberty and freedom. People around the world, not just racial minorities in the United States, want acknowledgment and appreciation of their contribution to the common culture as well as respect for their unique traditions.

Instead of viewing itself as a nation composed of ideas and ideals both developed indigenously and commandeered from a wide variety of people and cultures, America continues to see itself as Greco-Roman in its polity and Judeo-Christian in its theology. The point of this work is that we find common ground in recognizing and emphasizing the shared values of the civic traditions brought by those of European heritage as well as by those who are Asian,

Hispanic, African, and Native American in origin. Each of these traditions contains something of universal value; to confine ourselves to affirming and acknowledging the importance of only one is to deny access to the fullness of a changing but very rich national culture.

Both a national identity and a national culture still appear possible if we are willing to move away from our obsession with the notion of a received tradition and see our national identity as never fixed nor final but always in the making. Amitai Etzioni is one of many new American voices who argue that there is no reason to pressure people to give up their heritage, their hyphen, as long as pluralism operates within the strong framework of shared values. Etzioni describes our common values in *The Spirit of Community*, but we need to go one step further and acknowledge that these shared values can be found in the benevolent traditions of America's racial minorities as well.[2]

Some Americans look at the present emphasis on history and heritage and think they see a cult of ethnicity. With Crevecoeur, they want to know "what is the American," this new person.[3] What makes one an American is not genetics, ideology, or theology. It is the shared values of an emerging civic culture that emphasizes the multiple roots of the principles affirmed. Whether one relies on the teachings of Cicero, Confucius, Locke, or de Tocqueville, the communal ideals of the African village or the Native American tribe, what Americans share in common is a set of values grounded in at least four principles: (1) that citizens have rights and responsibilities that precede the state and the notion that the true patriot is one who is willing to protect his country from even his own government; (2) that society is distinct from government and that government is but one of several sectors that can, and should, promote the common good; (3) that a healthy society is one that protects the freedoms of speech, of the press, of assembly, and of worship; (4) that the rights of the minority are to be protected by the majority.

Even a casual review of Western political thought and the civic traditions of America's racial minorities reveal that the notion of civil society is still evolving. John Locke, for example, emphasized the rights and duties of citizens, but his notion of civil society was restrictive and exclusionary. John Stuart Mill, on the other hand, was interested in a more inclusive society. He extended the idea of rights to include women and working people who did not own property. Thomas Jefferson and other early Americans borrowed from Locke the idea that individual rights included life, liberty, and the pursuit of happiness. But it was many years before the notion of rights was applied to all Americans.

We are still left to untangle the various ways in which we understand ourselves and relate to each other. But as we come to know each other better, to understand and appreciate the many values we share in common, we have an opportunity to fuse elements of both our ideals and our traditions into a common effort to form the "more perfect union" our founders sought.

We need to depoliticize the public discussion of values, to make the emphasis on private virtue less partisan. William Bennett, former secretary of the U.S. Department of Education, is known for provoking controversy, but even he agrees that "we must not permit our disputes about thorny political questions to obscure the obligation we have to offer instructions to all our young people in the area in which we, as a society, have reached consensus: namely, on the importance of good character, and some of its particulars."[4] He offers ten virtues on which he believes there is general agreement: self-discipline, compassion, responsibility, friendship, work, courage, perseverance, honesty, loyalty, and faith.

This is a good list, but we cannot permit the discussion of values to focus only on the micro-ethics of private individual behavior. We need to be equally concerned with the macro-ethics of social institutions, including government, business, and voluntary organizations. Martin Luther King, Jr., reminded us often of the need to link the individual's duty to embrace the responsibilities of citizenship with the obligation to act in concert with others to ensure citizenship rights. He sought to transform both individuals and society.[5]

Those who talk most about promoting "good values" are often those who want simply to argue that someone else—poor people, Democrats, Republicans—have "bad values." If we can accept the existence of shared values across the wide spectrum of our diversity, we can move to the next step of practicing them in a complex, multicultural society.

A Universal Compassion

Of the many values needed in the social glue of community, compassion may have primacy. And here it is pleasing to see Bennett praising compassion, which he argues "takes its stand with others in distress" and "takes seriously the reality of other persons, their inner lives, their emotions as well as their external circumstance."[6] One can only conclude that our ability to develop and sustain community may depend to a large degree on our ability to develop and practice the associated virtues of compassion: empathy, altruism, and respect. The focus of this study has been on the benevolent traditions of America's racial minorities because it is often through involvement with the needs of others that we find the social cement that binds people together in community. When "their" problem becomes "our" problem, the involvement transforms a mere association into a new community of meaning and belonging. Thus, to be true to the benevolent traditions we have examined, a new paradigm of community must begin with empathy.

The capacity for empathy is universal. It needs to be nurtured. This ability to feel what another is feeling can be thought of as a fundamental plank in the blueprint for building community. When Adam Smith set out to develop a basic theory about how human beings could transact business with each other in an orderly and predictable fashion, he set forth the principle of empathy. Knowing what gives others joy and pain because we know what gives ourselves joy and pain became the unstated basis for his economic theory in *The Wealth of Nations*.[7] This is not surprising. Adam Smith is remembered most for what he had to say about economics, but he was a moral philosopher, not an economist. He wrote *A Theory of Moral Sentiments* before he wrote *The Wealth of Nations*. His economic theories were based on his idea about moral community, especially the notion that the individual has a moral duty to have regard for fellow human beings.[8]

Although developing empathy within the primary community is easier than extending it across secondary communities, all human beings operate with certain predispositions for social bonding. This predisposition toward community provides the capacity for transforming the passive virtue of empathy into the more active virtue of altruism. The altruistic impulse is also universal. But it too may remain passive until activated. The cultivation of an environment where members of one community can see others as human beings like themselves and can care about those of another group and want good things for them is a necessary prerequisite for both empathy and altruism. But altruism is not simply a matter of developing other-serving values. It has an element of enlightened self-interest as well. We promote the general welfare in order to be able to compete in an interdependent world economy, in order to provide for our progeny the quality of life we now enjoy.

Empathy and altruism must be accompanied by respect. The most important challenge in the present remaking of America may lie in finding the balance between respect for differences and respect for contributions to the common culture. It is right and good that we celebrate multiculturalism, but social inclusion requires that we do so in a way that does not diminish the role of racial minorities in fashioning the American culture. Nowhere is this need for inclusion more important, more challenging, and more provocative than in the canons that shape our intellectual ideas and moral ideals.

We must acknowledge that while the great books, ideas, and

personalities that have been the makers and interpreters of much of our history and culture—from Plato and Ptolemy to Faulkner and Hemingway—are irreplaceable, we must now make room for others. Michael Dirda, editor of the *Washington Post Book World*, reminds us that "Ours is no longer a civilization devoted exclusively to the high culture of the European past. The thinking of the East shapes our poets and physicists. We read avidly books by people named Mahfouz, Achebe, Abe, Allende, Oz."[9] The real issue is not whether these newly discovered writers are equal to Aquinas, Goethe, or Dante. The point is that they too help us understand the human condition, the struggle between good and evil, and speak to us forcefully of matters much on our mind. Sophocles, Kafka, and Kirkegaard will not disappear simply because others join them in the canon of Great Books.

Our notion of respect, interdependence, and civic consciousness cannot stop with the human community. The new paradigm must embrace the Native American vision of every part of the earth as sacred. What a difference it might have made to our natural environment if we had heeded Chief Seattle and adopted the Native American view of proportion and balance in our relationship to all other living things. For him, the survival of the human race depended on how we conduct ourselves in the biosphere. His notion of community was an interlocking system of mutually dependent parts, all of which play a unique role in the functioning of the system, and all of which are essential to the system's survival.

Native Americans who make this argument do not necessarily elevate nature or the rights of nature to a position equal to that of human beings, but they affirm a mutuality of interest and claims. They argue that there needs to be a sense of proportion and accommodation in the way human beings relate to the biotic community. We endanger our chances of survival as a human race, or at a minimum diminish the quality of life we enjoy, when we lose our sense of connection with the rest of creation and refuse to accommodate the needs that grow out of our interdependence.

Implicit in this view is both a reverence for all of life and a concept of human primacy. Especially important is for those who destroy other forms of life so that human life may continue to know fully that the destruction of nonhuman life is morally serious. The Native Americans had a theory of justice, a notion of morality, that embraced both human society and the natural order. The early European settlers, on the other hand, had a more limited concept regarding both the human community and the biosphere. The community which they embraced in their concern for justice excluded at varying times women, nonwhites, and those without property. Obviously, as they did not include the whole of the human community in their embrace, they certainly did not extend the concept of community to include nonhuman living things.

We argue, therefore, that a primary element in the articulation of a new paradigm of community must be the universal compassion of the Native American, the idea that reverence for life should apply to all life—animal, plant, and human. To destroy needlessly or exploit any part of nature is to defile the harmony and unity of the created order.

A Spiritual Vitality

Religious faith has the power to break down barriers between strangers and cultures, to provide meaning and grounding during times of rapid transformations, and to provide the spiritual glue that creates and nurtures social bonding. But it can also be a cause of hatred and polarization. Instead of providing bonding and communal vision, religion in America has become a battlefield where opposing absolutes are proclaimed and ambiguity disallowed. It is not the old struggle between such historically related forms of monotheism as Christianity, Judaism, and Islam, but a new holy war waged by groups trying to redefine the public culture. These groups are in many ways just as polarizing and pulverizing as the early Crusaders. The target of their enmity, however, is not other religions, but those within their own groups who do not fit their image of true believers. James Hunter, author of *Culture Wars*, argues that a cultural realignment is taking place that has tremendous historical significance and political consequences for the nation. On one side, according to Hunter, one finds the orthodox—people who believe in absolute, universal, eternal truths derived from divine revelation. Those on the other side Hunter calls "progressives"—people who believe that truth is relative, pragmatic, and evolving.[10] These new alliances cross the lines of the three faith systems of the Protestant, Catholic, and Jew that have so long shaped public culture; the tensions between them are now replaced by internal tensions within each. While it is disconcerting to find Hunter quoting Jerry Falwell, Pat Robertson, and Jimmy Swaggart as spokespersons for the orthodox, one cannot quarrel with his basic argument that these conflicts arise over fundamentally different conceptions of moral authority and different ideas about our obligations to each other and the nature of community.

Meanwhile, there is in all of our communities a yearning for something deeper than the fight over theological orthodoxy and the fear of a collapse of the Judeo-Christian consensus. There is a spiritual hunger that none of the orthodoxies seems to satisfy. It is not yet clear what role religion will or should play in the search for common ground, but there are many reasons to believe that the search for a higher level of being is a reflection of the human condition. And perhaps it is the search, rather than the answers, that provides the basis of our unity. Reuben Snake, the Native American religious leader, may have spoken with great wisdom when he contended that we began to lose our way when we allowed the Greek devotion to rationality to obscure our spiritual affinity with all of the created order.

Snake would be pleased with the observation of James Redfield, author of *The Celestine Prophecy*, that for half a century, a new consciousness has been entering the world, a new awareness that can only be called transcendent, spiritual.[11] If the popular reaction to Redfield's fictionalized account of the search for a manuscript with key insights into life is any guide, what one generation repressed, another generation may be seeking to recover. The previous generation lost itself in creating economic security. The present generation wants to recover the spiritual security sacrificed in the money chase.

If the emerging civic culture is also a spiritual culture, as now seems likely, it could thus become the dominant paradigm of the next century. For those of us who share the old values of caring and sharing, the task is to help introduce a new perspective, a new way of seeing ourselves, a new way of structuring our relationships. We may need to redefine the enduring purpose of the human journey. Everywhere we look in the world, we find institutions in trouble, people frustrated by their inability to find meaning. But at a time when people everywhere are alienated from the deepest roots of their being, even organized religion seems to be in crisis.

We can no longer proclaim one tradition or one theology as the national reality. Some of our citizens believe that every human being possesses the Buddhist nature that leads from narrow particularism to universal compassion and community. Others find the Confucian emphasis on good conduct and wisdom providing the opportunity for new social relationships and the ethic of social responsibility that genuine community requires. Christianity and Judaism have much to teach about respecting differences while seeking wholeness, but these two great traditions lose nothing when they acknowledge or accept the validity of a Buddhist or Confucian perspective as well. Islam, with its emphasis on charity as one of the pillars of the faith, will also be important to the emerging civic culture. The emphasis on civil society rather than the state, and the feeling of responsibility for the total community, provide a strong basis for the development of a paradigm of community based on shared values. It is no accident that tithing is more widespread among Muslims than among members of any other faith. The faithful are taught that giving and sharing are fundamental moral imperatives.

The search for meaning, the yearning for community based on

spirituality rather than old or new orthodoxies, is a phenomenon still evolving in contemporary America. The communal groups that grew out of the ferment of the sixties were a partial realization of this longing, but they do not fully encompass the paradigms needed to live together across deep and often bitter differences. The old communities brought together people who shared a worldview, a political philosophy, and a lifestyle. The new spirituality acknowledges differences and welcomes the heterodox while affirming and promoting a deeper unity. It calls for self-restraint in the pursuit of pleasure and emphasizes the connectedness of humanity. It is not disinterested in rival public theologies, but its primary interest is in providing healing and wholeness. Adherents to the new spirituality seek to stimulate what John Dewey called "the vital habits" of democracy, the ability to follow an argument, grasp the point of view of another, expand the boundaries of understanding, debate the alternative purposes that might be pursued. They want above all to appeal to, and stimulate, people's better nature. And in doing so, they remind us of the importance of spiritual energy in building and sustaining community.

A Compelling Vision

No community is possible without a compelling vision. It may be Martin Luther King's dream sustaining a movement or Cesar Chavez's vision of farm workers fashioning a new ethic of labor. It is still true that where there is no vision the people perish.[12]

Many Americans look back to a time of well-known visionaries in the universities, churches, synagogues, businesses, and government. Hard pressed to identify any such leaders today, they worry about the system of selection, the influence of the mass media, and the single-issue obsession that combine to restrict individuals with a compelling vision from emerging as leaders.

For a moment, this all seemed to be changing. But the euphoria we felt when people toppled old governments in Eastern Europe and when Nelson Mandela was released in South Africa has given way to caution and reality. We are learning once again that it is not enough to gain the release of political prisoners, to bring down repressive governments, or to crown new leaders. When expectations outstrip reality, initial high hopes can be transformed easily into frustration and disillusionment.

Although the present leadership climate may appear at first glance to be a leadership vacuum, it is more likely that we simply look in the wrong place for visionary leaders. If we have learned anything from those who are building new societies in Eastern Europe, Central America, and southern Africa, it is that the next generation of leaders is not likely to fit the traditional mold, nor are those leaders likely to be found in traditional places.

The days are over when we look for leaders with the right endorsements and the right credentials defined by an established elite. The leaders of the future will not come riding out of the sunset on white chargers—heroes without heroism. Many will instead be ordinary people with extraordinary commitments. Their styles will be different. Their accents will be different and so will their color and complexion. What most will have in common is a compelling vision.

Leadership is in many ways a moral activity. The best and the most compelling of the new leaders have a vision of a higher purpose, and they seek to inspire, motivate, and gain the commitment of others to carry out that vision. They are able to persuade others to try new ideas because they are social entrepreneurs who create an excitement about a mission or challenge.

As the demographics of society change, so too will the demographics of leadership. Many leaders of the future will come from the margins of society, from racial minorities who have learned to operate effectively in multiracial and multicultural settings.

With the decline of ideology, the emerging vision for society may well be a transformation of the 1980s emphasis on national patriotism into a new form of earth patriotism in which humanity seeks to live in harmony with itself, with nature, and with the cosmos. To call this a new environmentalism would be misleading, but it must be a simultaneous and multifaceted concern—with the natural environment and its creeping deserts and declining rain forests; with the moral environment that directs our relationship to one another, to nature, and to the planet; and with the social environment in which almost a quarter of the world's population is inadequately housed and where 700 million and 1 billion people live in poverty.

The demographic changes are creating a demand for a new group of visionaries who seek power in order to disperse it rather than simply hold it. The successful leaders of the future will likely be those who understand sharing power rather than simply possessing it. Those who seek power only to concentrate it will ultimately lose to those who seek power in order to diffuse it. Much attention has been given to individual and "lone ranger" leadership in American history. It remains a major theme of historical analysis and self-understanding. But in a society yearning for community, the most successful leader will be the one with a compelling vision.

Can the old and new Americans, the descendants of Europe and those whose roots are elsewhere, live together in community? Can they create something that is more than simply the sum of its individual parts? Can they shape a national identity? The need for diversity and inclusiveness cannot be overemphasized, but diversity does not create community. Many university administrators, corporate managers, and well-meaning civic leaders have learned through hard, and sometimes, bitter experiences that simply bringing diverse groups together does not create unity.

The new America is a web of myriad cultures and traditions. To keep American society whole, "one people, indivisible," we will need to enlarge our vision of what it means to be American. The old America sought to melt individuals of all nations into "a new race." The new America must be built and sustained by a different paradigm. While cultural and racial communities will remain the focus of identity for some time to come, the options available to us are not simply a melting pot or a Tower of Babel. There is a third way, a vision of community that respects boundaries while also transcending them. This may be the only way to maintain coherence and cohesion in a society that is integrating and fragmenting at the same time.

It is in the making and remaking of American society that we encounter the gap between American ideals and its reality, what the Swedish scholar Gunnar Myrdal described as an American dilemma. Our nation became great because it offered hope and help for individuals to transcend and transform society. Somehow along the way, we ceased to value the new communities equally. Their histories and cultures were no longer seen as simply different but as deviant. They were prohibited from sharing in the nation's resources and decision making. They were even restricted in how much say they had in the direction of their own communities.

The experience of racial minorities in transforming the notion of benevolence to include strategies for self-help, empowerment, and social reform is instructive for people around the world who are seeking to define or redefine the public role of private voluntary organizations. The beginning of the twentieth century was a watershed moment in the transition from the age of the individual to the age of the organization. Charity, which had been basically ad hoc, affective, and personal, gave rise to organized philanthropy, which is more systematic, cognitive, and calculating. Now, as we approach the end of the century, there are many who want philanthropy to become primarily charity again, to ameliorate the consequences of inequity, alienation, and hopelessness, rather than to support advocacy and social reform that seek to eliminate the causes.

The present debate about the social role of government and the public responsibilities of private individuals is really a debate about the nature of the social contract between a society and its people. It reflects the continuing dialectic and tension between private and public, the continuing concern about what is the proper mode and what is the management scale of public and private benevolence. Each of the traditions examined here embodies a vision of community that harmonizes the conflicting demands of individual interests and social good. The notion of social good may vary, as the boundaries of community vary, but each group shares in common the emphasis on some form of synthesis of private and public good.

The message of this examination of benevolent traditions is simple. For some time, we thought we could find common ground in our political culture, in citizen participation, and in our commitment to democratic ideals. More recently, we have sought common ground in our economic culture, emphasizing the need of all groups for jobs, the increasing urban/rural connection, and our common commitment to a market economy. It may be, however, that, given the way in which society is changing, we find common ground in the emerging civic culture with its emphasis on both a benevolent government and a benevolent people.

The effect of doing something for another person is powerful. When you experience the problems of the really poor or troubled by trying to help, you are far more likely to find common ground. And you are likely to gain a sense of self-worth, personal satisfaction, and meaning in the process. The genesis of community is in making the concern for others, making some form of civic engagement in behalf of the neighbor, a part of the human journey. The Confucianists are right. A society without benevolence invites its own destruction.

Notes

Preface

1. Robert Bellah and Associates, *Habits of the Heart* (New York: HarperCollins, 1985), p. viii.
2. *The New Encyclopedia Britannica*, Vol. 18, 1989, p. 638.

Introduction

1. Michel-Guillaume Jean De Crevecoeur, *Letters from an American Farmer*, Letter III (1782; reprint, Temecula, CA: Reprint Services, 1990).
2. *New York Times*, Thursday, June 29, 1993, p. A10.
3. Education Review, *Washington Post*, April 7, 1991, p. 13.
4. *New York Times*, Thursday, June 29, 1993, p. A10.
5. *New York Times*, Thursday, June 29, 1993, p. A10.
6. Alex Haley, *Roots* (New York: Doubleday, 1977).
7. John Naisbitt and Patricia Aburdene, *Megatrends 2000* (New York: Morrow, 1990).
8. Arthur M. Schlesinger, Jr., *The Disuniting of America* (Knoxville, Tenn.: Whittle Direct Books, 1992).
9. Dietrich Bonhoffer, *Letters and Papers from Prison* (New York: MacMillan, 1972), p. 17.
10. William Shakespeare, *Hamlet*, Act V, Scene 2, lines 381–382.
11. Howard Thurman, *The Search for Common Ground* (Richmond, Ind.: Friends United Press, 1986), p. xiii.
12. Alexis de Tocqueville, *Democracy in America*, Vol. 1 (New York: Knopf, 1945; reprint of 1840 edition), Ch. XIV, p. 7.
13. Robert Bellah and Associates, *Habits of the Heart* (New York: HarperCollins, 1985).

14. Gunnar Myrdal, *American Dilemma* (New York: Pantheon Books, 1962).
15. James D. Hunter, *Culture Wars: The Struggle to Define America* (New York: Basic Books, 1991).
16. Myrdal, *American Dilemma*.
17. Andrew Hacker, *Two Nations* (New York: Charles Scribner's Sons, 1992).
18. Hacker, *Two Nations*, p. 170.
19. Reinhold Niebuhr, *Man's Nature and His Communities* (New York: Charles Scribner's Sons, 1965), p. 85.
20. John Winthrop, "Models of Christian Charity." In Edmund S. Morgan (ed.), *Puritan Political Ideas, 1558–1794* (New York: Bobbs-Merrill, 1965), p. 92.
21. Quoted by Arthur M. Schlesinger in *The Disuniting of America*, p. 6.
22. Parker Palmer, *The Company of Strangers* (New York: Crossroad, 1981).
23. Robert B. Reich, *Tales of a New America* (New York: Times Books, 1987), p. 170.
24. Quoted by Charles Handy, *The Age of Paradox* (Boston: Harvard Business School Press, 1994), p. 259.
25. Handy, *The Age of Paradox*, p. 259.
26. Handy, *The Age of Paradox*, p. 260.
27. Donella H. Matthews, "Imagine a Global Village" (reprinted by United Church News, 700 Prospect Avenue, Cleveland, Ohio 44115–1100).
28. Lester Salaman of Johns Hopkins University has done pioneering work in this area.
29. Cornel West, *Race Matters* (Boston: Beacon Press, 1993).
30. *USA Today*, Friday, August 27, 1993, International Edition, p. 8A.
31. Derrick Bell, *Faces at the Bottom of the Well* (New York: Basic Books, 1992), p. x.
32. West, *Race Matters*, p. 20.

33. John Winthrop, "Models of Christian Charity." In Edmund S. Morgan (ed.), *Puritan Political Ideas, 1558–1794* (New York: Bobbs-Merrill, 1965), p. 92.
34. 1 Corinthians 12:25–26, Revised Standard Version.

Chapter One

1. Donald A. Grinde, Jr., and Bruce E. Johnson, *Exemplar of Liberty* (Los Angeles: American Indian Studies Center, 1991), p. xxii.
2. Hazel W. Hertzberg, *The Search for un American Indian Identity* (Syracuse, N.Y.: Syracuse University Press, 1971), p. 162.
3. David Archambault, "Columbus Plus 500 Years," speech delivered to the Rotary Club, Murray, Utah, April 6, 1992.
4. Jay Miller, "A Kinship of Spirit." In Alvin Josephy, Jr. (ed.), *America in 1492* (New York: Knopf, 1992), p. 306.
5. Miller, *America in 1492*, p. 306.
6. Friedrich Engels, *The Origin of the Family, Private Property and the State: In the Light of the Researches of Lewis H. Morgan* (New York: International Publishers, 1942), p. 87.
7. Jack Weatherford, *Indian Givers: How the Indians of the Americas Transformed the World* (New York: Ballantine Books, 1988), p. 162.
8. Weatherford, *Indian Givers*, p. 122.
9. Weatherford, *Indian Givers*, p. 136.
10. Eastman's address was published in *American Indian Magazine*, 1919, 7(3), pp. 145–52.
11. Quoted by Clara Sue Kidwell in *Foundation News*, May/June 1990, p. 27.
12. Weatherford, *Indian Givers*, p. 19.
13. LaDonna Harris and Jacqueline Wasilewski, "Contemporary Tribal Governance," a paper published by Americans for Indian Opportunity, Washington, D.C., 1992.
14. Harris and Wasilewski, "Contemporary Tribal Governance."

15. Harris and Wasilewski, "Contemporary Tribal Governance," p. 119.
16. Hertzberg, *The Search for an American Indian Identity*, p. 217.
17. Hertzberg, *The Search for an American Indian Identity*, p. 220.
18. Hertzberg, *The Search for an American Indian Identity*, p. 223.
19. Hertzberg, *The Search for an American Indian Identity*, p. 227.
20. Alexis de Tocqueville, *Democracy in America*, trans. by George Lawrence (New York: Doubleday, 1969), p. 287.
21. Hertzberg, *The Search for an American Indian Identity*, p. 13.
22. Hertzberg, *The Search for an American Indian Identity*, p. 113.
23. Hertzberg, *The Search for an American Indian Identity*, p. 115.
24. Hertzberg, *The Search for an American Indian Identity*, p. 114.
25. Dennis Tedlock and Barbara Tedlock, eds., *Teachings from the American Earth* (New York: Liveright, 1992), p. 83.

Chapter Two

1. Dennis Tedlock and Barbara Tedlock, eds., *Teachings from the American Earth* (New York: Liveright, 1992), p. xviii.
2. Quoted in John M. Rich, *Chief Seattle's Unanswered Challenge* (Seattle, Wash.: Pigott-Washington, 1932), pp. 32–33.
3. Rich, *Chief Seattle's Unanswered Challenge*, p. 33.
4. James Vernon Metcalfe, *Chief Seattle* (Seattle, Wash.: Catholic Northwest Press, 1970), p. 3.
5. Michael Schulman and Eva Mekler, *Bringing Up a Moral Child* (Reading, Mass.: Addison-Wesley, 1985).
6. Metcalfe, *Chief Seattle*, p. 11.
7. Jay Miller, "A Kinship of Spirit." In Alvin M. Josephy, Jr. (ed.), *America in 1492* (New York: Knopf, 1992), p. 306.
8. Miller, *America in 1492*, p. 307.
9. Miller, *America in 1492*, p. 307.
10. Miller, *America in 1492*, p. 308.
11. Metcalfe, *Chief Seattle*, p. 6.

12. Mel Boring, *Sealth* (Minneapolis, Minn.: Dillon Press, 1978), p. 28.

13. Boring, *Sealth*, pp. 34 ff.

14. Rich, *Chief Seattle's Unanswered Challenge*, pp. 35–37.

15. Rich, *Chief Seattle's Unanswered Challenge*, p. 42.

Chapter Three

1. Unless otherwise indicated, the words and opinions of Reuben Snake presented here are drawn from an interview conducted by the author in Santa Fe, New Mexico, on August 24, 1992.

2. Hearings on Peyote, House Subcommittee on Indian Affairs, U.S. Congress, 1918, Part 1, pp. 88–89.

3. Paul Radin, *The Winnebago Tribe*, 37th Report, Bureau of American Indian Anthology (1915–1916), (Washington, D.C.: Government Printing Office, 1923), p. 389.

4. Hazel W. Hertzberg, *The Search for an American Indian Identity* (Syracuse, N.Y.: Syracuse University Press, 1971), p. 248.

5. Hertzberg, *The Search for an American Indian Identity*, p. 243.

6. Weston La Barre, *The Peyote Cult* (Norman: University of Oklahoma Press, 1989), p. 7.

7. LaDonna Harris and Jacqueline Wasilewski, "Contemporary Tribal Governance," a paper published by Americans for Indian Opportunity, Washington, D.C., 1992, p. 52.

8. Jack Weatherford, *Indian Givers: How the Indians of the Americas Transformed the World* (New York: Ballantine Books, 1988), pp. 120–121.

9. From Douglas Loycock, "Peyote, Wine, and the First Amendment." *The Christian Century*, 1989, *106*(28); and from Snake interview.

10. Hertzberg, *The Search for an American Indian Identity*, p. 7.

Chapter Four

1. Unless otherwise indicated, the information and quotes in this chapter come from Zikala-Sa, *American Indian Stories* (Lincoln: University of Nebraska Press, 1985).
2. Quoted in Hazel W. Hertzberg, *The Search for an American Indian Identity* (Syracuse, N.Y.: Syracuse University Press), p. 208.
3. *American Indian Magazine*, 1916, 4(1), 57.
4. Hertzberg, *The Search for an American Indian Identity*, p. 174.
5. Edward E. Hipsher, *American Opera and Its Composers* (1927; reprint, New York: Da Capo, 1978).
6. Letter from Zikala-Sa to Carlos Montezuma, May 2, 1901, Papers of Carlos Montezuma, Wisconsin State Historical Society.

Chapter Five

1. John H. Bracey, Jr., August Meier, and Elliott Rudwick, eds., *Black Nationalism in America* (Indianapolis, Ind.: Bobbs-Merrill, 1970), p. 97.
2. See, for example, *The Myth of the Negro Past* by Melville J. Herskovits (Boston: Beacon Press, 1958); *The African Background Outlined* by Carter G. Woodson (New York: Negro Universities Press, 1968); and *Black Folk, Then and Now* by W.E.B. Du Bois (New York: Holt, 1939).
3. See Peter Wood's detailed study of Africanisms in colonial South Carolina in his work *Black Majority: Negroes in Colonial South Carolina from 1670 through the Stono Rebellion* (New York: Norton, 1974).
4. Robert Harris, "Early Black Benevolent Societies, 1780–1830," *The Massachusetts Review*, Autumn 1979, 20(3), p. 613.
5. Harris, "Early Black Benevolent Societies," p. 613.
6. Harris, "Early Black Benevolent Societies," p. 608.
7. Thomas L. Webber, *Deep Like the Rivers: Education in the Slave*

Quarter Community 1831–1865 (New York: Norton, 1978), p. 63.

8. Webber, *Deep Like the Rivers*, p. 63.

9. Webber, *Deep Like the Rivers*, p. 237.

10. Webber, *Deep Like the Rivers*, p. 237.

11. Webber, *Deep Like the Rivers*, p. 68.

12. Webber, *Deep Like the Rivers*, p. 243.

13. Charles Wesley, *In Freedom's Footsteps*, International Library of Negro Life and History (New York: Publishers Company, 1968), p. 186.

14. Wesley, *In Freedom's Footsteps*, p. 187.

15. Wesley, *In Freedom's Footsteps*, p. 187.

16. Ira Berlin, *Slaves Without Masters* (New York: Pantheon Books, 1974), p. 302.

17. Berlin, *Slaves Without Masters*, p. 315.

18. Alicia D. Byrd, *Philanthropy and the Black Church* (Washington, D.C.: Council on Foundations, 1990), p. 10.

19. Byrd, *Philanthropy and the Black Church*, p. 10.

20. "Giving and Volunteering in the United States," a national survey by Independent Sector, Washington, D.C., 1992.

21. *Newsweek*, May 18, 1992, p. 34.

Chapter Six

1. Robert Reinders, "The Free Negro in the New Orleans Economy, 1850–1860," *Louisiana History*, Summer 1965, p. 274.

2. John W. Blasingame, *Black New Orleans, 1860–1880* (Chicago: University of Chicago Press, 1973), p. 10.

3. Blasingame, *Black New Orleans*, p. 154.

4. Blasingame, *Black New Orleans*, p. 56.

5. Blasingame, *Black New Orleans*, p. 58.

6. Howard A. White, *The Freedmen's Bureau in Louisiana* (Baton Rouge: Louisiana State University Press, 1971), pp. 64–78.

7. Blasingame, *Black New Orleans*, p. 167.
8. Blasingame, *Black New Orleans*, p. 167.
9. Blasingame, *Black New Orleans*, p. 147.
10. *New Orleans Louisianan*, March 20, 1875.
11. From the dedication ceremony for the Lafon Nursing Home of the Holy Family, New Orleans, La., October 21, 1973.
12. J. M. Murphy, "Thomy Lafon," *The Negro History Bulletin*, Vol. VII, 1943–1944 (Washington, D.C.: The Association for the Study of Negro Life and History, 1943), p. 6.
13. Blasingame, *Black New Orleans*, p. 188.

Chapter Seven

1. Marjorie R. Longwell, *America and Women* (Philadelphia: Dorrance, 1961), p. 190.
2. Longwell, *America and Women*, p. 191.
3. Mary White Ovington, *Portraits in Color* (New York: Viking Press, 1927), p. 133.
4. Rayford W. Logan and Michael R. Winston, *Dictionary of American Negro Biography* (New York: W.W. Norton, 1983), p. 626.
5. Longwell, *America and Women*, p. 196.
6. L. H. Hammond, *In the Vanguard of a Race* (New York: Council of Women for Home Missions and Missionary Movement of the United States and Canada, 1922), pp. 113–114.
7. Longwell, *America and Women*, pp. 196–197.
8. Hammond, *In the Vanguard of a Race*, p. 114.
9. Ovington, *Portraits in Color*, p. 134.
10. Hammond, *In the Vanguard of a Race*, p. 115.
11. Abraham L. Harris, *The Negro as Capitalist* (Gloucester, Mass.: American Academy of Political and Social Science, 1968), p. x.
12. Sylvia G. Dannett, *Profiles of Negro Womanhood. Vol. 1, 1619–1900* (Yonkers, N.Y.: Educational Heritage, 1964), p. 197.
13. Dannett, *Profiles of Negro Womanhood*, p. 197.

14. Alexis de Tocqueville, *Democracy in America*, vol. 2 (New York: Knopf, 1945; reprint of 1840 edition), p. 106.

15. Edward Needles, *Ten Years' Progress; or a Comparison of the State and Condition of the Colored People in the City of Philadelphia from 1837–1847* (Philadelphia: Merrihew & Thompson, 1849), p. 3.

16. Paul Avrich, ed., *Mutual Aid: A Factor of Evolution* (New York: New York University Press, 1972), pp. 13, 246.

17. Ralph Ellison, *Shadow and Act* (New York: Random House, 1964), p. 316.

18. Margaret Mead and Muriel Brown, *The Wagon and the Star: A Study of American Community Initiative* (Chicago: Rand McNally, 1967), pp. 13, 19.

Chapter Eight

1. Unless otherwise noted, the source of information and quotes in this chapter is A'Lelia Perry Bundles, granddaughter of Madame Walker and author of *Madame C. J. Walker* (New York: Chelsea House, 1991).

2. *The Madame C. J. Walker Beauty Manual* (Indianapolis, Ind.: The Madame C. J. Walker Manufacturing Company, 1928), p. 16.

3. *The Literary Digest*, 1917, 55(15), 75 (New York: Funk and Wagnalls, 1917).

4. Roi Ottley, *Black Odyssey* (New York: Charles Scribner's Sons, 1948), p. 242.

Chapter Nine

1. Stanford Lyman, "Conflict and the Web of Group Affiliation in San Francisco's Chinatown 1850–1910," in *The Asian American: The Historical Experience*, ed. Norris Hundley, Jr. (Santa Barbara, Calif.: Clio Books, 1976), p. 27.

2. Stanford Lyman, *Chinese Americans* (New York: Random House, 1974), p. 32.

3. Stanford Lyman, "Conflict and the Web of Group Affiliation," p. 42.

4. Robert Lee, "The Confucian Spirit," *Foundation News* (Washington, D.C.: Council on Foundations, 1990), *31*(3), p. 33.

5. Robert Lee, *Guide to Chinese American Philanthropy and Charitable Giving Patterns* (San Rafael, Calif.: Pathway Press, 1990), p. 142.

6. Lee, *Guide to Chinese American Philanthropy*, p. 30.

7. Harry H. L. Kitano, *Japanese Americans: The Evolution of a Subculture* (Englewood Cliffs, N.J.: Prentice-Hall, 1969), p. 61.

8. Kitano, *Japanese Americans*, p. 80.

9. Kitano, *Japanese Americans*, p. 19.

10. Bill Hosokawa, *The JACL in Quest of Justice* (New York: William Morrow, 1982), p. 22.

11. Nancy Weiss, "Contrasts in the Community Organization of Chinese and Japanese in North America," in *The Asian in North America*, ed. Stanford Lyman (Santa Barbara, Calif.: ABC-Clio, 1977), p. 123.

12. Nancy R. London, *Japanese Corporate Philanthropy* (New York: Oxford University Press, 1991), pp. 15–16.

13. London, *Japanese Corporate Philanthropy*, p. 11.

14. London, *Japanese Corporate Philanthropy*, p. 12.

15. London, *Japanese Corporate Philanthropy*, p. 11.

16. *Washington Post*, July 5, 1992, p. A1.

17. Brian Lehrer, *The Korean Americans* (New York: Chelsea House, 1988), p. 87.

18. *Introduction to Vietnamese Culture* (San Diego: Multifunctional Resource Center, San Diego State University, 1987), p. 50.

19. *Introduction to Vietnamese Culture*, p. 42.

20. Charles C. Munzy, *The Vietnamese in Oklahoma City: A Study in Ethnic Change* (New York: AMS Press, 1989), p. 66.

21. Munzy, *The Vietnamese in Oklahoma City*, p. 38.

22. Munzy, *The Vietnamese in Oklahoma City*, p. 172.

23. Paul Ong, *The State of Asian Pacific America* (Los Angeles: UCLA Asian American Studies Center, 1993), p. 11.

Chapter Ten

1. The material for this profile of Le Ly Hayslip comes primarily from a personal interview by the author on June 13, 1992; Hayslip's book *When Heaven and Earth Changed Places*, coauthored with Jay Wurts (New York: Penguin Books, 1990); and newsletters from the East Meets West Foundation, San Diego.
2. Greg Martin, *Seiko Times* (Santa Monica, Calif.: SGI-USA Publications, August 1993), p. 30.
3. Martin, *Seiko Times*, p. 30.
4. Martin, *Seiko Times*, p. 30.

Chapter 11

1. The quotations from Okura in this chapter are taken from an interview by the author, March 8, 1994, except where noted as originating in a printed source.
2. Bill Hosakawa, *JACL in Quest of Justice* (New York: William Morrow, 1982), p. 317.
3. Bill Hosakawa, *Nisei* (Rahway, N.J.: Quinn & Boden, 1969), p. 191.
4. Hosakawa, *Nisei*, p. 318.
5. Hosakawa, *Nisei*, p. 224.
6. Hosakawa, *Nisei*, p. 281.
7. Hosakawa, *Nisei*, p. 281.

Chapter Twelve

1. Robert Lee, *Guide to Chinese American Philanthropy and Charitable Giving Patterns* (San Rafael, Calif.: Pathway Press, 1990), p. 10.

2. Except where otherwise indicated, the source of information and quotes in this chapter is Wang's autobiography, Eugene Linden and An Wang, *Lessons* (Reading, Mass.: Addison-Wesley, 1986); p. 225.

3. Robert Lee, *Guide to Chinese American Philanthropy*, p. 135.

4. Robert Lee, *Guide to Chinese American Philanthropy*, p. 135.

5. Robert Lee, *Guide to Chinese American Philanthropy*, p. 35.

6. Robert Lee, *Guide to Chinese American Philanthropy*, p. 21.

7. Robert Lee, *Guide to Chinese American Philanthropy*, p. 25.

8. Robert Lee, *Guide to Chinese American Philanthropy*, p. 25.

9. *Foundation News*, May/June 1990 (Washington, D.C.: Council on Foundations), p. 32.

10. *Foundation News*, May/June 1990 (Washington, D.C.: Council on Foundations), p. 33.

11. Robert Lee, *Guide to Chinese American Philanthropy*, p. 36.

12. Robert Lee, *Guide to Chinese American Philanthropy*, p. 41.

Chapter Thirteen

1. Jose A. Hernandez, ed., *Mutual Aid for Survival: The Case of the Mexican American* (Malabar, Fla: Robert E. Krieger, 1983), pp. 84–84.

2. Emory S. Bagardus, *Mexican Americans in the United States* (Los Angeles: University of California Press, 1934), p. 50.

3. Hernandez, *Mutual Aid for Survival*, p. 86.

4. Nancy L. Gonzalez, *The Spanish American of New Mexico* (Albuquerque: University of New Mexico Press, 1969), p. 58.

5. Gonzalez, *The Spanish American of New Mexico*, p. 62.

6. Margarita Melville, "Latino Nonprofit Organizations," in Herman E. Gallegos and Michael O'Neill, (eds.), *Hispanics and the Nonprofit Sector* (New York: The Foundation Center, 1991), p. 104.

7. Melville, *Hispanics and the Nonprofit Sector*, p. 105.

8. Gonzalez, *The Spanish American of New Mexico*, p. 76.

9. Gonzalez, *The Spanish American of New Mexico*, p. 77.

10. Gallegos and O'Neill, *Hispanics and the Nonprofit Sector*, p. 83.

11. Gallegos and O'Neill, *Hispanics and the Nonprofit Sector*, p. 89.

12. See the discussion of the historic role of immigrant clergy by William C. McCready in *Hispanics and the Nonprofit Sector*, ed. Herman E. Gallegos and Michael O'Neill (New York: Foundation Center, 1991), p. 88ff.

13. Hernandez, *Mutual Aid for Survival*, p. 8.

14. Hernandez, *Mutual Aid for Survival*, p. 15.

15. Hernandez, *Mutual Aid for Survival*, pp. 15–29.

16. Hernandez, *Mutual Aid for Survival*, p. 100.

17. Gallegos and O'Neill, *Hispanics and the Nonprofit Sector*, p. 20.

18. Virginia Korrel, *From Colonia to Community: The History of Puerto Ricans in New York City, 1917–1948* (Westport, Conn.: Greenwood Press, 1983), p. 154.

19. Lisandro Perez, "Philanthropy Among Cuban Americans: The Demographic, Social, and Cultural Factors Relevant to the Development of Organized Philanthropy Among Cuban Americans," paper presented at Researchers Roundtable seminar, Council on Foundations, Washington, D.C., 1989, p.11.

20. Perez, "Philanthropy Among Cuban Americans," p. 11.

21. Perez, "Philanthropy Among Cuban Americans," p. 21.

22. Perez, "Philanthropy Among Cuban Americans," p. 4.

23. Paul Ylvisaker, "The Future of Hispanic Nonprofits" in Gallegos and O'Neill (eds.), *Hispanics and the Nonprofit Sector*, pp. 163–164.

24. Bradford Smith, *Asian and Hispanic Philanthropy* (San Francisco: Institute for Nonprofit Organization Management, University of San Francisco, 1992), p. iii.

Chapter Fourteen

1. Unless otherwise indicated, the information and quotes provided in this chapter come from Martin McMurtry, *Mariachi Bishop* (San Antonio, Tex.: Corona, 1987).

2. Joseph P. Fitzpatrick, *One Church, Many Cultures* (Kansas City, Mo.: Sheed and Wood, 1987), p. 132.
3. Fitzpatrick, *One Church, Many Cultures*, p. 132.
4. Fitzpatrick, *One Church, Many Cultures*, p. 132.
5. Moises Sandoval, *On the Move: A History of the Hispanic Church in the United States* (Maryknoll, N.Y.: Orbis Books, 1990), p. 84.

Chapter Fifteen

1. The material in this chapter is taken from an interview with Sister Isolina conducted by the author in Ponce, Puerto Rico, on February 21, 1994.

Chapter Sixteen

1. Unless otherwise indicated, the information and quotes in this chapter are taken from Winthrop Yinger, *Cesar Chavez: The Rhetoric of Nonviolence* (Hicksville, N.Y.: Exposition Press, 1975).
2. Melvyn Dubofsky and Warren Van Tine, eds., *Labor Leaders in America* (Chicago: University of Illinois Press, 1987), p. 355.
3. Margarita Melville, "Latino Nonprofit Organizations," in Herman Gallegos and Michael O'Neill (eds.), *Hispanics and the Nonprofit Sector* (New York: The Foundation Center, 1991), p. 107.
4. Melville, *Hispanics and the Nonprofit Sector*, p. 107.
5. Melville, *Hispanics and the Nonprofit Sector*, p. 107.
6. Melville, *Hispanics and the Nonprofit Sector*, pp. 107–108.
7. Ray B. Browne, *Heroes and Heroines* (Detroit: Gale Research, 1990), p. 75.
8. Browne, *Heroes and Heroines*, p. 75.

9. Browne, *Heroes and Heroines*, p. 74.

10. Dubofsky and Van Tine, *Labor Leaders in America*, p. 35.

11. Cletus E. Daniel, "Cesar Chavez and the Unionization of California Workers," in Melvyn Dubofsky and Warren Tine, eds., *Labor Leaders in America* (Urbana: University of Illinois Press, 1987), p. 350.

12. Dubofsky and Van Tine, *Labor Leaders in America*, p. 359.

13. *Washington Post*, Sunday, April 24, 1993, p. B6.

14. "Text of Mrs. Huerta's Speech at Capitol Rally," *Delano Record*, April 28, 1966, p. 9.

Conclusion

1. "Black Like All of Us," *Washington Post*, Sunday, February 7, 1993, p. C2.

2. Amitai Etzioni, *The Spirit of Community* (New York: Crown, 1993).

3. Quoted in Arthur M. Schlesinger, Jr., *The Disuniting of America*, pp. 1–2.

4. *Washington Post*, January 18, 1994, p. A19

5. *Washington Post*, January 18, 1994, p. A19.

6. *Washington Post*, January 18, 1994, p. A19.

7. Adam Smith, *The Wealth of Nations* (Buffalo, N.Y.: Prometheus Books, 1991).

8. Adam Smith, *The Theory of Moral Sentiments* (Indianapolis, Ind.: Liberty Classics, 1982).

9. Education Review, *Washington Post*, April 7, 1991, p. 17.

10. John Davidson Hunter, *Culture Wars: The Struggle to Define America* (New York: Basic Books, 1991).

11. James Redfield, *The Celestine Prophecy* (New York: Warner Books, 1993).

12. Proverbs 29:18 King James Version.

Recommended Readings

Native Americans

Barnett, H. G. "The Nature of the Potlatch." *American Anthropologist*, July-September 1938, *40*, 349–357.

Belshaw, Cyril S. *Traditional Exchange and Modern Markets*. Englewood Cliffs, N.J.: Prentice-Hall, 1965.

Benedict, Ruth. *Patterns of Culture*. New York: Penguin Books, 1934.

Driver, Harold E. *Indians of North America*. Chicago: University of Chicago Press, 1961.

Gill, Sam. *Native American Traditions*. Belmont, Calif.: Wadsworth, 1983.

Hassrick, Royal B. "Teton Dakota Kinship System." *American Anthropologist*, July-September, 1944, *46*, 338–347.

Jacobs, Wilbur. *Diplomacy and Indian Gifts*. Stanford, Calif.: Stanford University Press, 1950.

Josephy, Alvin M. *America in 1492*. New York: Knopf, 1992.

Katz, William Loren. *Black Indians*. New York: Atheneum, 1986.

Kidwell, Clara Sue. "Indian Giving." Paper presented to Researchers Roundtable seminar, Council on Foundations, Washington, D.C., 1989.

Kidwell, Clara Sue. "True Indian Giving." *Foundation News*, Nov./Dec. 1990, pp. 27–29.

Marshall, Murdena, and Novack, Yvonne. "The Roots of Philanthropy." Unpublished paper. Graduate School of Education, Harvard University, no date.

McNickle, D'Arcy. *Native American Tribalism*. New York: Oxford University Press, 1973.

Rickard, Jolene, and Edelstein, Michael. "Prospects for Planned Giving Among Native Americans." Paper presented to Researchers Roundtable seminar, Council on Foundations, Washington, D.C., 1989.

Rosman, Abraham, and Rubel, Paula G. *Feasting with Mine Enemy: Rank and Exchange Among Northwest Coast Societies*. New York: Columbia University Press, 1971.

Tedlock, Dennis, and Tedlock, Barbara. *Teachings from the American Earth*. New York: Liveright, 1992.

Thorpe, Dagmar. "Native Americans in Philanthropy." Paper presented to Researchers Roundtable seminar, Council on Foundations, Washington, D.C., 1989.

Weatherford, Jack. *Indian Givers: How the Indians of the Americans Transformed the World.* New York: Ballantine Books, 1988.

African Americans

Adams, Russell L. *Great Negroes: Past and Present.* Chicago: Afro-Am Publishing, 1969.

Bakewell, Danny J. X. "The Brotherhood Crusade: A Conceptual Model." *The Black Scholar,* March 1976, 7(6), 22–25.

Berlin, Ira. *Slaves Without Masters.* New York: Pantheon Books, 1974.

Birmingham, Stephen. *Certain People: America's Black Elite.* Boston: Little, Brown, 1977.

Blasingame, John W. *Black New Orleans 1860–1880.* Chicago: University of Chicago Press, 1973.

Browning, James. B. "The Beginnings of Insurance Enterprise Among Negroes." *Journal of Negro History,* October 1937, 22(4), pp. xxx.

Byrd, Alicia D. *Philanthropy and the Black Church.* Washington, D.C.: Council on Foundations, 1990.

Carson, Emmett D. "The Charitable Activities of Black Americans: A Portrait of Self-Help?" *The Review of Black Political Economy,* 1987, 15(3), 98–111.

Carson, Emmett D. "Despite Long History, Black Philanthropy Gets Little Credit as 'Self-Help' Tool." *Focus,* June 1987, 15(6), 3, 4, 76.

Carson, Emmett D. "Pulling Yourself Up by Your Bootstraps: The Evolution of Black Philanthropic Activity." Paper presented at the National Conference of Black Political Scientists in Atlanta, Georgia, April 22–25, 1987.

Carson, Emmett D. "Contemporary Trends in Black Philanthropy: Challenging the Myths." Paper presented to Researchers Roundtable seminar, Council on Foundations, Washington, D.C., 1989.

Curtain, Philip D. *The Atlantic Slave Trade: A Census.* Madison: University of Wisconsin Press, 1969.

Darling, Marsha. "We Have Come This Far by Our Own Hands: African-Americans Self-Help, Mutual Aid, Benevolence and Charitable Giving." Paper presented to Researchers Roundtable seminar, Council on Foundations, Washington, D.C., 1989.

Du Bois, W.E.B., ed. *Some Efforts of American Negroes for Their Own Social Betterment.* Atlanta: Atlanta University Press, 1906.

Du Bois, W.E.B. *Black Folk, Then and Now.* New York: Holt, 1939.

Franklin, John Hope. *From Slavery to Freedom: A History of Negro Americans*. New York: Knopf, 1961.

Giddings, Paula. *When and Where I Enter: The Impact of Black Women on Race and Sex in America*. New York: Bantam Books, 1984.

Harris, Abram. *The Negro as Capitalist: A Study of Banking and Business Among American Negroes*. Gloucester, Mass.: American Academy of Political and Social Science, 1936; reprint College Park, Md.: McGrath Publishing, 1968.

Harris, Robert. "Early Black Benevolent Societies, 1780-1830." *Massachusetts Review*, Autumn 1979, 20(3).

Herskovits, Melville J. *The Myth of the Negro Past*. Boston: Beacon Press, 1958.

Holloway, Joseph E. *Africanisms in American Culture*. Bloomington: Indiana University Press, 1990.

Kessel, Felicia. "Black Foundations: Meeting Vital Needs." *Crisis*, December 1989, 96(10), 14–18.

Lerner, Gerda. "Early Community Work of Black Club Women." *Journal of Negro History*, April 1974, 59(2), 158–167.

Loewenberg, Bert James, and Bogin, Ruth, eds. *Black Women in Nineteenth-Century American Life: Their Words, Their Thoughts, Their Feelings*. University Park: Pennsylvania State University Press, 1976.

Mbiti, John. *Introduction to African Religions*. New York: Anchor Books, 1970.

Petry, Ann. *Harriet Tubman: Conductor on the Underground Railroad*. New York: Pocket Books, 1955.

Reid-Dove, Allyson. "Making Your Money Work for Them." *Black Enterprise*, June 1979, 19(11), 321–328.

Robinson, Dinah. "Black America and the Psychographics of Giving." Paper presented to Researchers Roundtable seminar, Council on Foundations, Washington, D.C., 1989.

Robinson, Wilhelmena S., ed. *Historical Negro Biographies*. International Library of Negro Life and History. New York: Publishers Company, 1967.

Rury, John L. "Philanthropy, Self Help, and Social Control: The New York Manumission Society and Free Blacks, 1785–1810." *Phylon*, 1985, 46(3), 231–241.

Spencer, C. A. "Black Benevolent Societies and the Development of Black Insurance Companies in Nineteenth-Century Alabama." *Phylon*, 1985, 46(3), 251–261.

Washington, Booker T. *A New Negro for a New Century*. Miami: Mnemosyne Publishing, 1900.

Webber, Thomas L. *Deep Like the Rivers: Education in the Slave Quarter Community 1831–1865*. New York: Norton, 1978.

Wesley, Charles. *In Freedom's Footsteps*. International Library of Negro Life and History. New York: Publishers Company, 1968.

Wood, Peter H. *Black Majority: Negroes in Colonial South Carolina from 1670 through the Stono Rebellion*. New York: Norton, 1974.

Woodson, Carter G. *The African Background Outlined*. New York: Negro Universities Press, 1968.

Asian Americans

Directory of International Corporate Giving in America, 1991. Rockville, Md.: The Taft Group, 1991.

Hosokawa, Bill. *The JACL in Quest of Justice*. New York: Morrow, 1982.

Hoy, William. *The Chinese Six Companies*. San Francisco: Chinese Consolidated Benevolent Association, 1942.

Kitano, Harry H. L. *Japanese Americans: The Evolution of a Subculture*. Englewood Cliffs, N.J.: Prentice-Hall, 1969.

Lee, Robert. *Guide to Chinese American Philanthropy and Charitable Giving Patterns*. Pathway Press: San Rafael, Calif.: 1990.

Levine, Gene N., and Rhodes, Colbert. *The Japanese American Community: A Three-Generational Study*. New York: Praeger Publishers, 1981.

London, Nancy R. *Japanese Corporate Philanthropy*. New York: Oxford University Press, 1991.

Lyman, Stanford M. *Chinese Americans*. New York: Random House, 1974.

Lyman, Stanford M. "Conflict and the Web of Group Affiliation in San Francisco's Chinatown, 1850–1910." In Norris Hundley, Jr., ed., *The Asian American: The Historical Experience*. Santa Barbara, Calif.: Clio Books, 1976.

Multifunctional Resource Center. *Introduction to Vietnamese Culture*. San Diego: San Diego State University, 1987.

Munzy, Charles C. *The Vietnamese in Oklahoma City: A Study in Ethnic Change*. New York: AMS Press, 1989.

Rutledge, Paul. *The Vietnamese in America*. Minneapolis: Lerner Publication Company, 1987.

Strickland, Carol. "Two Hundred Million and Growing: How Team Tokyo Has Focused Its Funding." *Foundation News*, Nov./Dec. 1990, pp. 28–33.

Weiss, Nancy. "Contrasts in the Community Organization of Chinese and Japanese in North America." In Stanford M. Lyman. ed., *The Asian in North America*. Santa Barbara, Calif.: ABC-Clio, 1977.

Latinos

Camarillo, Michael. "Mexican Americans and Nonprofit Organizations: An Historical Overview." In Herman E. Gallegos and Michael O'Neill, eds.,

Hispanics and the Nonprofit Sector. New York: The Foundation Center, 1991.

Cortes, Michael. "Latino Philanthropy: Some Unanswered Questions." Paper presented to Researchers Roundtable seminar, Council on Foundations, Washington, D.C., 1989).

Hernandez, Jose Amaro. *Mutual Aid for Survival: The Case of the Mexican American.* Malabar, Fla.: Robert E. Krieger, 1983.

Korrel, Virginia. *From Colonia to Community: The History of Puerto Ricans in New York City, 1917–1948.* Westport, Conn.: Greenwood Press, 1983.

McCready, William. "Organized Religion and Nonprofit Activities Among Hispanic People in the United States." In Herman E. Gallegos and Michael O'Neill, eds., *Hispanics and the Nonprofit Sector.* New York: The Foundation Center, 1991.

Melville, Margarita B. "Latino Nonprofit Organizations: Ethnic Diversity, Values, and Leadership." In Herman E. Gallegos and Michael O'Neill, eds., *Hispanics and the Nonprofit Sector.* New York: The Foundation Center, 1991.

Perez, Lisandro. "Philanthropy Among Cuban Americans: The Demographic, Social, and Cultural Factors Relevant to the Development of Organized Philanthropy Among Cuban Americans." Paper presented to Researchers Roundtable seminar, Council on Foundations, Washington, D.C., 1989.

Index

A

African American(s), 73–117; African roots of benevolent traditions, 73–74, 76–77; aristocrats, benevolence of, 84, 87, 94; and civil rights movement, 81; civil society institutions of, 84–85, 86; concept of community, 73–74, 173–74, 104–105; extended family concept, 74–75, 77; mutual aid and voluntary societies, 8–9, 74–75, 77, 83–84, 100, 106; in post–Civil War New Orleans, 87–95; and racism, 67, 75; as recipients of charity, 90–91, 106; slave quarter communities, 77–80; support for political and social movements, 80–81, 82; traditional secret societies, 76–77; universal compassion of, 76; voluntarism and giving tradition of, 81–82, 85. *See also* Black church

African Masonic Lodge, 74

African-Seminole Alliance, 30

Alianza Hispano Americana, 177

All Peoples Christian Center, Los Angeles, 121

Allen, R., 75–76

American Indian Association, 30

Asian Indians, benevolent traditions of, 122

Asian-American(s): diverse cultural backgrounds, 121–123; population growth since 1980, 135. *See also* Chinese Americans; Filipino Americans; Japanese Americans

Asian Exclusion Act of 1924, 121–122

B

Bell, D., 17

Bellah, R., 5

Bennett, W., 217, 218

Berlin, J., 161, 164

Black church, 81–84, 111; as center for philanthropy and voluntarism, 81–82; economic development programs, 82–83; involvement in civil rights struggle, 82

Bonhoffer, D., 3

Bonnin, R. T., 63

Breedlove, Sarah. *See* Walker, Madame C. J.

Buddhist vision of community, 138–139

Bunche, R., 215

Bureau of Indian Affairs, 33, 34

C

Cambodian immigrants, 122

Carlisle Indian School, 66, 67

Catholic Church: benevolent practices, 174–175, 185; and Cesar Chavez, 207–208; and Cuban Americans, 182; *personalismo* in religious practice, 186–187; and Reconstruction, 92; as source of empowerment, 187, 190

Charity, versus philanthropy, 227

Chavez, Cesar, 178, 187, 188–189, 203–211; childhood as migrant worker, 204, 205–206; personal sacrifices, 209; public attacks on, 211; religious faith and theology, 207–208; religious support for, 207–208; self-education, 207

251

Chinese American(s), 123–126,
    159–167; benevolent practices, 126;
    clan authority, 123–124; and Confu-
    cian ethic, 125–126; family founda-
    tions, 163–164; fraternal orders (*hui
    kuan*), 89, 124–125; immigrants, 121,
    123–125; secret societies, 125; social
    service organizations, 163–164
Christianity: and Korean Americans,
    132; and Native American Church,
    52, 53
Churches. *See* Black church; Catholic
    Church
Cisneros, H., 189
Civil society: as civic participation, 58;
    and good society concept, 9; as inclu-
    sive society, 68, 217
Clinton, Bill, 57
Community, 11–20; Buddhist vision of,
    138–139; and caring impulse, 11, 13;
    conceptual and demographic changes
    in, 12–14; functional changes in,
    14–15; geography as boundary in,
    12–13, 16; racism and nativism as
    barriers to, 16–17; as Winthrop's city
    on a hill, 19, 213. *See also specific eth-
    nic community*
Community, new paradigm of, 213–228;
    concept of good society in, 9–10, 228;
    natural environment in, 220–221;
    shared values in, 213–218; spirituality
    and religion in, 221–224; universal
    compassion in, 218–221; vision and
    visionary leaders in, 224–228
Community Service Organization
    (CSO), 207
Confucian ethic, 125–126, 161, 167
Consolidated Bank and Trust Company,
    101
Council of Energy Resource Tribes
    (CERT), 34
Cuban American(s): as exile group, 181,
    182–183; philanthropy, community
    and political focus of, 181
Cuban American National Foundation
    (CANF), 181

D

Dakota tribe, 69
Daniel C. E., 210
De Tocqueville, A., 9, 105
Democratic process, and private benevo-
    lence, 15

Dirda, M., 220
Disraeli, B., 13
Doctor White Community Center,
    Brooklyn, New York, 197, 198
DuBois, W.E.B., 98, 109
Dukakis, M., 167
Dwamish Confederacy, 37, 38

E

East Meets West Foundation, 142
Eastman, C., 26–27
Edwardson, C., 55
Ellison, R., 106
Engels, F., 25–26
Etzioni, A., 216

F

Ferre, Sister Isolina, 193–202; approach
    to community revitalization,
    196–202; calling to serve the poor,
    194–196; community projects in
    Puerto Rico, 199–202; work with
    youth gangs, 197–198
Filipino Americans: immigrants' status as
    U.S. nationals, 121–122; and United
    Farm Workers' strike, 122, 210
Fisher, D., 70
Fitzpatrick, J., 186
Flores, Patrick (archbishop of San Anto-
    nio), 185–192; appointment as first
    Mexican-American bishop, 187–188;
    commitment to poor, 188, 190; orga-
    nized philanthropy of, 191; political
    activism of, 188–190; support for
    Cesar Chavez, 188–189; vision of
    community, 185–186, 189–190
Flores, Pete, 191–192
Forten, J., 84
Franklin, B., 26
Free American Society, 74

G

Global village, neighborhood as, 13–14
Great Society programs, 18

H

Hacker, A., 6
Haley, A., 2
Handy, C., 13
Hayslip, Le Ly, 137–145; adolescence in
    Vietnam, 140–141; Buddhist beliefs,

138–139; entrepreneurial success, 141; philanthropic activities of, 142–143

Hernandez, J. A., 171, 176

Hispanic American(s), 171–211; advocacy orientation of volunteer groups, 183; benevolence as church-centered, 174–175; concept of la raza, 172–173; confraternidades (lay brotherhoods), 8, 176–177; familial relationship as primary, 171–172; generosity and social solidarity of, 171; idea of community, 171; individual giving as sharing, 183; religion of, 186–188 (See also Catholic Church); social activism of 1960s, 203; social class distinctions, 173–174. See also Cuban Americans; Mexican Americans; Puerto Rican Americans

Huerta, Dolores, 211

Humphries, S., 84

Hunter, J. D., 5–6, 221–222

I

Immigrants, and assimiliation myth, 1–2, 7

Independent Order of Saint Luke, 100–101

Indian Welfare Committee, 65

Iroquois, 23, 25, 26

J

Jackson, M., 85–86

Japanese American(s), 126–130, 147–157; civic habits of, 127; civic and patriotic organizations, 128–129; concept of community and kinship, 127–130; participation in civil rights movement, 147–149; value system of, 154–155

Japanese American Citizens League (JACL), 129, 147–149

Japanese Association, 128–129

Jones, A., 75–76

Jones, J., 84

Jung, C., 13

K

Kerrey, R. T., 54

King, Martin Luther, Jr., 147, 149, 217–218

Kitano, H., 127

Korean American(s): churches, as social agencies, 132; family obligation, 132; immigrants, 122, 130–131; tradition of thrift (keh), 131

L

La Alianza Federal de Mercedes, 178

La Barre, W., 53

La Liga Puertoriquena e Hispana, 180–181

Lafon, Thomy, 87–89, 91–94, 95; benevolence of, 88, 90–91; and Catholic Church, 91–93; honors for, 92–93

Lamere, O., 31–32

Laotian immigrants, 122

Leadership: and ethnic identity, 204–205; as moral activity, 225; visionary, 224–228

Lee, R., 125, 161, 163

London, N., 130

Lopez Tijerina, R., 178

Los Penitentes, 176–177

Louisiana Equal Rights League, 89–90

M

Marx, K., 25–26

Matthews, D., 13

Mead, M., 107

Mekler, E., 39

Melting pot myth, 1–2, 7

Melville, M., 204

Metcalfe, J. V., 38

Mexican American(s), 175–179; confraternidades (lay brotherhoods), 176–177; importance of familial relationships, 172; in labor and civil rights movements, 177, 178; mutual aid groups (mutualistas), 171, 175–178; self-help groups of early settlers, 8l and social reform groups, 178

Mexican American Cultural Center (MACC), 190

Mexican American Legal Defense Fund, 178

Migrant farm workers, 206. See also Chavez, Cesar

Miller, J., 25

Mitchell, E. D., 98

Montezuma, C., 70

Mooney, J., 49–50

Myrdal, G., 5, 6

N

Naisbitt, J., 3
National Council of American Indians, 65
National Council of La Raza, 178
National Hispanic Scholarship Fund, 191
National Origin Quota System, 18
Native Americans, 21–70; aboriginal tribes, democratic and egalitarian nature of, 26; benevolence as sharing and honoring, 9, 24, 27–29; concept of community, 23, 40–46; cultural disposition, 23–24; fraternal and social clubs, 30–31; gambling operations as self-help, 35; Ghost Dance, 32–33; giveaway and potlatch, 27–29, 38–39; leadership by negotiation and example, 40–41, 54–55; powwow, 55; reformist and political organizations, 31–32; religious and spiritual beliefs, 24–25, 37, 49, 69 (See also Native American Church); self-help enterprises, 34–36; sharing and reciprocity in, 24, 27–29; urban, benevolent practices of, 30–34, 36. See also Seattle
Native American Church, 33–34, 49–50; and anti-peyote campaigns, 53–54; and Christianity, 52, 53. See also Peyote religion
Nativism, 17–18
Natural environment: in Native American cosmology, 23–25; in new paradigm of community, 220–221
Neighborhood: as community, 12–13, 16; as global village, 13–14
New Orleans Freedman's Aid Association, 90
Niebuhr, R., 7

O

Okura, Patrick, 147–157; activist role in relocation camp, 149, 150, 151; childhood, 151–152; discriminatory experiences at UCLA, 152–154; and integration of Civil Service, 150–151; philanthrophy of, 156–157; on present state of race relations, 155; vision of community, 154–155
Okura Mental Health Leadership Foundation, 156

P

Paine, T., 11, 25
Palmer, P., 12
Parker, Quanah (Commanche chief), 53
Patterson, O., 214
Perez, L., 181
Peyote religion, 33, 50, 51, 53, 68–69; 1990 Smith decision effect on, 57. See also Native American Church
Pluralism and multiculturalism, 3–5; dangers of, 214, 219; and new tribalism, 5, 14. See also Community, new paradigm of
Poro of Sierra Leone, 77
Portes, A., 2
Prescott, L., 35
Private benevolence, limitations of, 15
Public relief, and newly freed blacks, 90–91
Pueblo tribes, worldview of, 24–25
Puerto Rican American(s): concept of self-help organizations, 179–180; mutual aid societies, 179–181; religion and superstition in, 194
Puerto Rican Brotherhood of America, 179–180

R

Racial minorities: benevolent traditions, universality of, 8–10; and ethnic identity, 2–5, 14, 216
Racism, 6–7, 17, 75
Rawls, J., 13
Redfield, J., 222
Reich, R., 12–13
Reinders, R., 87
Religion, polarizing conflicts of new holy war, 5–6, 221–224. See also Black church; Catholic Church; Christianity; Native American Church; specific ethnic group
Rich, J., 44
Rillieux, R., 87
Rodriquez, R., 2
Roosevelt, E., 103
Ross, Fred, 206

S

St. Luke's Penny Savings Bank, 101
St. Paul African Methodist Episcopal Church, St. Louis, 111

Schlesinger, A., 3
Schulman, M., 39
Seattle (Suquamish chief), 37–47; great speech of, 45–46; idea of community, 38, 40–46; moral character of, 38, 39–40; relationship with whites, 42–44
Simmons, Gertrude. See Zikala-Sa
Sioux, 59, 67
Sister Isolina. See Ferre, Sister Isolina
Smith, Adam, 218–219
Snake, Reuben A., 49–58; faith and theology of, 50–51; as tribal leader, 54–55; vision of community, 52
Sociedad Progresista Mexicana (Mexican Progressive Society), 177–178
Society of American Indians (SAI), 31, 63–64, 65, 66, 68
Spirituality, in new paradigm of community, 221–224. See also Religion
Stevens, I. I., 44
Stone, O., 143
Suzuki, A., 121

T

Tecumseh, Chief, 58
Teepee Orders, 30–31
Thurman, H., 4–5
Triad Society, 125
Trinkle, E. L., 103–104
Trotter, W. M., 110
Tubman, Harriet, 81

U

Underground Railroad, 80–81
United Farm Workers (UFW), 122, 210–211

V

Values: as common ground for community, 214–216; compassion and empathy as, 218–221; and respect for natural environment, 220–221; of social institutions, 217–218
Velasco, Carlos I., 177
Vietnamese American Association (VAA), 134
Vietnamese Americans, 132–134; central role of family, 132–133; as refugees from Viet Nam war, 122, 133–134, 137–145. See also Hayslip, Le Ly

Voluntary groups: advocacy versus service orientation in, 202; as means of economic survival, 8

W

Walker, C. J., 113
Walker, Madame C. J., 109–117; creation of Walker Hair Care Method, 115–116; as entrepreneur, 112–114, 115–116; involvement in service and civil rights organizations, 114–115; philanthropy and political activities of, 110, 115, 116–117
Walker, Maggie, 97–107; charitable endeavors of, 105; concept of black community, 104–105; early accomplishments of, 98–99; entrepreneurial philosophy of, 101–103; as founder of St. Luke's Penny Savings Bank, 101; as leader of Independent Order of Saint Luke, 100
Wang, An, 159–167; childhood in China, 160, 162, 164–165; philanthropy of, 159, 160, 161; view of civic responsibility and community, 159–160, 162, 164
Wang Center for the Performing Arts, 159
Wang Laboratories, 161–162
Wang, Fred, 159
Washington, Booker T., 97, 109, 110
Weatherford, J., 29, 55
Webber, T., 77
West, C., 17
When Heaven and Earth Changed Places, 143–144
Winnebago tribe, 49, 52, 54–55
Winthrop, J., 19, 213

Y

Ylvisaker, P., 183
Yuen, Moon, 163
Yinger, W., 207

Z

Zikala-Sa, 59–70; as advocate of Indian self-determination, 65–66; childhood of, 59–61; community service of, 63–64; as political activist, 64–66; religion of, 69–70; vision of community, 70